Henry Hardy

Nazareth against Nice

Or an impartial Review of the Existing Churches, their Creeds and Principles, from the Stand-Point of the Written Word of God

Henry Hardy

Nazareth against Nice

Or an impartial Review of the Existing Churches, their Creeds and Principles, from the Stand-Point of the Written Word of God

ISBN/EAN: 9783337255015

Printed in Europe, USA, Canada, Australia, Japan

Cover: Foto ©Lupo / pixelio.de

More available books at **www.hansebooks.com**

NAZARETH against NICE,

OR

AN IMPARTIAL REVIEW OF THE EXISTING CHURCHES, THEIR CREEDS AND PRINCIPLES,

FROM THE

STAND-POINT OF THE WRITTEN WORD OF GOD.

BY ICONOCLAST.

"This is life eternal, that they might know thee, O Father,—the only true God,—and Jesus Christ whom thou has sent."
John's Gospel, 17: 3.

"To us (the Christian Church) there is but One God, the Father; and One Lord, Jesus Christ."
Paul's 1st to Corinthians, 8: 6.

"The knowledge of the truth, For there is One God, and One Mediator between God and men, the Man Christ Jesus."
Paul's 1st to Timothy, 2: 4 and 5.

"A SECOND REFORMATION, and it must be an extensive one, remains to be attempted and achieved by our sons, such as shall bring the Church home to its resting place upon the foundation of the Apostles and Prophets, Jesus Christ himself being the chief corner-stone."
Isaac Taylor.

"Ye shall know the truth, and the truth shall make you free."
Christ.

WASHINGTON, D. C.
1887.

Entered, according to act of Congress, in the year 1887, by HENRY HARDY, in the Office of the Librarian of Congress, at Washington.

*Thomas McGill & Co.,
Printers and Stereotypers,
Washington, D. C.*

ADVERTISEMENT.

The object of the following pages is to place the general reader—usually not well furnished with time and opportunity for controversial inquiry—in a position to judge intelligently concerning the doctrines and opinions of the leading churches or sects of Christendom, and thus, measurably at least, to ascertain the merits or demerits of each in particular.

Nothing is more sure than that there is not a church existing, any more than an individual, without some, and occasionally, grievous faults. If, in Apostolic days and the Seven Churches of Asia there was no little to reprove, who will presume that among the warring sects of these less favored times there is not much that demands a fearless and healthy scrutiny? From faults and blemishes all churches and all men are in duty bound to seek to be as free as possible, yet, great is the pity, the too common habit is not merely to extenuate or excuse errors but to elevate them into merits. In this way, religion, the great purifier, is made to miss its quality as a curative of the spiritual and moral disorders of the human race. God's boundless and unceasing mercies are, however, always at hand to provide in His Holy Word both balm and physician for even this sad situation. Thither we must repair, and thereunto, in every difficulty and doubt, apply, with a faithful exercise of our God-given faculties, without fear, favor or affection for whatever is mortal or earthly. The truth as it is in Jesus, which comprehends the earlier truth of Moses and the Prophets, is the one criterion of these pages. Their humble author calls no man that is or ever was upon the earth his spiritual Father: he calls no man spiritual Master save the one Master from whom all Christians derive their honored name. He therefore gratefully rejoices in that liberty wherewith Christ has made his people free. On those like-minded, grace, mercy and peace from God the Father and the Lord Jesus Christ our Saviour, are fraternally invoked.

CONTENTS.

Ambrose	58	Consubstantiation	119
Anselm	68	Creed, Apostles'	40
Apostle John	24	Creed, Nicene	41
Arius	44	Emperor Constantine	43
Calvin, John	106	Emperor Theodosius	57
Castalio	109	Fathers, Early	59
Christ, sinless	50	Impanation	120
Church, Baptist	125	Incarnation	27
R. Catholic	5	Knox, John	114
Congregationalist	68	Leeser, Rabbi	150, 159
Disciples of Christ	63	Logos, The	24
Episcopal of England	7	Massacre, St. Bartholomew	116
Episcopal of U. S.	8	Milton, John	101
Jewish	143	Neander	10
Lutheran	117	Servetus	112
Methodist	165	Theophilus	76
Presbyterian	96	Webster, Daniel	9
Unitarian	183	Whately, Dr.	65
Universalist	176	Wise, Dr. I. M.	159
Confession, Westminster	97	Zwingli, Ulric	121

NAZARETH against NICE.

THE CHURCH OF ROME, commonly called the Roman Catholic, whereby it stands distinguished from the Greek Catholic Church—likewise "so-called"—is the oldest church organization west of the Atlantic Ocean. It claims to date its origin from the alleged presence of Peter, the chief or leader of Christ's Apostles, in the ancient City of Rome, after a round of services in his apostolical capacity in Samaria, in Syria, throughout Palestine and back as far as the country of the Euphrates. But the New Testament makes no record of this alleged Peter's visit to Rome as it does of Paul's residence in that capital by reason of a special mission from above. If Peter really visited Rome it must have been very near the close of his earthly career; and as to his Roman bishopric, fond assumption is most probably its sole basis. Had the claim been made for Paul instead of Peter there would have been color in it; but however the fact might be, inasmuch as it holds no place in the Divine Records, it can have no religious significance whatsoever.

As a question of practical interest to accountable beings it matters not by what means, right or wrong, designed or fortuitous, the great fabric of Romish hierarchical supremacy was reared or maintained. What does the Roman Church teach to-day? is the real consideration now before us.

The system of the Roman Catholic Church is synonymous with the Papacy, because the Papa, or Pope, too readily styled by the votaries of that church the "Holy Father," is the central figure and pivot on which the whole fabric turns. The Pope is also known by the title of Supreme Pontiff, a word drawn from profane history and designating the office of Chief Priest in Pagan Rome. No Roman Catholic will hesitate about calling the Pope his "Holy Father," or will question for a single instant his supreme spiritual authority. The system is saturated with this unlawful homage or worship, so as to make it patent upon its forehead and name, and not to be possibly gainsayed or mistaken. But how does all this comport with the teachings and commands of the Word of God?

We read in the Gospel of Matthew (23:9) the pointed

command of Christ to his disciples, "Call no man your Father upon the earth: for one is your Father who is in heaven." Here is a direct prohibition by the Lord and Master of Christians forbidding precisely that practice which is habitual with every individual member of the Romish clergy and laity, and which is, moreover, blindly supposed by millions of them to be an act of acceptable service! Could such be possible were the reading and study of the Word of God enjoined upon those people as a duty and a privilege? Perhaps not one in ten thousand entertains the smallest notion that such a prohibitory command anywhere exists. How, indeed, should they know, when the study of the Bible is the reverse of encouraged among them?

The circumstance must be regarded as very significant that a vast organization, claiming to be the sole Christian Church, should be designated by themselves and others by that one single word which proclaims them flagrant transgressors of Christ's positive command! But for all others, where the warning is so instant and plain, only the wilfully blind can be led astray.

If we follow onward from the great text above quoted, we shall alight upon a kindred ordinance of the Saviour with which the Romish system, with its infinity of human doctors and teachers, of decrees and dogmas, is in naked antagonism. "One is your Master, namely, Christ; and all ye are brethren;" not popes, fathers, prelates, cardinals or priests, but "brethren."

It is because these great and explicit injunctions of the Son of God have been ignored that a thousand fallacies and delusive doctrines and practices have dishonored the religious history of about 1500 years. We cannot recount them all, but may ask, in the words of a man of great insight and wisdom, "What have *we*, with the New Testament in our hands, to do with a vast medley of superstitions, such as the 'tremendous sacrifice' of the Mass; the adoration of the Mother of God; prayers for the dead or prayers to them; or the intercession of saints; or the seven sacraments; or holy water, holy oil, holy vestments, and crossing of the forehead; the worship of images, pictures, and relics; penance, purgatory, or auricular confession; indulgences or works of supererogation; monkery and celibacy and lying miracles? The modern Christian, Bible in hand, throws off these follies and abominations as a man would rend from his shoulders a fool's chequered coat that had been forced upon him."

No two systems of doctrine and practice could be more

mutually repugnant than the system of Peter as developed in his Epistles and the Acts of the Apostles and the system of the Roman Catholic Church. That church has about the same right and title to claim Simon Peter for its patron that the Czar of Russia would have if he were to claim that the opinions and writings of Thomas Jefferson furnish the basis and justification for his (the Czar's) arbitrary despotism.

ONE of the principal results of the great disruption that took place about the time of the Lutheran reformation was the formation of THE ENGLISH NATIONAL CHURCH under peculiar circumstances. Mixed up with a popular and genuine indignation at the rapacity and corruptions of the Papal hierarchy and a desire to be rid of them, were the personal purposes of the headstrong and wayward English king, Henry the Eighth, who would suffer no restraint upon his ebullient passions and desires, even in their wildest moods. His marriage to six wives; the divorce of two of them and murder of two, with executions, by the scaffold and the fagot, often of the cruellest description, and in numbers perhaps exceeding the average of a hundred a month during his long reign of thirty-eight years, for the most part in punishment of heresy and misbelief only of doctrines and dogmas of the pedant king's own propounding, will give some distant idea of the works and ways of this royal monster, who was said never to spare man in his anger or woman in his lust.

Doubtless the Tudor dynasty, to which Henry belonged, were a bloody race, but so also bloody were the times in which they reigned, from which it is only equitable that the times should bear their due share of our modern detestation as well as pity. King Edward the Sixth, the gentle son and youthful successor of the sanguinary Henry, spilled human blood in some unnecessary instances, and his royal sister, the Bloody Mary, deluged England with Protestant gore. Elizabeth, great and distinguished for many qualities that became a ruler, followed in the family track, yet with fewer instances of barbarous cruelty; but under her the secular power asserted its claim to supervise and control the "Estate ecclesiastical and spiritual," thus confirming an innovation of her father's which has ever since caused scandalous comment and disapproval at home and abroad. With varying fortunes in the reigns of the Stuarts, James the First; Charles the First; the Protector Cromwell; Charles the Second and James the Second, down to the Revolution under William the Third, the two antagonistic Papal and Protestant parties were alternately up and down; but finally, the Protestant interest prevailed, subject to the domination, as just remarked, of the state authority, which continues to this day operative in England and Wales, but not in Scotland or Ireland, or the several British colonies.

In looking back upon the rugged ages through which Christian ideas and principles were struggling with worldly aims and desires, it will be the part of a cautious wisdom to note the reformatory work that was to be done, and to consider the only agencies sufficient to perform it. To break up the firm-set sod that had been depositing and hardening for centuries, required no superficial or dainty manipulation, but bold and resolute force exerted in thorough earnest. Henry the Eighth was such a rough and sturdy ploughman, and Martin Luther, it will be remembered, would not have been the right man in the right place with a spirit and temper only pliant and smooth. The exigency provided the men.

William and Mary's accession to the English throne, with William's military successes in Ireland over the forces of the ex-king James the Second, confirmed the Protestantism of the English church as by law established, having the sovereign for its spiritual head. Its theology is displayed in thirty-nine Articles, reduced from forty-two, but which the Episcopal church of the United States has of late further reduced to thirty-five "Articles of Religion." Some of these Articles we propose candidly to consider.

The First Article is in the words following: "There is but One living and true God, everlasting, without body, parts or passions; of infinite power, wisdom and goodness; the Maker and Preserver of all things, both visible and invisible. And in unity of this godhead there be three persons of one substance, power and eternity: the Father, the Son, and the Holy Ghost."

This first article consists of two sections or clauses, each inconsistent with the other. The former section teaches monotheism; the latter Tritheism; but neither of them the Trinity, though the caption to the article calls for it. To the former every true Christian, Jew, and Mohammedan will yield a ready assent, because it declares "there is but one living and true God, without body or parts," and therefore sole and indivisible, a veritable unity. The latter sentence rather furtively substitutes "godhead" for "God"—two words by no means synonymous or equivalent, for under a "unity of godhead" innumerable individuals might be comprised as well as only three, "godhead" not being like "God," a strictly singular and personal name, but a neuter noun of multitude. So the idolatrous Hindoos "allege that the three hundred and thirty millions of gods, whom they enumerate, are subordinate agents, assuming various offices in preserving the harmony of the universe under *One godhead*, as innumerable rays issue from one sun." So thought Dr. Isaac Watts when he sang of the

"Counsels of peace between th' Almighty Three,
Conceived at once and signed without debate
In perfect union of the Eternal Mind."

Thus the latter part of the first article inculcates Tritheism, a form of belief which, however unfounded in fact and Scripture, is not illogical, and but slightly violates the laws of language or of the mind.

Not so the "Trinity" proper, which the article by its heading professes but fails really to teach, because it has no existence anywhere; neither in heaven, nor in earth, nor in the mere imagination. There may indeed be collocations of words arbitrarily set together by uninspired and therefore unauthorized men, such as are written in the so-called Athanasian creed, and are supposed by some to describe the Trinity; but when an intelligible explanation of them is asked, the would-be instructor invariably retreats behind the screen of "mystery," declaring the Trinity not a doctrine to be examined by analysis but to be implicitly taken as a whole.

Monotheism is intelligible; Tritheism is intelligible; but the Trinity, which is nothing other than a vain effort to combine or compromise with the other two, is wholly unintelligible and incomprehensible, and has been so confessed by not a few of its votaries. I find a story, and it might be a true one, appended with something of triumph to an argument for the Trinity. It is about as follows: The distinguished statesman, the late Daniel Webster, was one day leaving an Episcopal Church, when he was accosted by an acquaintance thus: "Then you attend that church?" "Sometimes," answered Mr. Webster. "So you believe that three and one are the same thing?" again queried the acquaintance. "I believe, sir," replied Mr. Webster, "that neither you nor I understand the arithmetic of heaven."

Whilst we cannot but admire the dexterity of Mr. Webster in thus answering impertinence with a puzzle, he plainly said nothing that could help the Trinity, for if the language in which the commands of heaven are couched is to mean something else than the just human interpretation of it, the Bible thereby becomes a mass of insoluble riddles. Especially would this be the case with numbers. If, for instance, the six days in which God created the heavens and the earth mean not six but some other number, then the Sabbath was not appointed for the seventh day, as Jews and Christians have always supposed. So the tribes of Israel were some other than twelve, and the Apostles, though each one is separately named, might have been of any number more or less than what we call the "twelve." We may be sure that Mr. Webster intended nothing more serious by his shrewd reply than a well-bred rebuke to over-intrusiveness. The solemnity with which the little circumstance was introduced into a theological discussion shows, however, the extreme paucity of weighty arguments for the doctrine of the Trinity.

The distinguished historian of the Christian church, Augustus Neander, in treating of the doctrine of the Trinity, honestly confesses, Nicenist as he was, that "the doctrine of the Trinity does not strictly belong to the fundamental articles of the Christian faith, as appears sufficiently evident from the fact that it is expressly held forth in no one particular passage of the New Testament, for the only one in which this is done,—the passage relating to the three that bear record (1st John 5:7)—is undoubtedly spurious, and in its ungenuine shape testifies to the fact how foreign such a collocation is from the style of the New Testament."

It is scarcely less than solecistic to speak of the Trinity, or the doctrine of the Trinity, in the singular number. Sometimes singular, sometimes plural, it is characterized by ambiguity. The conceptions about the Trinity, or the "doctrines" of it, are about as numerous as the planets in our system. The bishops and learned doctors of the English Episcopal Church profess this, that, or the other theory as each one's notion might determine. Thus, Dr. John Wallis, profound as a mathematician, took the Sabellian view, or, as it is called, The Modal Scheme, which "represents the Father as the sole person, and the Son and Spirit as attributes, or emanations from Him. It compares the divinity to the sun, of which the Father would be analogous to the substance, the Son to the light, and the Holy Ghost to the heat." This comes near monotheism.

It is supposed that Archbishop Tillotson was of this way of thinking.

Not very different from this in effect is Bishop John Pearson's idea. He regards the Father as the fountain of deity and the centre of its attributes, which are communicated with fulness to Christ and the Holy Ghost. He says "there can be but One person originally of himself subsisting in that Infinite Being, because a plurality of more persons so subsisting would necessarily infer a multiplicity of Gods." Bishop George Bull, perhaps, thought this way. Dr. Thomas Burnet supposed the Father to be self-existent, the Son and Spirit dependent on the Father, yet so that the Father's perfections are theirs also, constituting them divine and proper objects of worship. Dr. Robert South insisted that there was but one infinite, eternal mind, and three *somewhats*, not distinct intelligences, but called by different names, as modes, faculties, &c. He engaged in controversy with Dr. William Sherlock, dean of St. Paul's, whose opinion was that each of the three persons in the Trinity is distinct from the others and each *a* god, but that the three have a common consciousness, so that each one has the same attributes as the other two unitedly. This controversy was settled in favor of neither, but brought upon both the charge of heresy in daring to attempt to explain an inexplicable mystery. Dr. Thomas Burgess, bishop of St. David's, (a stout stickler, by the way, for the interpolated verse 1st John, 5:7,) supposes the three divine persons to constitute One God, but that the three persons are not three beings, but only one being, because there cannot be more than one omnipresent Being; therefore the three are not severally but jointly omnipresent, and so One God. Dr. Daniel Waterland, who held several church preferments and was an ardent controversialist, kept closely to the Athanasian creed—that the Trinity consists of three distinct and equal persons, each uncreate, incomprehensible, eternal, almighty, each God and Lord, yet together only One God and One Lord. Still there is discrepancy; for the Father is said to be neither made nor created nor begotten; the Son, though neither made nor created, is begotten; and the Holy Ghost, neither made nor created nor begotten, is "proceeding." This creed amounts to no more than a bold effort to reconcile the essential differences of monotheism and tritheism by sheer stress of robust assertion. *Vox et preterea nihil.*

There is a theory advocated by Rev. John Howe, that the Trinity consists of three persons severally possessing all the attributes of deity, yet so united as to be One God, as the bodily, sensitive, and mental faculties are united in a single man. The justly renowned Richard Baxter was not well inclined to make definition of the Trinity, but thought the three divine persons to be wisdom, power, and love, as in man there may be three faculties of vital power, intellect, and will; or in the sun, motion, light, and heat. Francis Gastrell, bishop of Chester, believed the three names of the persons in the Trinity to indicate a three-fold distinction in the divine nature, yet not inconsistent with its essential unity. He is quoted as saying that "each of the names includes the *whole* idea of God and something more. So far as they express the nature of God they all adequately and exactly signify the same. It is the additional signification which makes all the distinction between them." What those several somethings are, and what they amount to when aggregated, must be equal to nothing, because the three persons when united are not supposed to be more than One God. What is *something* before union becomes *nothing* when multiplied by three at the instant of union.

It will be seen, then, that when anybody speaks about the Trinity and desires to be rightly understood, he should indicate which of the several doctrines, or theories, he alludes to.

A number of years ago a series of sermons were preached in the city of Boston by ministers of different denominations, each "plainly declaring why he is compelled to hold and teach his creed." The Methodist declared his "belief in the existence of One God, and that he is clearly revealed to us in the Bible under a three-fold distinction or personality—the Father, Son and Holy Ghost." He made no attempt to demonstrate the alleged *clearness* of the "revelation;" but taught under a considerably obscure phraseology that there are three persons in the One God, that is to say, three persons in One person, because the word "God" is unipersonal. He did not avail himself of the usual resort to the word "godhead," which is a word of multitude similar to company or partnership, and may include within it three, or thirty, or three millions, or any number of objects whatsoever. His statement was therefore self-contradictory as well as scripturally unsustained.

The Baptist minister "insisted upon the essential unity of God, but not so as to reject the Trinitarian doctrine." This, at least, showed a disposition to be accommodating. He did not undertake to explain how an "essential unity" (whatever that might be) could comport with an actual triplicity of contained yet separate units, each unit being distinct from and in every respect equal to each of the others. He then went on to say, as if inwardly acknowledging the unsatisfactoriness of his statement, that his church "placed no stress whatever upon the numerical idea, because we do not believe that God can be measured by any human arithmetic," for which last idea he was most probably indebted to Mr. Webster. But in saying and doing thus, the minister and his church, however strong they might feel under Mr. Webster's backing, happen to differ very widely with Moses and the Prophets and with Christ and his Apostles, for in every instance in which those great teachers gave pointed instruction, or doctrine, concerning the being and manner of being of the Most High, the number One is solely and with "stress" set forth as descriptive thereof. How thoroughly the unit principle pervades all the great and distinguishing features of the Christian religion can be readily judged from Paul's comprehensive account of it in Ephesians 4:3 to 6, ending with "One God and Father of all, who is above all, and through all and in you all." Throughout the New Testament the "One God" is also designated, as if to obviate all misapprehension and mistake, "the Father."

The Trinitarian Congregationalist Minister summarily excludes all from the name of Christian who do not "pay divine honors to Jesus Christ;" who do not "pray" to him and "render him divine worship." Such proscribed parties, he says, are not "evangelical" and not "Christian."

Notwithstanding, may we meekly and respectfully dare to call into question these stern disparagements, and ask an appeal from them to the "'law and the testimony'"?

Where in the whole Bible can a command be found "to pay divine honors to Jesus Christ," that is to say, honors as to God? A sincere, hearty and practical obedience to Christ's commands, as being primarily the commands of God, is everywhere enjoined, but "divine honors" nowhere. Let us place ourselves in the presence of Christ himself. At the well of Sychar, Christ taught (John 4:21 to 24) the worship of the Father, for that the "*true* worshippers worship the Father in spirit and in truth, for the Father seeketh such to worship Him." If some other besides the Father, Christ himself, to wit, was entitled to the "divine honor" of supreme worship, why did Christ keep silence when he should have spoken out? If he was not afraid to utter the truth, and the *whole* truth, Why did he confine all *true* worship to the worship of the Father alone? Was it for any other reason than that the worship of the Father, and the Father only, was the truth and the *whole* truth in the matter? What Christ taught might be "unevangelical" in the view of a Congregationalist minister, but there it stands indelible, "graven in the rock forever."

Again, in Matthew 6:6, Christ directly enjoins that prayer be made to the "Father who is in secret," for that the Father will "openly reward" His sincere petitioners. In the 9th verse Christ solved the problem by a plain direction concerning prayer, viz., *to whom* and *how* it should be offered. He says, "After this manner pray ye, Our Father, who art in heaven, hallowed be thy name," &c., &c. No Jesus Christ, no Holy Ghost, but the Father only; all the nouns, pronouns and verbs being in the singular number.

If we look further, and especially into the Gospel by St. John, which is strangely supposed by some to favor the doctrine of Christ's deity, we shall be confronted with very pointed testimony. In John, 15:16, Christ tells his disciples that "Whatsoever they should ask of the Father in his name the Father would give it to them," which plainly is that they must ask gifts from the Father whilst praying to Him in the character of believers in Christ. In John 16:23 Christ makes a yet more distinct and decided step away from the idea of his own supremacy by admonishing his disciples that "in that day," or subsequently to his resurrection and corporeal retirement from the earth, they should "Ask him nothing," for "Verily, verily, whatsoever they should ask of the Father in Christ's name, the Father would give it to them." Are we then to be denounced because we understand that in these and similar instructions it was Christ's express design to warn his followers of that time and all coming ages against making prayer to him, or in any way rendering him that supreme worship which is due to God alone? His whole drift and purpose seem to have been diametrically opposite to the views entertained by our Trinitarian Congregationalist.

Beyond what absolutely belonged to Christ as the envoy, the ambassador, and representative on earth of God Most High, Christ sought no honors or distinctions. The only honor which Christ valued was what came to him from God. (John, 8:54.) And it was great and glorious. (2d Peter, 1:17.)

The New Testament furnishes no instance where the apostles ever paid "divine worship" to Christ as to God, though to their hearts' cores they loved and venerated Christ as the Lord and Master of all Christians, the Saviour and the visible final Judge of the World. The Congregationalist minister who puts his "paying divine honors" to Christ on the ground of what is said in 1st Corinthians 1:2 about "calling upon the name of Jesus Christ our Lord," greatly overshoots the mark, forbearing to look at the very next verse, which would have corrected his error, and forgetting the Apostolic intimation in chapter 8th, verses 5th and 6th, of the same Epistle, that how numerous soever might be those who are called gods and lords, whether in heaven or in earth, yet "to us (Christians) there is but One God, the Father, and One Lord, Jesus Christ." To call Christ "Lord" is to speak as a Christian should speak; to call him God is to speak without a justifying reason from the Book of God. More even than this: it should be remembered that even when we denominate Christ by the secondary title of "Lord," which he rightly claimed to be his due, it is not to be done without an ulterior reference to the superintending provisions and mercy, and therefore "to the *glory* of God the Father." (Philipp., 2:11.)

If it were permissible to worship the image of God instead of God Himself, then it might be lawful to worship Christ supremely, for Christ is the moral image of God. But nowhere is such a liberty granted. God "will not give His glory to another." Man is commanded to worship God alone, "no other God," Exod., 34:14, and with the profoundest humility, 1st Cor., 14:25, and Nehemiah, 8:6. We shall fulfil our duty and pay just honors to Christ when we do whatsoever he commanded, believe in what he *really* said, and carry in our hearts a due sense of the immense obligation we owe him. To exceed these lawful limits and accord to him the honors and worship due only to God, may subject us to be ranked among idolaters instead of Christians.

The second clause of the first Church article affirms the Father, Son, and Holy Ghost to be of "one substance," meaning thereby one essence or material, but it deigns no information as to how or where the asserted fact was discovered, or why the Bible has failed to testify about so prime a point of belief. There is, however, some verbal ambiguity, for it is doubtful whether by "one substance" we are to understand one connected whole, so that the three must be considered in combination, or whether by "one substance" is intended the *same* substance," or essence, so that the three may still be personally disconnected and their persons individually limited and separate. In this latter sense, which seems to be that intended, neither of the persons can be infinite, for his infinity is bounded by the equal personalities of the two others. Dr. Burgess saw this plainly.

But to recur. With regard to the bold and unsustained assertion relative to the composition of the godhead and the "unity of the substance" of the same, it is to be said that in spirit and letter it is at flagrant war with some of the most impressive teachings of God's Word. The Divine Being announced Himself to the Israelitish people by Moses as the "I AM," the Self-existent ONE,—not three, as according to Dr. Watts, &c.—and by Christ, the great Heaven-sent teacher, as "*A Spirit*" and not a "substance," and to be "worshipped in spirit and in truth." Any language, therefore, which savors of materiality is the reverse of appropriate when applied to the nature of God, and we may securely assume it as certain that the wide departure from the true Christian doctrine, and which departure so unhappily obtained in the third and fourth and succeeding centuries of the Christian era, was mainly due to the low conceptions which so easily prevailed among the Gentile as distinguished from the Hebrew converts to Christianity. We may, perhaps, derive hence some intimation of the reason why in conveying His authoritative truth to mankind, the Divine Being chose to send it by the minds, mouths, and pens of the children of Abraham rather than by Gentile channels. Nearly every one of the books of even the New Testament was written by a Jew.

One stands astounded at the squabbles and contentions of those reeking centuries when the texture of the inscrutable godhead formed the ground of strife; when men who were far worse informed than the children of our schools upon the topics of natural history and philosophy and general science, undertook with an irreverent rashness to formulate (as we have it in the Nicene and Athanasian creeds) dogmas about the nature and interior organization of the Most High, as if the divine anatomy were spread *in extenso* before them.

That there are in the universe and in the Bible what are therein denominated the Father, the Son and the Holy Spirit, is a truth of unsurpassable gravity and importance. What these existences *are* and what they *are not* are two matters amply revealed in the Divine Word. Of the Father—undoubtedly the Jehovah of the Old Testament—we learn by the mouths of Christ and his Apostles that He is the "only true God," or that the Father, and the Father only, is God. Of the Son we are taught by the same divine oracles that he was brought into being at a specified period, not yet 1900 years ago, through a special exertion of the divine influence upon the person of a Jewish maiden, and because of this divine paternity he has always been justly called the Son of God. Of the Spirit, very commonly denominated the Holy Ghost, we are scripturally informed that it "proceedeth from the Father," as it ever has done and ever will do, and as it especially and signally did when by its means (Luke, 1:35) a commencement was made of the being of him named Jesus, the Son of God and Saviour of the world.

Nor does God's holy word refuse to the candid and inquiring mind a true knowledge of the nature—so far as comprehensible by our faculties—of God, of His Son and of His Spirit. God the universal Creator and Father, is an eternal Spirit, more boundless than the universes of matter and of mind, filling, sustaining and controlling them throughout. The heaven of heavens cannot contain Him. The Son, who by reason of his being the divinely appointed leader and king of the present and future world of regenerate men, became the *Anointed* or the CHRIST, declares to us upon his personal word and official authority (Luke, 24:37 to 43) that he is not a spirit, but a being such as ourselves; that is to say, a soul encompassed by bodily organs, hands, feet, &c., and that spirits are *not* so endowed. The Holy Spirit, or Holy Ghost, proceeding from the Father, is therefore pure spirit, the closest emanation and outpouring from God and the immediate instrument of His Divine Will. All three are instructively referred to in Acts 5: 29 to 32. It was because the soul and spirit of Jesus were anointed and interpenetrated by this Holy Ghost, not only that he was constituted to be the Christ, but was kept throughout his life upon earth entirely free from sin; in a word, it was because Jesus was ever full of the Holy Ghost that he enjoyed that greatest of conceivable blessings and distinctions, viz., the "dwelling in the bosom of the Father," and was empowered to speak as never man before spake, to work the mightiest miracles and to rise triumphantly from the dead. (See Isaiah, chap. 11th.) That Spirit from whose overshadowing influence Christ originally sprang; which filled his moral and intellectual nature throughout his whole life on earth "until the day in which he was taken up," and thus enabled him "to give commandments unto the Apostles whom he had chosen," was, doubtless, the same agency through which, even in heaven, "God gave unto him that Revelation which he sent and signified by his angel to his servant John." By that same Spirit also did Jesus, "the first begotten of the dead and the Prince of the kings of the earth," speak unto the churches. In every respect that Divine Spirit, always originally proceeding from the Father but mediately through the Son,

> "Lives through all life, extends through all extent;
> Spreads undivided; operates unspent."

The English word "Spirit" or "Ghost," in the phrases "Holy Ghost" and "Holy Spirit" of the Old and New Testaments, is the translation of a word that in Greek means "what has been breathed," that is to say, "breath." In Latin, the same. The primary idea evidently is that the Spirit of God, or the Holy Ghost, is an emanation from the Divine personality, analogous to the breath of man, or man's utterance, expressive of his will. When it is said in the first of Genesis that "the Spirit of God moved upon the face of the waters," it is as if it were written "the breath of God went forth upon the face of the waters." How fraught that "breath of God" was with irresistible efficiency and perfectness in all respects, all can understand. David, in the 33d Psalm, says: "By the word of the Lord were the heavens made and all the host of them by the breath of His mouth"—the breath being the medium by which the irresistible word was conveyed. And in Job, 38:4, "The Spirit of God hath made me, and the breath of the Almighty hath given me life." When man was formed from the dust of the earth God "breathed into his nostrils the breath of life, and man became a living soul"—the Divine breath or Spirit bearing life along with itself.

Now, God being himself a Spirit, the Holy Ghost is a spiritual procession from His person, and not a separate deity; it is God's avenue for action upon and communication with all beings and things exterior to Himself, and is always in constant outflow to the whole spiritual and material creations. With this divine and all-efficacious Spirit Jesus Christ was "anointed" or endued. It was afterwards entrusted to Christ's direction, for after his resurrection he *breathed* on his disciples, saying, "Receive ye the Holy Ghost." On the great day of Pentecost the Holy Ghost was freely shed forth, doubtless through the hands of Christ; and on other occasions. The same Spirit was likewise confided to the hands of the Apostles for distribution among converts to Christ—Acts, 8:17; 11:17; 15:8. It would be nothing short of profane absurdity to suppose that the Apostles Peter and John could communicate a divine personality, that is to say, God in his proper person, to the Samaritan believers.

We perceive, then, that in so far as to the Father and the Son they are *not* of the "same substance." Equally wrong is it to say that they are of the same "eternity," (referring to the eternity that is past,) for whilst God, as "the Ancient of days," has lived for ever and ever, Christ His Son came first into existence so lately as the days of Herod King of Judea, through the aforesaid originating power of the Holy Ghost. Thus it does not appear that the second part of the first Episcopal "Article of Religion" was prepared with due respect and consideration for the Word of God. Moses and the prophets, Christ and his Apostles and Evangelists, seemed to have weighed very lightly as against the tumid interpolations by the Nicene council into the good old Apostles' creed, and that other effusion without a known parentage, mis-called the Athanasian, of which the American Episcopalians thought too dubiously to admit it into their prayer-book.

A vigorous writer, indignant at the utterly undue homage still paid to the out-put from the tumultuous assemblages at Nice and Constantinople, thus remarks: "It is bad enough that the church should have inherited her chief formulas of belief from such an age and such a reign as that of Constantine; a reign hideous with guilt; an age so surrendered to depraved morals and misdirected intellect, that, if ever there could be in Christendom an incapacity for discerning spiritual truth, it must have been then. But to make such a time the rule for all others,—to dignify by the name of "the Catholic faith" the propositions which emerged from its wranglings by outvoting or outreaching the rest; to scorn, in comparison, the light of recent thought, and constrain the modern Anglo-Saxon to put back the index of his Christian consciousness to the hour when Athanasius triumphed,—is a weak rebellion against providential tendencies, and an irreligious scepticism of God's perpetual inspiration."

By way of covering his own unscrupulous machinations at the council of Nice, it was a subsequent remark of Athanasius that "God spoke to the world through that council." He could in truth have added that in so speaking there was unspoken nearly all that had been spoken before by Moses and the Prophets; by Christ and his Apostles. The poet Moore, well read in ancient learning, frankly admits, Roman Catholic that he was, in a note to his poem on Intolerance, that "the corruptions introduced into Christianity may be dated from the period of its establishment under Constantine; nor could all the splendor which it then acquired atone for the peace and purity which it lost."

The second Episcopal article is remarkable for its robustness of speech and confidence of expression, as if it exultingly hoped to compel assent by sheer force of loud-sounding phraseology. A little examination will, nevertheless, show out of what so much exceeding boldness took its rise. Professors of the Nicene faith have always betrayed a propensity for nestling their dogmas in the few difficult spots or dark passages of the volume of Scripture. A hundred texts—plain, clear, positive and direct—appear to weigh nothing in point of conclusiveness against some one, or two possibly, of a figurative and hence somewhat obscure character, which they can interpret to suit themselves. In the case before us the reliance is upon the two or three brief verses introductory to the Gospel by John. The bulk of the Gospel goes for almost nothing.

Upon this contracted footing, misunderstood and misinterpreted, Nicenists are fain to erect their system, of which the second article under consideration furnishes a fair example. They construe it to mean that the Son—whom we call Jesus Christ—existed in co-equality with the Father from all eternity, or that there never was a moment in the history of the Father when the Son was not present with Him in absolute and equal fulness of Divine power and perfection. They, therefore, feel authorized in declaring Christ to be "very and eternal God," composed of "one" or the same "substance," or material, with the Father, so that the Father begat the Son out of Himself as early as the Father possessed His own being.

Now, every one acquainted with the Gospels in their full extent—the first three of which were certainly well known to John when in the closing years of the first century he wrote his own—will recollect how it was that Jesus, afterwards the Christ, came to be called the Son of God. His primitive title to that distinguished name grew out of the fact (Luke 1: 35) that the Holy Ghost, or the emanant influence of the Most High, had, taking *locum genitoris*, originated his being. Another ground for his bearing the title was the audibly divine endorsement of the fact just stated, by the acknowledgment of Jesus as His beloved Son immediately following Christ's baptism by John the Baptist, (Matt., 3: 17; Mark, 1: 11; Luke, 3: 22); and a third and, if possible, yet stronger reason when he was declared "the Son of God with power,"—"the Son of God *with power* by his resurrection from the dead." On still another ground, though a more general one, none so worthy as Jesus to be called the Son of God (Romans 8:14), "For as many as are led by the Spirit of God, they are the sons of God," and by the Spirit of God Christ was always led.

On these several and assuredly sufficient accounts, and for no other reason whatever, the scriptures denominate Jesus the Son of God. But the second article ignores all these intelligible, reasonable and scriptural statements, and sets up Christ's title to sonship upon what it probably deems far better grounds, as being infinitely anterior and more sublime. That sonship, says the article, (and all Nicenists, Papal and Protestant, join the accord,) began from "everlasting." Thus they undertake to locate the date. Neither do they hesitate to define the manner in which Christ at first became a "Son." He was, they say, "begotten" (whatever that might mean) "of" or by "the Father," leaving no other inference, if they do not directly say it, than that the Father begat the Son out of His own, that is, the Father's "substance," without the concomitancy of any other being.

Not desiring to push this scrutiny into Nicenist dogmatism any farther just here, let us ask, if such teachings be be true, how comes it to pass that the Bible nowhere inculcates them? Why did the Divine Being, in His most benignant condescension to the Israelitish people, omit to inform Moses (Exodus 3:14) as to the actual circumstances of the celestial sovereignty, and instead of saying as He did, "I AM hath sent thee," why did he not the rather say "WE ARE have sent thee," thereby paying due honor to the co-deified Son, and reporting the case as it truly was? It would have been equally effective with the yet untaught Israelites.

Why again, if the throne of heaven was from all eternity occupied by more than one divine person, did God strictly command his people to listen while it was proclaimed (Deut., 6:4), "The Lord our God is One Lord;" and why did He, after repeatedly declaring through his prophets that He was the "Holy *One*" of Israel, put the question (Isaiah, 44:8), "Is there a God beside me? Yea, there is *no* God; I know not any." Also, "I am Jehovah, and there is none else; there is no God beside me;" and in Deut., 32:39, "I, even I, am He, and there is no God with me." Are we to suppose that all this and vastly more of the same character that could be readily quoted was a mass of misleading and mistake, calculated to produce wrong impressions that would have to wait for correction the greater part of two thousand years, or till after Athanasius had superseded Sinai and the temple at Jerusalem by decrees issued from the palace of a semi-Pagan emperor in a semi-heathen land? Who with God's holy word in his hands and a ruling desire to know God's holy truth in his heart, will suppose any such thing?

It has been remarked that Nicenists had seized upon the three brief verses at the commencement of John's Gospel whereon to build their peculiar system, with substantially no regard to the great multitude of explicit statements of doctrine and duty which go to make up the whole remainder of that Gospel, the other Gospels, and the Bible at large. Though they have thus seized upon those verses they have no valid title to them. Their policy was to assume or beg the question of the identity of the Word, not with the Son of God of the New Testament, who was born at Bethlehem, but with the Son,—that is to say, the "God-the-Son"—who, according to their creeds, was begotten infinite ages before the beginning of time, and reigned in heaven forever afterwards as "very and eternal God," in common and equal majesty with his Father.

Overlooking, then, for the present, the consideration that there would thus inevitably be more Gods than One, the question before us will be to inquire whether the Word mentioned in the aforesaid verses was meant by John for a person endowed with the full round of faculties and properties that duly attach to personality, or was simply an utterance-forth or expression of the divine mind and will sent out into the surrounding universe, furnished with all appropriate divine forces to do His bidding. Contrariwise from the Nicenists, we take the ground that the Word was not a person, but what it was claimed to be, viz., a Word, or utterance forth, analogously to the decree, mandate, order, ukase, or firman of an earthly potentate, and instinct with every divine power and virtue. Of course, we do not indicate that it was but a single word, for, from the Infinite God—analogously with rays from the single sun in the sky—words have forever proceeded in infinite directions and on infinite errands to the infinitely numerous objects of his love and care.

The first five verses of the preface to the Gospel of John, literally translated from the Greek, are after this wise:

"In the beginning was the word, and the word was

with God, and the word was God. The same was in the beginning with God. All things came to pass through him (or it), and without him (or it) not one thing came to pass of what did come to pass. In him (or it) was life, and the life was the light of men. And the light appears in the darkness, and the darkness did not apprehend it." The words (him or it) are inserted because in Greek the noun for "word" is masculine; in Latin, it is neuter.*

Now, it cannot be said that this language is quite so plain, explicit, and matter-of-fact as the introductions to the other gospels, for which reason, as we have already observed, the professors of the Nicene faith seem somewhat naturally to take to it. It is not absolutely certain what John meant by "the beginning," whether of the universe, of this world, of the Christian dispensation, or of what.

The Nicenist doctrine is that the "Word" is not to be understood as an impersonal utterance of the divine mind and will, but as a distinct living being or person, fully equipped with all the attributes of personality, and they add that the word is the Son, participating and equal in divine majesty and glory with the Father, of whose own substance or material he (the Son) was by the Father begotten. Have they, however, a just right to add this? The Evangelist John does not authorize it. If, for argument sake, we temporarily adopt the Nicene idea that the "Word" is the synonym for the "Son," then John teaches and repeats that the "Word" was in the beginning "with God." Thus John will have introduced two originally cotemporaneous and independent Gods, of which the Word is set forth as the more operative and efficient, and not a syllable or a hint is uttered about his being the "Word of the Father," or "begotten of the Father from everlasting." John's language does not call for these concessions to God the Father, who, it cannot be denied, is made, on the Nicene hypothesis, to appear far less advantageously creative and energetic than the Word or Son, which, by the way, may help us to account for the disparagement of the Father in comparison with the Son, so common as to

---

*The proem, or first fourteen verses of John's Gospel, looks much like the responsive part of a dialogue with the questions omitted. Had we the supposed questions, all would, doubtless, be easy. There are in the Gospel eight hundred and eighty-five verses, wherefore the proem constitutes about a sixty-third part of the whole. It is obvious that this fractional part must not be interpreted in conflict with the mass of the Gospel, and that this little which is in some degree obscure must not dominate the much which is clear and unmistakable. The real purpose of the Gospel is disclosed in chapter 20: 31.

be wellnigh universal in Nicene writings, worship, and song.*

From all which we must conclude that the dictum of the opening of the Second Article has no color of support from the preface to John's Gospel so far as to the dogma of the "Son's being the Word of the Father, begotten from Everlasting of the Father, the very and eternal God, of one substance with the Father." We, therefore, unhesitatingly reject it, as unscriptural and a mere human invention, imposed upon mankind in days of ignorance, intolerance, and corruption. We advise its rejection by all who in these happier times prefer the truth, the whole truth, and nothing but the truth in matters of religion as well as everything else.

The Apostle John, by general consent, was at the time he wrote his Gospel a resident of the maritime city of Ephesus, in Asia Minor. He was by nation a Jew, and lived under the influence of christianized Jewish ideas and opinions during the latter half of his long life. Wherever he went or lived, and especially when in the cosmopolitan city of Ephesus, he was witness to continual differences and discussions about the *Logos*, that is to say, the Word, in connexion with the creation and ordering of the visible world. Of much that he heard he necessarily disapproved, so that when he came to write his Gospel he at once solved the perplexing problem by advancing *in medias res* with the sceptre of divine inspiration in his hand, and in a few brief but authoritative sentences, showed that the "Word," so much debated about, was no separate divinity, but was God himself, in the midst of His attributes, the God of the Jews and the Creator and Giver of all that was and is good and great, visible and invisible.

In this way John brought all speculation back to the

---

*The following is an extract from a sermon delivered in a church in the city of Washington on January 3d, 1886, imbibed, doubtless, by the large congregation as if it were the veritable milk of the word:

"As it would have profited us nothing to have been born unless we had been redeemed, it follows how much greater was the work of redemption than of the creation, and so much greater is the name of Jesus than the name of Jehovah. Jehovah is the principle of being, the source and principle of life, but Jesus is the source and principle of grace, of glory, and of salvation. Jehovah was the vanquisher of Pharaoh, but Jesus is the vanquisher of the devil and of hell. The one was the lawgiver of the Old Testament and of the Jews, the other of the New Testament. Jehovah led the people of Israel through the Red Sea into the land of Canaan, but Jesus, by his most precious blood, has conducted us from sin to innocence, from earth to heaven, and most fitting it is that the Christian world should be mindful of him who has loved us so much. * * * In every act of his life Jesus proclaimed himself the God and Saviour of the poor."

great Mosaic and Christian principle that God was and is in Himself the beginning and the end of all things, the "all in all." And then, further on, when, by a single, bold, but most appropriate and comprehensive figure, he demonstrated how the full volume of divine wisdom had been poured into the individual soul of the only-begotten Son,—he gave the highest possible credential to Christ's Messiahship and just authority over the opinions, consciences, and lives of mankind.

The Second Article goes on next to say that "the Son, the very and eternal God, of one substance with the Father, took man's nature in the womb of the blessed virgin, of her substance." This intimates that the "very and eternal God-the-Son," after having become a voluntary occupant of the womb of the blessed virgin, took her substance into union with his own. If the question be asked how much of the substance of God-the-Son was then taken, the article answers that it was his "whole and perfect nature," that is to say, his entire godhead. This, "joined" to the "whole and perfect nature" derived from the virgin, constitutes the "one person," Christ, who is therefore described as "very God and very man." Hence, it must be concluded, according to the article, that the union between God-the-Son and the virgin Mary, was, in point of fact, a veritable marriage union, paralleled in the case of human couples that become united in the bonds of matrimony. Under the influence of this doctrine the effusiveness of some of the Roman Catholic divines of France breaks forth in praises of the degree of ravishing beauty which the purity and holiness of the virgin had reached, causing God-the-Son to hasten the period of the Incarnation. One of these ecclesiastics (Pere Gratry) distinctly says that it was the Son's "love for Mary which more than anything else led him to descend from heaven."

But what is most remarkable in all this Nicene or Episcopal doctrine, is the total absence of God the Father (either in His own immediate personality or through the medium of the Holy Ghost) from the whole proceeding.

If we compare the Second Article of the Protestant Episcopal Church with the statements of the Gospels on the subject of Christ's generation, the discrepancy between the two will be very marked. Luke says, "And the angel answered and said unto Mary, The Holy Ghost shall come upon thee and the power of the Highest shall overshadow thee; therefore also that holy thing which shall be born of thee shall be called the Son of God." But, according to the Nicene dogma, in which Roman Catholics and most Protestant sects coincide, neither the Father nor the Holy Ghost was the actual parent of Jesus Christ. That parent, according to those authorities, was God-the-Son, so that, analogously to human relationships, God the Father was only Christ's *grandfather*, and, especially in the Episcopal article, the Holy Ghost was altogether dispensed with and out of the question.

There is no reason to suppose the very unlikely circumstance that the Apostle and Evangelist John would teach in his very brief passing preface a doctrine so conflicting and variant from the entire body of his Gospel, as that there are more Gods than One, or other persons in the godhead than the Father. The word he speaks of is therefore no other than the word of God, which, whatever might be the date of the "beginning," has ever and will ever utter itself forth to every intelligent and sentient being in the universe.

This Word, never apart from the divine personality, contains within itself all the authority, force and practical essentiality of God himself; it is therefore before His presence, or "with" Him, and cannot be distinguished from Him. It is, in fact, to all that is exterior to it, God, and has never been otherwise. Thus the true God has never been an inactive or restful deity, selfishly satisfied with His own supremacy and unassailable happiness, and unconcerned about the world's welfare, like what is described concerning Brahma or the Jupiter of old, but a Divine Parent of unutterable love, perpetually sending forth whatever is needful for the well-being of His manifold offspring.

Such, we believe, to be a great aim of John's teaching. Why should it not be, consistent as it is with the majesty and honor of the Most High, and with the dictates of well-regulated human reason at its best estate? This Divine Word, or Utterance, has ever been instinct with life and light, and especially to the spiritual being of men. In the fulness of time God gathered the rays thus scattered into a focus, with the purpose of illustrating their excellence and value by a living example begotten, born, reared and prepared for the sublimest earthly office under the very auspices of God himself. So perfect was that oracle and that example that by an easy and perspicuous figure of speech, yet a figure that rather strengthens than weakens the meaning behind it, the divine word became enshrined in the flesh, or embodied in the material person of

Jesus, the Christ, so as to be identified with him. That wonderful production, the Epistle to the Hebrews, strikes off this pregnant truth with instructive brevity in its introductory statement: "God, who at sundry times and in divers manners spake in time past unto the fathers by the prophets, hath in these last days spoken unto us by his Son." There we have it, gathered as it were into a nutshell—God's all-abounding wisdom, will and word, formerly spread through many minds of seers and prophets, now gathered to a focus in the teachings and life of Jesus Christ.

No Protestant who steadily rejects the Roman Catholic interpretation of the Saviour's words at his breaking of the bread and giving of the cup at the last supper, can consistently stumble at John's beautiful figure, "the Word became flesh," that is, was planted into humanity. Yet, setting personal consistency and John's true meaning aside, a doctrine, too mythological for a Bible truth, and called the *Incarnation*, has been allowed to grow out of it and to engage an exceedingly deep interest in many Protestant minds. It is true that the word "Incarnation," that thus captivates, has no place in the Bible, in which respect it resembles its *congener*, the Trinity; for the Bible having no cognizance of the things signified, had no occasion for names to distinguish them. As the ablest Nicene doctors fail to explain it, the doctrine of the Incarnation falls under the congenial category of mystery. It may be remarked that Hilary, bishop of Poictiers, in France, a luminary of Nicenian times, says of the Incarnation, that it "consisted in Christ's self-emptying of himself, and his assumption of human nature." "In this process," says Hilary, "he lost none of his divine nature, and even during the humiliation he continued to reign everywhere, in heaven and on earth." How Christ, or any being whatever, could empty himself of himself and still part with nothing of what he had been, may be plain to Nicenian intellects, but by every other class of minds must be regarded as a self-contradiction. Again, could that be properly called a "humiliation" which was a "continual reign everywhere in heaven and on earth"? With all the display of wisdom on this subject, the professors of it have never deigned to point to the sources of their information.

To all who read the scriptures with a prevailing desire to understand them aright, there will be no real difficulty in the prologue to John's Gospel, especially when it is faithfully translated and not forced into a service which it would not itself elect. The mere English reader must, nevertheless, be warned against a mistranslation in the 10th verse, which should be read, "He" (or it), referring to the true light, "was in the world and the world got its existence through (or, because of) him (or it), and the world knew him (or it) not," which appears fairly to teach that when Christ, in whom the true light shone, (and for whose final and perpetual dominion as head of his redeemed church the earth itself was constituted,) came into the world, his presence was not generally recognized. He came amongst his own proper people, the Jews, but was not nationally accepted, yet those spiritually-born few who did accept and believe in him, received from him, by the baptisms of water and the Spirit, power to become sons of God. In the 14th verse John speaks of Christ in the flesh as the "only begotten of the Father," whilst, as we have seen, the Protestant Episcopal Church, in its Second Article, assigns to the Christ in the flesh an origin not from the Father but from the "very and eternal" Son!

To obtain a just understanding of the introduction to John's Gospel it will be necessary to read with attention the Epistles by the same writer. They will, we doubt not, amply confirm the view that the Father only is God and Jesus Christ is truly his Son. Of one verse in the first Epistle the general reader must have a care. The seventh verse of the fifth chapter was not written by John, but was in some unknown way interpolated into the sacred text between three hundred and four hundred years ago. The motive we do not assign, but of its effect it can surely be said that the counterfeit has been a chief prop to the popular belief of the Trinity. The recently Revised Version omits it, for of late years its character has become increasingly bad; though there are those who regret the expunction of so handy a witness to the great leading dogma.

The Third Episcopal Article states that during the brief interval between the death and resurrection of Jesus "he went down into hell," meaning not the grave, nor that invisible state which was called by the ancient Greeks "Hades" and the Hebrews "Sheol," but the place of perpetual torment and everlasting despair, scripturally designated "Ge-Hinnom," or "Gehenna," and occasionally, Tophet. Bishop Pearson, an honored light of the English Episcopal Church, speaks as follows in his Exposition of the Creed: "1st. The soul of Christ, really separated from his body by death, did truly pass unto the places below where the souls of men departed were. I conceive the end for which he did so was that he might undergo the condition of a dead man as well as of a living. He appeared here in the similitude of sinful flesh, and went into the other world in the similitude of a sinner. In the interim between death and resurrection there is nothing left, at least known to us, but to satisfy the law of death. This he undertook to do, and did. 2d. By the descent of Christ into hell all those which believe in him are secured from descending thither; he went unto those regions of darkness that our souls might never come into those torments which are there. By his descent he freed us from our fears, as by his ascension he secured us of our hopes. He passed to those habitations where Satan hath taken up possession and exerciseth his dominion, that having no power over him, we might be assured that he should never exercise any over our souls departed as belonging to him. * * * Because there was no sin in Christ, and he had fully satisfied for the sins of others, which he took upon him, therefore as God suffered not His Holy One to see corruption, so he left not his soul in hell, and thereby gave sufficient security to all those who belong to Christ of never coming under the power of Satan, or suffering in the flames prepared for the devil and his angels."

Such is an exposition of the article, but it is questionable whether the subject had not better be left in that silence which is observed towards it in the Apostles' Creed, as that creed was in its original and authentic shape before it was meddled with by Nicenist fingers at the provincial council of Aquileia, A. D. 381. In this view this much may be said, that when the Saviour gave up the ghost upon the cross he commended his spirit into his Father's hands. Can we identify the going into the Father's hands with a descent into the pit that is bottomless? Again, to the penitent and believing thief on his cross, Jesus said, "To-day shalt thou be with me in Paradise." We have no disposition to protrude any solution or explanation of our own in the matter. *Non nobis componere lites.*

The Fourth Article professes firm faith in Christ's resurrection and reassumption of the body complete in all its parts; with which body he subsequently ascended into heaven, where he now sits and will sit until he shall come to execute a final judgment upon the whole human race, not because he is God, but for the very reason that he is man. (John, 5: 27.) In connection with this article it may not be inappropriate to call to mind that the Christ who thus ascended was, by his own declaration, (Luke,

24:39), "he, himself," and not a mere spirit, but an organized human being, capable of audible speech, of eating and drinking, of being touched and handled, and of being seen by the eyes of men, like any other material body, when he was taken up from the mount called Olivet, a short distance east of Jerusalem. It can further be said, on the irrefragable testimony of the Word of God, that Jesus was not only seen by human eyes in the act of ascending up on high, but has been seen since, even when in heaven itself; seen there as "the Son of man," "standing on the right hand of God." (Acts, 7: 55 and 56.) Believers in the Trinity may have reason to ask their theologues how it came to pass that Stephen, in beholding through the opened heavens "the glory of God," did not, like Dr. Watts in his "Sight of Christ," discern "the Almighty Three"? The Holy Ghost, as appears by the sacred record, was at the time down in Stephen's heart, inspiring it with spiritual supports, whilst the martyr saw up in the celestial realm, not God, indeed, but "the glory of God, and the Son of man standing on the right hand of God," a separate object of vision. No such person or being as "God-the-Son" was anywhere descried. No such person was there.

Stephen's account of what, for more sakes than his, he was granted to see in that heavenly home of bliss and glory, cannot be placed on the credit side of Nicenism. The testimony against Nicenism is ocular and direct—in fact, irresistible.

Nor does Stephen's personal evidence stand alone upon the face of the Scripture record. The great-souled Paul, the Apostle of the Gentiles, who preached the gospel not after man, for he did not receive it from man, neither was taught it, but by the revelation of Jesus Christ,—the mighty Paul has also furnished us with an interior view of celestial circumstances. He describes how he had been caught up to the third heaven, into Paradise, where he heard unspeakable words which it was not lawful for him to utter. He tells us, elsewhere, probably from his personal knowledge, that within the city of the Living God, the heavenly Jerusalem, there dwell an innumerable company of angels. That there is in it the general assembly and church of the first-born, who are written in heaven; God the Judge of all, and the spirits of just men made perfect. There is Jesus, the mediator of the new covenant, and the blood of sprinkling, that speaketh better things than the blood of Abel.

Does Paul tell of any Trinity in Paradise? Not a syllable about it. He speaks of God, the Judge of all—one God and no more; of Jesus, in no respect as God or a part of God, but as the mediator of the new covenant, which only mediator he describes (1st Tim., 2: 5) as "the man Christ Jesus." We may hence securely conclude that there is no Trinity either in heaven or in the Bible, and no where else save in creeds, the work of ill-advised men in wrong-headed and demoralized times. That a crowd of very fallible men, having the priceless treasure of the Old and New Testaments and the excellent compendium of the Apostles' creed within their reach, should assume to set up a counter-creed and compel devotion to it under peril of loss of liberty and life, amply justifies the condemnation of them and their work to the censure of right-minded men as long as the human race shall endure.

Article Fifth, which says that "The Holy Ghost, proceeding from the Father and the Son, is of one substance, majesty and glory with the Father and the Son, very and eternal God."

We have Christ's conclusive testimony that the Holy Ghost "proceedeth from the Father," (John, 15: 26,) and is sent by the Father in Christ's name, and as all the divine agencies relating to salvation were at the period of the consummation of Christ's earthly ministry given unreservedly into his hands (Matt., 26: 18), the Fifth Article is not to that extent unscriptural, if it be concurrently understood that the Holy Ghost not only proceeds from—but originates with—the Father, and that in the Son it is only derivative. The Nicene creed, which was commenced at the council of Nice in the year 325, but was not completed till the year 381 by the council of Constantinople, defined, under the decision of two ecumenical, or general, councils, the Holy Ghost as "proceeding from the Father." This was the accepted belief of the Christendom, so called, of that day and for an indefinite number of years thereafter, but history informs us that in the fifth and sixth centuries more or fewer of the Spanish churches added the words *filioque*, meaning "and from the Son," and were followed in this by most of the Gallican, or French, churches. The matter was discussed in the council of Gentilly, near the city of Paris, in the year 767. Though the Latin churches were generally favorable to the interpolation, the Greeks angrily antagonized it as being not only surreptitious but, doubtless, a misrepresentation of the truth. In the early part of the next century the dispute broke out afresh and so hotly that the Emperor Charlemagne was requested to interfere. Councils were held in France and at Rome itself in the presence of Pope Leo the Third. The Pope decided, somewhat amusingly, that whilst the words *filioque* were interpolated and ought to be omitted from the creed, they still spoke the truth. The final result was that the interpolation was retained in the Roman or western branch of the church, and so we have it at this day and in this country in Article Fifth of the Protestant Episcopal Church, as well as in the creeds and confessions of most of the other churches. The Greek churches throughout the east of Europe and elsewhere retain the creed as delivered at Constantinople in the year 381. One of the chief grounds of dissension between the Greek and Roman branches of the Nicene profession was this same interpolation, and it helped largely towards their final disseverment. Thus what was designed for a bond of union proved a pregnant cause of lasting separation.

We have not, at this distance from the era of those contentions, any fully satisfactory account of the reasons which influenced the Greek Nicenists in their view of confining the procession of the Spirit to the Father only. They might have thought, and it would seem justly, that as the Holy Ghost was announced in the gospels to have been the paternal originator of Christ's being, it would wear a very unreasonable and unscriptural appearance to declare that the parent proceeded from the offspring! Yet so said the Romanists, and so echo most of the Protestant creeds and churches of our freer and more enlightened day.

It is pretty clear that this Fifth Article was prepared with little or no reference to the Scriptures, but with a view to conformity with the articles that precede it. What Christ was and is as to *substance* we have already heard upon his own decisive authority. He was truly a "substance," "a glorious body" (Philipp., 3: 21), and not a spirit in its accepted sense. The Holy Ghost is *not* substance, but spirit only, of which the very name gives evidence. The Son and the Holy Ghost cannot, therefore, be of "one substance."

The Holy Ghost, being the Spirit of God himself, necessarily partakes of God's supreme "majesty and glory." The Son, as the celestially dignified and glorious Lord his followers will ever delight to confess him, was yet seen by Stephen standing apart from "the glory of God." Paul also advertises us that when we confess Christ to be

"Lord" (Philipp., 2:11) we must do it "to the glory of God the Father."

The Sixth Article applauds the Holy Scriptures as "containing all things necessary to salvation," prompting the inquiry, Why, then, do you frame compulsory creeds and formularies out of the mandates of assemblages of uninspired men, tinctured with not a few ideas and notions that if originated at this day would consign them to general pity or contempt? Why paint the lily, or the rose, or attempt to refine pure gold, as the churches have done in a religious sense times without number almost ever since the days of the Apostles? The new doctrines and systems that have been propounded must have been to alter, either by addition or subtraction, the written Word of God; in either case, and still more in both, the efforts were criminal, and the result divinely condemned in advance.

Many things that the Nicene churches teach are neither read in the Scriptures nor can be honestly proved thereby; they should not, therefore, be required of any man as articles of faith, much less be thought necessary to salvation. Speaking of the period when the Nicene creed was framed under the auspices of the Emperor Constantine, the distinguished Neander, the historian of the Christian church, says that "with the year 325 Christian history closed, and Church history began."

The Seventh Episcopal Article speaks of "Christ as the only mediator between God and man, being both God and man." It is undoubtedly read in Scripture that Christ is the "one mediator between God and man," but in vain will any one seek for a single syllable that will justify the allegation that Christ is "both God and man." The statement is totally unsustained. Contrariwise, the Apostle to the Gentiles distinctly testifies in his first Epistle to Timothy (2:5) that the "one mediator" is simply "the *man* Christ Jesus." Now it so happens that the phraseology of that text is peculiar, and found nowhere else in the whole Bible. What, then, could have possessed the framers of the article to hazard a statement so directly in contradiction of the Apostolic declaration, and at the same time so readily exposed? Why make an averment that one opening of the New Testament would disprove?

The phrase "God-man" is one of those expressions much in vogue among Nicenists, consisting, like "Trinity" and "Incarnation," of a mingling of the unscriptural and the impossible. Properly, then, what is meant by the word "God-man"? It is taken to mean a supposed being compounded of God and man—part one and part the other. Where now, in point of fact, in the heavens, or the earth, or the waters under the earth, where in the wide universe outside of Nicenism or the older mythology, has such a prodigy been actually witnessed? From beginning to end of the Bible not a thought is entertained of any such incompatible entity, though, if there really were such, there would be no place from Genesis to Revelations where he could be more appropriately introduced than in 1st Timothy, 2:5. Mediating between God and men, it might look as if he should partake of the nature of both, (and that is the notion of the article,) but, when quitting fancy, we address ourselves to truth and fact, the "one mediator" is by nature and revelation simply "man." But some may still ask, How could Christ be suited for the office of mediator if he did not possess a nature in common with both the covenanting parties, God and man? The answer is, That Christ's mediatorship does not rest upon his being part deity and part humanity, but upon that unblemished righteousness and holiness which link him to God. Not nature, but character and spirit is the bond of union between God and Christ. Christ's being always led by the Spirit of God made him the Son of God. The writer to the Hebrews, quoting prophetically concerning Christ, says: "Thou hast loved righteousness and hated iniquity; therefore God, thy God, hath anointed thee with the oil of gladness above thy fellows." Therefore; for that reason; viz., the loving righteousness and hating iniquity. Who does not perceive that this view is far higher and more ennobling than the extravagant and unscriptural figment of a God-man?

The testimony of the Bible, without which we care not to move a step, is ample on this head, though we have only space for a very small part of it. In describing himself, Christ never claimed to be a God-man. His disciples and all the Jews, his contemporaries, regarded him as by nature a man, a "teacher come from God, for," said Nicodemus, "no man can do these miracles that thou doest except God be with him," in which sense Christ was the Emmanuel, or token of the divine presence. Arguing against the maliciously hostile Jews, Christ said of himself (John, 8:40): "But now ye seek to kill me, a *man* that hath told you the truth which I have heard of God." On the memorable day of Pentecost, when the Holy Ghost was visibly vouchsafed to an extent never before or since, the leading Apostle, Peter, lifted up his inspired voice and announced to the assembly of apostles and disciples—and to us and the people of all time—that "Jesus of Nazareth, a *man* approved of God among you by miracles and wonders and signs which God did by him in the midst of you, as ye yourselves also know, ye have taken and by wicked hands have crucified and slain; whom God hath raised up and made both Lord and Christ." It required no more than a human nature, or rather, that was exactly what *was* required, in conjunction with unsullied righteousness in heart and life, to befit Jesus for a dignity surpassing all the magnates of the earth, viz., the Lord of the redeemed, here and hereafter, and the anointed Christ of God. Into his name and faith three thousand of the people were then and there baptized.

On an occasion not long after, Peter declared that Jesus was a prophet like unto Moses, whom nobody ever supposed to be other than a man. Still again (Acts, 4: 10 to 12) Jesus Christ of Nazareth is proclaimed to all the people of Israel as the one out of whom there can be no salvation, "for," said Peter, "there is none other name under heaven given among men whereby we must be saved." In Acts 5: 28 Jesus is shown to have been preached and understood at Jerusalem by the Jewish priests and people as a man, in whose name and doctrine the Apostles taught. The Apostle Paul, when addressing the Athenians from Mars hill, declared that he by whom God will judge the world in righteousness is "that man" whom God has for that purpose ordained. In Paul's masterly Epistle to the Romans (5: 15) he teaches that God's gracious gift of redemption comes through the medium of "one man, Jesus Christ,"—not by reason of Christ's being God, in whole or in part, but because of the "righteousness" and "obedience" of that one man through the continual indwelling in him of the Divine Spirit, imparted "not by measure." It was Christ's moral quality, and not the impressed constitution of his nature, that gave him his lofty place in the counsels and purposes of the Most High. "Since by man came death, by *man* came also the resurrection of the dead; for as in Adam all die, even so in Christ, the second and spiritual Adam, shall all be made alive. But every *man* in his own order: *Christ* the first fruits, afterwards *they that are Christ's* at his coming," meaning that Christ and they that are Christ's are alike human. Nor will this lofty moral excellence be always confined to the man Christ only, for, by the goodness of God, they who are in a condition to "receive abundance of grace and of the gift of righteousness shall reign in life by one, Jesus Christ." (Also Rev., 3: 21.) We therefore see how very unfounded is the idea which prevails in Nicenist teachings, that it is "the presence of the divine nature in Christ's person which gives infinite worth and efficacy to his sacrifice," so that the question presents itself whether the Christ of Nicenism is not a merely imaginary being, and not the true Christ of the Bible, the human offspring of the Spirit of God and the pure young woman of Nazareth? And, as a corollary, might not an unreal Christ involve, to a greater or less extent, an unreal Christianity? Professors of Nicenist doctrines seem to be generally reaching after the substance, essence, matter, or nature (*ousia*) in God and in Christ, whereby they lose the infinitely more profitable moral and spiritual considerations with which we have really almost all to do. Human investigations into the divine nature, as considered apart from the divine character, must be inevitably fruitless. That divine nature is an infinite deep, which no human plummet can sound. Is it not irreverent as well as foolish to attempt, by mortal searching, to find out God? And is it much less of a fatuity to allege, concerning the person of Christ, a state of things about which the scriptures have nothing to say except to contradict it? As to who and what Christ is, we shall surely err if we depart from the plain and positive declarations of the Bible. The philosophy of his constitution must arise directly out of the facts vouchsafed chiefly in the gospels, and must not grow out of analogies hypothetically drawn from the order of common nature. The Spirit of God is the instrument of the will of God, and that will is subject to no analogies, but is absolutely and for ever supreme. "With God all things are possible." It was His will to originate a new creation with Christ for the "second man," the "last Adam," the spiritual progenitor of the everlasting age; so that Christ was none the less human because the Spirit of God, "the power of the Highest," furnished his parentship. Whatever, from a worm to an archangel, it is the will of God to produce, His Spirit can originate. He willed Christ to be man, and a man he was. (Refer in particular to Hebrews 5: 7, 8, and 9.)*

---

* Paul suffered persecution because he preached "Christ crucified." (Gal., 5: 11.) The "offense of the cross" interfered seriously with conversions to Christianity, especially from Judaism. It was a forbidding trial with many to pass forward and onward from Moses to Christ, with the indelible recollection of the latter's ignominious fate. Even before the crucifixion, the haughty Pharisees said, "We know that God spake unto Moses, but as for this (Jesus), we know not whence he is." Utterly unrighteous and unjustifiable as was the infliction of death upon the great

There is another Nicenist phrase which is quite common, and is found in the Second Article, that God-the-Son (for it must have been a being anterior to Jesus Christ) "took man's nature upon him." The indulgence in language implying that one kind of being has taken or may take upon it the nature of beings of another kind, as if it were little more difficult than an exchange of coats or cloaks, may be allowed as a verbal *divertissement*, but cannot be accepted as a practical reality. It involves considerations beyond any human mastery.

If it were meant to say that Christ, like ourselves, was a participant of human nature, there could be no objection, for that will be both intelligible and scriptural, especially if it be understood at the same time that neither Christ nor ourselves could possess any prior choice as to what we were or are to be, and the only choice in the matter lies with our common Maker. But Nicenism does not say that. It undertakes to assert that the God-the-Son of its creed, and not the Holy Ghost, was the male parent of Jesus; and not only so, but that he designedly became his own child, or, at all events became indissolubly united in person with his own child, leaving, as we have already remarked, God the Father quite apart and unrelated to Jesus nearer than as a grandparent. Familiarity with the notions of ancient heathen mythology may smooth the way for the reception of, or rather acquiescence in, transformations from divinity to humanity, or even to animality, but with all whose bed-rock of religion is Bible-doctrine, such metamorphoses pass for nothing. We may give no place in our minds to the grossness of Jupiter, Neptune and Pluto, the Pagan three; nor set value on the avatars or incarnations of Vishnu, or Crishna, the most active and important of the Hindoo Triad, Brahma, Vishnu and Siva, yet ideas energize the teachings and writings of Nicenist theologians which, not being properly derivable from the pages of the Hebrew and

---

Benefactor, for which the Jewish nation were alone responsible, it still wore a public and official stamp, and this had a strong effect upon numerous Jewish people in the succeeding age or two, keeping them from embracing and professing the Christian faith. We cannot but suppose that the same recollection carried much weight with the confluent masses of Gentiles of a hundred names in the following two or three centuries, and that it had a repellent effect upon their minds. Without justifying, this might go far to account for, the adoption of the policy by certain of the cotemporary Christian leaders of declaring Christ to be more than human, and substantially divine—lifting him, in fact, out of what he is, in the plain and simple Apostles' creed, into the glittering refulgence with which the Nicene composition surrounds him. This scheme has surely had its sufficient sway. Let us, then, return to the wiser sobriety of gospel truth.

Christian scriptures, bear hardly deniable marks of ethnic and, especially, Hindoo origin.

We are told, too, that, speaking of Christ, "two whole and perfect natures were joined together in one person." This statement, when we attempt to realize its meaning, is found none of the easiest. Not that there is any difficulty in understanding how two distinct objects can be united into one organism, for that is common enough in the world; but then there is always some approach, more or less perfect, to equality in the two objects. In the alleged case of the two natures in Christ no such equality can be predicated. Christ's person does not appear to have exceeded the limits of ordinary personality, yet according to the aforesaid dogma that personality comprises the infinity which more than fills the universe with its countless millions of suns and attending planets and satellites, far the greater part of which has never yet glimmered into human vision. Can infinity and a speck be joined together in a speck? Astounding, if true; yet, while reason is staggered, it is utterly unknown to the Bible.

Neither does our knowledge of the universe, of this world, or of God's Word, furnish a syllable about one kind of being "assuming," or joining with, the nature of another kind of being. Every being in the universe, we may reverently include even the Ineffable Creator, and every one of His creatures, is what he or she is, either by original constitution or by divine ordination, and that nature once appointed remains forever. Every something and somebody that we see or have knowledge of is itself, himself or herself, and not something or somebody else. To this effect the Apostle Paul, in his revelation of the last things, quite pointedly speaks: "All flesh is not the same flesh; but there is one kind of flesh of men, another flesh of beasts, another of fishes, and another of birds. There are also celestial bodies and bodies terrestrial; but the glory of the celestial is one and the glory of the terrestrial is another. There is one glory of the sun and another glory of the moon and another glory of the stars; for one star differeth from another star in glory." He refers all to God, who has given to every several existence such body or constitution as it has pleased Him, and to every body its own proper constitution. Similarly, (Ecclesiastes, 3: 14,) "I know," says the Preacher, "that whatsoever God doeth it *shall be forever;* nothing can be put to it, nor anything taken from it; and God doeth it that man should fear before Him." A single thought remains: Can it be possible that whilst God has made so fixed and immutable the works of his hands, that considerable part of Himself which Nicenism claims God-the-Son to be should have been so subject to change as from one nature to become *two*, and to re-enter heaven after the date of Christ's resurrection a differently constituted being from what he had previously been from all eternity? If God the Father, God the Son, and God the Holy Ghost had been always equal before, that equality must have been disturbed when the "two whole and perfect natures were joined together in the one person" of God-the-Son. Deity then comprehended two natures where previously it had but one. It was no longer "one substance."

The Eighth Episcopal Article declareth after this wise, that "The Nicene creed and that which is commonly called the Apostles' creed ought thoroughly to be received and believed: for they may be proved by most certain warrants of Holy Scripture."

Our Saviour, who well knew what was in man, hesitated not to strike at that tendency which is apt to pervade men in high ecclesiastical authority to control the minds of the common people by proposing codes and systems favorable to their own views and purposes. He quotes the prophet Isaiah as speaking for God against such, and saying (Mark, 7:6 to 13) "In vain do they worship me, teaching for doctrines the commandments of men." Now, if the Old and New Testaments were deficient in lessons that teach what is requisite for human faith and practice, there might be justifying reasons why the want should be supplied from human sources, but since "all scripture given by inspiration of God is profitable for doctrine, for reproof, for correction and instruction in righteousness, to the end that the man of God may be perfect, thoroughly furnished unto all good works," it would appear to be neither necessary nor wise to leave those holy, safe, and sufficient precincts for the superfluous devices of men. Such devices, notwithstanding any pretensions they might set up, may be intended rather to supersede than to assist scripture,—which, by the way, can work its course without such assistance. The Nicene creed, for which the Church of England and her daughter, the Protestant Episcopal Church of the United States, testify in terms of the strongest commendation, was not constructed till one-quarter of the fourth century after Christ had passed away. It was not even then finished but was put upon the anvil of the council or synod of Constantinople over fifty years after, or within twenty years of the beginning of the fifth century, and there received its finishing stroke, except, that in order to get it as now read in the prayer books, it was made to carry an interpolation fabricated by some of the churches of Spain, and then continued by the whole Latin Church, though always resisted by the Greek and Eastern churches. The Nicene creed takes its name from the place of its birth at Nicæa, or Nice, in Bithynia, not far from the city of Constantinople, out of an assembly of three hundred and eighteen bishops sent on a call from the Roman Emperor Constantine to meet there in his palace in the year 325. The especial object of the meeting was to attempt a settlement of the differences that had arisen in the Church of Alexandria, in Egypt, between two of its clergy, Athanasius and Arius, as to the nature and dignity of Christ. Athanasius contended for the deity of Christ as being equal to the deity of the Father; Arius held that while Christ was the most distinguished and glorious of all derived beings, far above angels and archangels, he was still second to the Father from whom he had sprung. Our information relative to the behavior of the members and the general circumstances of the council is but meagre, yet enough seems to be known to show that the proceedings were considerably tumultuous and disorderly, with no little violence and cruelty in its decisions, which were unfavorable to Arius and his friends. For differing with the majority they were condemned to banishment, and threatened with death in case they continued to promulgate their opinions.

Instead of referring for a right settlement of the controversy to the teachings of the Word of God in the Bible, the council undertook to erect a standard of its own in the shape of an authoritative creed. In constructing this it availed itself of the long-enjoyed popularity of a compendious confession of Christian faith, called the Apostles' creed, though perhaps not with absolute accuracy. The council took the outline of this time-honored summary as the pattern for its own; but by filling in with garish and extravagant expressions, the new product came forth rather a travesty and perversion. If we read the Apostles' creed as the Nicene council found it, and compare it with the subsequent Nicence production, the truth of this will appear. The Apostles' creed originally ran thus: "I believe in God the Father Almighty, and in Jesus Christ his only Son our Lord, who was conceived by the Holy Ghost, born of the Virgin Mary, suffered under Pontius Pilate, was crucified and buried: the third day he rose from the dead.

He ascended into heaven and sitteth on the right hand of the Father; from thence he shall come to judge the quick and the dead. I believe in the Holy Ghost, the holy church, the forgiveness of sins and the resurrection of the body. Amen."

The Nicene creed is after this wise:

"I believe in one God, the Father Almighty, maker of heaven and earth, and of all things visible and invisible;

"And in one Lord Jesus Christ, the only begotten Son of God, begotten of his Father before all worlds; God of God, Light of Light, very God of very God, begotten, not made, being of one substance with the Father; by whom all things were made; who, for us men and our salvation came down from heaven and was incarnate by the Holy Ghost of the Virgin Mary and was made man, and was crucified also for us under Pontius Pilate. He suffered and was buried; and the third day he rose again, according to the scriptures, and ascended into heaven, and sitteth on the right hand of the Father; and he shall come again with glory to judge both the quick and the dead; whose kingdom shall have no end.

"And I believe in the Holy Ghost, the Lord and giver of life; who proceedeth from the Father; who with the Father and Son together is worshipped and glorified; who spake by the prophets. And I believe one Catholic and Apostolic Church. I acknowledge one baptism for the remission of sins; and I look for the resurrection of the dead and the life of the world to come. Amen."

It will be noticed that the Apostles' creed is a plain, concise statement of the principal articles of the Christian's faith, no one of which can be dispensed with. Some have supposed, and with probability, that it was constructed for use in baptisms as an expansion and exposition of Christ's purpose in the command Matt., 28:19, which was a quite proper and congenial duty for Apostles to perform. There is nothing in the creed which is out of conformity with the preaching and writings of the Apostles. We may therefore accept its several particulars as authentic truths, and the creed as a whole for satisfactory testimony relative to what *was* and what was *not* the belief of the Apostles themselves. It evidently comprises the general, that is to say, the catholic, belief for the most of all the time from the Apostolic era in the first century to a good distance into the fourth century, or almost three hundred years. Nicenist authority reports that what was called "Monarchianism" "was the ruling principle" of the popular faith, and that it held "vigorously and formally to the unity of God," even though there might be wide differences upon other points.

From expressions dropped by prominent parties in those ages the inference is just that they felt it necessary to have some other foundation than the Bible and the Apostles' creed for the new faith they had devised. Thus Athanasius, the champion and chief constructor, declared that the Homoonsion, or Trinity, "was the only true foundation for the absoluteness of the Christian religion." And the council of Ephesus, convened by the Emperor Theodosius the Second, and held in A. D. 449, looked upon the "Nicene creed as the only and immutable foundation of orthodox doctrine;" in other words, it looked upon the gaudy epithets which the council of Nice had foisted into the frame-work imitated from the Apostles' creed as the "only foundation of orthodox doctrine." To be sure, this council of Ephesus was not a remarkably reputable body as to order and decency of behavior, for it got the title of the "Robber Council" from the scandalous and even murderous scenes presented there; yet its loyalty to "orthodoxy," as Athanasianism or Nicenism delights to be called, was never questioned.

The Apostles' creed follows the gospels in ascribing the origin of Christ's being to the miraculous agency of the Holy Ghost at a definite point of time, being utterly silent, like the gospels, about any pre-existence of either Christ's body, soul, or spirit. The Nicene creed, on the other hand, asserts Christ to have been "begotten of the Father before all worlds," that is, from all eternity, which, as there is no divinely authenticated history of what took place "before all worlds," the Nicene assembly promulgated conjecturally, or as guess-work, upon their own responsibility.

The Apostles' creed adheres to the New Testament in naming Christ as "Lord," but the Nicene outstrips all records and lifts Jesus higher than to the highest honors of deity, calling Him "God of God," "Light of Light," "very God of very God, begotten, not made, being of one substance with the Father"—all upon its own dogmatic assertion.

The Nicene next says that "Christ came down from heaven and was incarnate by the Holy Ghost of the Virgin Mary, and was made man." But this is not consonant with the Second Article of the Protestant Episcopal Church, which latter does not include any agency of the Holy Ghost in producing the incarnation, needing no other interposition than that of God-the-Son. It must be confessed that the aid of the Holy Ghost, whilst God-the-Son is present "in his whole and perfect nature," appears to be entirely superfluous; besides which, no explanation is furnished of the procedure whereby the Holy Ghost effects by his own action on the person of Mary an incarnation of a third object, God-the-Son, distinct from both. There certainly seems to be one paternal agent too many, producing a very complicated result upon the statement in the creed. From all this the Apostles' creed stands clear.

Alluding to Christ's kingdom, the Nicene creed says: "Whose kingdom shall have no end." It is presumed that the creed here refers to Christ's *mediatorial* kingdom. If that be so, a greater than Athanasius, speaking by the Holy Ghost, states that after certain happenings, "then cometh the end, when Christ shall have delivered up the kingdom to God, that is, the Father; when he shall have put down all rule and all authority and power; for he must reign till he hath put all enemies under his feet. But when he saith all things are put under him, it is manifest that He is excepted who did put all things under him. And when all things shall be subdued unto him, then shall the Son also himself be subject unto Him that put all things under him, that God may be *all* in *all.* Christ's mediatorial kingdom, very durable as it will most likely be, will therefore, nevertheless, "have an end."

If the Nicene had stated that in the redeemed and perfected world, which is to follow the present probationary state, the Lord Jesus would be king over the whole earth for ever and ever, it would have asserted a profound Scripture doctrine and undoubted truth. Christ will be Lord and king forever over this restituted globe; vice-gerent under the One God of the universe.

In the second paragraph of the creed as generally printed, it is read that the Holy Ghost "proceedeth from the Father and the Son." For the last three words the Nicene council is not responsible, as before shown. They were first appended by some of the Spanish churches, which seem to have had an early bias for extravagant and unscriptural notions, and have held to them ever since.

So much for the Nicene creed; what have Nicenist writers testified about its authors? "The council was gathered at the instance of the Emperor Constantine, who was much annoyed and puzzled by the discussions of the Christians among his subjects, by their perpetual squabbles about doctrines, and the fanatical hatreds thereby engendered. In the Roman Empire the most different religions lived peacefully beside each other, and here was a religion which could not live in peace with itself. For political reasons, however, unity and harmony were necessary, and in A. D. 325 the emperor convened a council at Nice to settle the dispute between Athanasius and Alexander on the one hand and Arius and his followers of the same city on the other. The council consisted of 318 bishops, selected by their superiors, the metropolitans and patriarchs, out of about 1900 bishops then in the empire. Its president was Hosius of Corduba, in Spain, but the emperor generally attended the sessions in person. It was the first time that the Christian church and the Roman state met each other face to face, and the impression was very deep on both sides. When the emperor stood there, among those 318 bishops, tall, clad in purple and jewels, with his peculiarly haughty and sombre mien, he felt disgusted at those coarse and cringing creatures who one moment scrambled sportively around him to snatch up a bit of his munificence, and the next moment flew madly into each other's faces for some incomprehensible mystery. The result of the council was, as before intimated, unfavorable to Arius and his friends, who would not consent to acknowledge that the Son was Omo-ousios, or of the *same identical* substance or material with the Father; though a portion of them were willing to grant that he was Omoi-ousios, or of a *similar* substance. The emperor, appearing much under the influence of Hosius, who adhered to the Athanasian party, decreed that all must comply with the decision of the majority, and henceforth believe and teach the creed as it had been drawn up, or submit to penal consequences, banishment and death. Arius refused, and was banished to Illyria, (the Botany Bay of those times,) his books were burnt, and his fellow-believers branded as enemies to Christianity. There was in the creed, as it came from the council, an anathema or condemnatory sentence. This anathema Eusebius of Nicomedia and Theognis of Nicæa would not sign. They were, therefore, deposed from their bishoprics and banished. Two Egyptian bishops, Theonas and Secundus, also refused to subscribe, and were sent to Illyria.

"After the council of Nice, Constantine conversed more and more frequently and intimately with the bishops, and his interest in Christianity grew with his years. Through his close intimacy with Eusebius, bishop of Cesarea, and the well-known historian of the early Christian church, Constantine was induced, about the year 328, to recall

Arius from banishment and to order his restoration to the Church of Alexandria. But this was strenuously resisted by Athanasius, who was, in consequence, himself banished to Gaul, or France, whilst Arius and his party were reinstated and received to the communion of the Church. The bulk, however, of the Christian people of Alexandria were partisans of Athanasius, and refused Arius a place among the presbyters, when in 336, Arius having had his faith approved by the synod of Jerusalem and one other city, the emperor invited him to Constantinople, and issued an order to Alexander, the bishop of that city, to admit him to his communion.

"On the Sunday appointed for the formal and full admission of Arius a procession was formed between the imperial palace and the church of the Apostles. In this procession the aged Arius, now in his 80th year, took his place, but when on the way was suddenly seized with an illness and compelled to step aside. Very soon a copious hemorrhage supervened; the smaller intestines and some parts of the liver and spleen passed from him, and death quickly closed the scene. His private and moral character were unimpeachable, but his antagonists declared his death to have been a judgment from heaven, whilst his friends regarded it as the result of poison administered by or through his sectarian foes. If poison, it must have been virulent in kind and probably large in amount. Athanasius is reported to have been among those who declared the death of Arius due to the special judgment of heaven. The conclusion of modern thought has been that Arius fell 'a victim to the resentment of his enemies, and was destroyed by poison, or some such violent method.'"

With regard to Constantine, he finally went over to the Arian opinions and was baptized not long before his death by the Arian bishop of Nicomedia. A Nicenist author of the present day remarks that Constantine's "conversion from Paganism to Christianity was a change of policy rather than of moral character. Long after that event he killed his son Crispus, his second wife, several other of his relatives and some of his most intimate friends, in passionate resentment of some fancied infringement of his rights. In his relation to Christianity he was cool, calculating, always bent upon the practically useful, always regarding the practically possible. He retained the office and title of Pontifex Maximus to the last, and did not receive Christian baptism until he felt death close upon him. He kept Pagans in the highest positions in his immediate surroundings, and forbade anything which might look like an encroachment of Christianity upon Paganism. With Christianity, not as a power of this world, he hardly ever came to understand it."

Returning now to the Eighth Article, we cannot but express surprise that two creeds, essentially antagonistic, should be declared provable "by most certain warrants of Holy Scripture." In the English Episcopal church service there is a third creed much longer and more elaborately wrought out than the Nicene, but to the same general effect. It goes by the name of the Athanasian creed, but is not rightly so called, for Athanasius never saw or heard of it. This creed was not in existence till some hundreds of years after the time of Athanasius. It was first written in Latin, whereas Athanasius spoke and wrote in Greek, and the methods of expression are not his. Some thirty years ago this creed was made the subject of earnest discussion in England, from which the conclusion seemed to be that the creed could not be traced higher up than the ninth century. Hilary, a bishop of Arelate, or Arles, in the southeast of France, a Nicene champion, was long thought to have been its author, but he seems to have lived much too early. The creed was not adopted at Rome till the middle of the tenth century. Its putative author, Athanasius, rightly called by his Nicenist disciples "the father of orthodoxy," was born a year or two before the beginning of the fourth century. He appears to have been a man of strong, overbearing temper, extremely tenacious of any purpose he had in view, eloquent and able, and endowed with popular talents which he exerted with effect among his own people. He suffered persecutions as he also countenanced them, but showed no excess of the milk of human kindness. He is described by a modern professor of his doctrines as "a man of one idea and one passion—the eternal divinity of Christ—which he considered the corner-stone of the Christian system." Taking his disciples at their word, it results that so-called "orthodoxy," the synonym of Nicenism, could not have originated till considerably within the fourth century after Christ. Thenceforward the church and her bishops triumphed over Christ and his Apostles for many following centuries.

We cannot wonder, then, that the simple scriptural teachings of the Apostles' creed were far too tame and unsophisticated for the demands of the high-strung theology abetted by Athanasius, nor that his ardent appetite craved some such above-proof results as he and his co-workers produced out of the laboratory at Nice. He is even imperious in his requirements upon the divine nature, for he considers that "the redemption and salvation of man *demand* that God has not only revealed himself to man through Christ, but has become man in Christ,—has been incarnated." Thus again it is seen how prone Gentile blood was to drop down into low and unworthy views of the divine nature. They inherited a propensity for believing in the metamorphosis of deity into humanity, and some of them—the Egyptians, for instance, of and among whom Athanasius was born—of deity into animality. Such, too, were the Hindoos with their "avatars" or incarnations of their gods, and especially of Vishnu, the second in the Hindoo triad. The Jews, on the contrary, profiting by their disciplinary sojourn in Babylon, were free from this taint. There were those of them that had their *cabala* full of grotesque and absurd fictions enough, yet they always maintained the most reverent distinction between the nature of the Uncreate and of the mortal. Even the Samaritans, close neighbors as they were of the Jews, had permitted so much idolatrous mixture into their religious ideas and services that the Saviour pronounced them to be "worshippers of they knew not what," in contrast with his own Jewish fellow-countrymen who *did* "know what they worshipped," and from among whom "salvation" was to arise.

The Fifteenth Article is as follows, so far as we can consider it: "Christ, in the truth of our nature, was made like unto us in all things, sin only excepted, from which he was clearly void both in his flesh and in his spirit. He came to be a lamb without spot, who, by the sacrifice of himself, once made, should take away the sins of the world; and sin (as St. John saith) was not in him."

Passing over the verbal discrepancy between this article and the Nicene creed—the one saying that Christ was "made" and the other that he was "begotten, *not* made" —we remark, that when similarity subsists between two objects, or sets of objects, each is like the other. If Christ was made like unto us in all things, sin only except," we are "made like unto Christ in all things" except as to sin. How does this agree with what is told us in the first, second, and other articles? It is therein declared that Christ is a person, consisting of "two whole and perfect natures, joined together never to be divided," and that one of these natures is "very God." Are we, as men, similarly composed of two distinct natures? Who, among the best of mankind, will pretend to be, in part, "very God," and so like unto Christ? Of course, nobody. Thus the alleged "likeness" fails at once, and in a most important respect, for "godhead" and "manhood" are essentially dissimilar. We are human *only*. Christ, say Nicenists, is *both* divine and human. The two are, therefore, on Nicene principles, extremely dissimilar—as dissimilar as they can be. The articles necessarily become self-contradictory. If, now, moreover, to the dissimilarity between Christ and mankind, (Nicenely speaking,) in that Christ is part divine and man is not, there be added the further very essential dissimilarity affecting both of Christ's natures, the result is that Christ is "like unto us" in *nothing* of real importance, instead of "in *all* things." It incidentally occurs to be remarked, just here, that if Christ was "made" sinless, his excellence therein was not spontaneous, and was in so far defective in merit, for he merely obeyed the law of his nature. He could not avoid being good. His sinlessness was automatic, and the merit of it goes back to his Maker.

The Fifteenth Article further says that Christ "came to be a lamb without spot," leaving it in doubt whether he came of his own will and motion, or was sent by another. The article appears to preponderate towards the former meaning, for it adds, as the object of his coming, that he "should, by the sacrifice of himself once made, take away the sins of the world." Upon this point Christ's own testimony is that he "came not of himself, but was sent by God." (Luke, 7: 28 and 29.) What Christ finally turned out to be he undoubtedly came to be, but he was not the author of his mission. That author was God his Father. Had Christ been the author of his own mission, his shrinking, though only momentary, from before the terrors which confronted him,(Matthew, 26: 39; Mark, 14: 35 to 41; Luke, 22: 42 to 44,) besides testifying to an inward frailty, would have betrayed a great falling-off in the designer of the more than nobly gigantic undertaking of a self-sacrifice for the sins of the world. It might have subjected him to the scorn of the universe. But Christ has never encountered the world's scorn ; on the contrary, the admiration, wonder, and praise of all mankind. And this has proceeded upon the understanding that Christ was not carrying out a design of his own, but was obeying to the letter the sovereign mandate of his heavenly Father. Christ did not send himself. (Luke, 4: 43.)

But there is another aspect of the case which is of paramount concern : The Holy Ghost, speaking through the mind and pen of the Apostle Paul, says (Heb., 4: 15) that "we have not a high priest which cannot be touched with the feeling of our infirmities, but was in all points tempted as we are, yet without sin." Nicenism says that this high priest is the God-man, part God, who, according to the Apostle James, "cannot be tempted of evil;" and part man, who, says Nicenism, was "made clearly void of sin both in the flesh and spirit," that is to say, the God-man was invulnerably protected; for as God he was untemptable; as man, impeccable. At what point, then, could he be so tempted as to be put in danger? Where in the close texture of his impregnability could he be "touched with the feeling of our infirmities so as to be in all points tempted as we are"? Through what crevice, suture, or spot could the keen and subtle apex of the tempter's spear impinge upon his sense? The God-man had no such crevice or opening; he was, therefore, untouched. Suppose for a moment that Adam and Eve had been so well defended; we have no reason to think they would ever have fallen.

Now, was such a being as the God-man a fair and suitable pattern or exemplar for tried, tempted, and exposed humanity, open to the more or less fierce assaults of the world, the flesh and the devil? Could there, in truth, be a being less fit and fair? Match a cripple, lame from birth and afterwards covered with festering sores, to contend for the prize of swiftness with a Dexter or Maud S, under the certainty in case of defeat of eternal damnation; you would have an equally just and righteous case of probation. If the God-man is set before us as an example to imitate, how could the best among us ever hope, not to equal, indeed, but to come within sight of him? Does such a being as the Nicenist God-man answer to the description in the Hebrews? He does not, but is essentially different. His innate, inherited perfection could not be touched with the feeling of human frailty so as to be affected by it as we are. If such an exemplar were offered us he would operate as a discouragement; the wisdom and justice of God would be open to arraignment, and the impossibility of imitating him would tend to justify failure and discourage efforts to be virtuous.

We conclude, then, that Jesus, the Christ of the New Testament, was not a God-man, in the Nicene sense. The appendage of the godhead constitutes the disqualification of the latter. It puts him out of the reach of human imitation and sympathy, for he would not be a proper subject for probation. Before starting in the race he would be already at the goal. The indispensable elements in a truly just exemplar must be the possibility of his going wrong joined with a mightier inward disposition to keep right. For this there must be a firm faith in and reliance upon God as Supreme lawgiver. This element must be in the soul either by intuition, or education, or direct gift. In due time there come the winds and storms of temptation to test its fixedness and strength, with the result either of overthrowing or of newly validating and fitting it for higher services and possibly more violent strains and endurance.

In what has been herein freely stated there will be nothing to ground an inference that Christ is regarded as a sinner such as we are, or a sinner at all. That he was sinless whilst most powerfully and severely tempted, constitutes one of the most valuable points of the real Christian faith. And it most deeply interests us to ask the reason for this. That reason lies in the fact that Christ kept the Holy Spirit of his Father perpetually resident in his soul, so as to be always under its guiding influence. When about to encounter the arch-enemy in that conflict in the wilderness he went "full of the Holy Ghost." He was "led by the Spirit;" yes, "driven" by it. After the struggle was over, Jesus "returned in the power of the Spirit into Galilee," and in his memorable first sermon at Nazareth he announced that "the Spirit of the Lord was upon him." So, throughout his whole life on earth, his body was a veritable temple of the Holy Ghost. On "the day on which he was taken up to heaven, after his resurrection, he gave commandments unto his Apostles through the Holy Ghost," promising them that best of gratuities, that they too should "be baptized with the Holy Ghost not many days hence." And even the "Revelation which God gave unto him" went forth unto the churches of Asia through the "sayings" of that "Spirit" which proceeded eternally from the Father.

As with Christ, so with his Apostles. When they first went forth they announced the "pouring out of the Spirit upon all flesh" that inappreciable "gift of the Holy Ghost." When Peter, the leader of the Apostles, spoke to the rulers of the people, he was "filled with the Holy Ghost," and so were all the "multitude of them that believed." (Acts, 4: 31.) Stephen, the first Christian martyr, "a man full of faith and the Holy Ghost," looked up thereby steadfastly into heaven and there beheld the glory of God, and Jesus standing on the right hand of God.

Here, then, is the great secret by which erring and sinful

humanity may become "like unto Christ." Besides a sincere and earnest desire to get the better of temptation to sin, and a hearty exertion of our own powers and opportunities to evade its assaults, there will be prayer and supplication for the most helpful aid of that Holy Spirit which was ever present with the Lord Jesus. There is an interesting recital of the operation of the Spirit in the tenth chapter of the first book of Samuel. One no better, we may suppose, than the general run of men, was suddenly changed in heart and transformed into another man. Saul had been instructed by the old prophet Samuel to do certain things. He obeyed, and the Scripture says, "that when Saul had turned his back to go from Samuel, *God gave him another heart*, and all those signs came to pass that day. And when they came thither to the hill, behold a company of prophets met him, and *the Spirit of God came upon him*, and he prophesied among them." It is not to be thought that in all, or perhaps in any, modern cases consequences of obedience to whatever is known to be right will be thus sudden and complete, yet God is as much present and just as near to every single one of *us* as he was to Saul. And faith and trust in God will, sooner or later, remove all mountains of difficulty and obstruction. Let us, then, "come boldly unto the throne of grace, that we may obtain mercy and find grace to help in time of need," and be filled with the Holy Ghost. "Ask and ye shall receive; seek and ye shall find; knock and it shall be opened unto you," for God giveth the Holy Spirit to them that in sincerity ask Him. To Christ, indeed, He gave it "not by measure."

The Nicene doctrines require us to acknowledge that the Lord Jesus Christ is "very and eternal God" and equal partaker with his Father of supreme divinity and glory. How then will it sound to reverent ears to hear the relation of a struggle, contest, or conflict between the "very and eternal God" on the one part, and Satan, the arch-fiend, on the other, lasting many days in the wilderness? But we proceed.

Two points suggest themselves in connection with the topics of the Fifteenth Article which need to be spoken of before closing. The first is to ask whether, on the supposition of Christ's inherent, and therefore involuntary, sinlessness and impeccability, the temptation in the wilderness would not lose most, if not the whole, of its genuineness and value? If Christ was untemptable as God and impeccable as man, was not the scriptural account of the conflict between him and Satan a mere illusory show, somewhat like what is called "a sham battle"? Against an opponent so panoplied as Christ is represented to have been, Satan's antagonism could amount to nothing. Just as much was known of the event before it occurred as afterwards, for Satan was no match for a combination of absolute perfection and impregnable sinlessness. Most surely, then, the Nicenist theory is inconsistent with the letter and spirit of the gospel history of Christ's temptation in the wilderness.

If, however, secondly, setting Nicenism aside, the conflict be regarded in the light of Christ's potential failure, it becomes a topic fraught with the most interesting moral and religious considerations. By his example through that successful struggle he taught mankind the inexpressible value of what we may designate muscular spirituality, or in all cases and to the last extremity grasping the principle of allegiance to the word and will of God. In those trying moments Christ's memory carried him back to those pithy commands in the book of Deuteronomy, delivered almost fifteen hundred years before to the Israelitish people when about to be established in the promised possession. They were guides for Israel; they were guides for Christ; they are guides for us and for the people of all times.

Let us now transfer our thoughts to that other scene of dread temptation a little before the close of the Saviour's sojourn upon the earth. His temptation was then through and through to the basis of his soul and being. Again he overcame; and *why?* Because of his loving faith in God. Even the unregenerate bystanders and witnesses of his passion saw and understood, at least in its outline, the active principle in the spirit of Christ. Said they, "He trusted in God." This unfailing trust was maintained by the steady indwelling of the Holy Ghost, that perpetual companion, Christ's solace and stay. All his life on earth it was with him, save perhaps during those anguished moments, "about the ninth hour," when he cried aloud with all the force his overtaxed nature could command, "My God, my God, *why* hast Thou forsaken me?" Perhaps, for we would not dogmatize, that visiting spirit was temporarily withdrawn, and Christ was left, as to his own apprehension he never had been before, *entirely alone.* Blessed be God, those moments of bereavement were not many, and Christ had become inherently strong.

In the earlier scenes of this last and sorest trial Christ's thoughts were not concentrated upon himself alone; they were shared by the best interests of his disciples. Though, in the consciousness of his being human, and therefore subject to temptation, he prayed most earnestly that the awful cup of bitter trial might be removed from him, yet, whilst the boiling waters of affliction were surging around him, he laid his hand upon the rock of his rest in God, that loving rest, and then exclaimed, "Nevertheless, not *my* will, but *Thine*, be done." At Gethsemane he imparted to his disciples a knowledge of the key by which alone they could escape from the moral and spiritual perils that environed them. "Pray," said he, "that ye enter not into temptation." Borne down by the strain upon their physical organization with weariness and sleep, they required again the admonition, "Watch and pray that ye enter not into temptation." He propounded to them what he exercised himself, and when the agony was at the direst his only resort was still more earnest prayer! Once more he urged upon his disciples the sorrowing question, "Why sleep ye? Rise and pray, lest ye enter into temptation."

During all this scene of unparalleled exigency and trial Christ fell not back upon the help of any deity indissolubly joined to him in the same person as "very and eternal God." He seems to have known of no such partner of his being, who, if he existed at all, must have been infinitely near him, the half of his very soul. Such an existence then, Christ, at the precise point and critical instant of his necessity, completely ignores, and confines his petitions to his Father alone. Why direct his cries and prayers to the God in heaven if there were a part of himself, so "joined to him as never to be divided," a God who was that Father's equal in power and every other divine attribute? Would it not involve a slight, a disrespect, an indignity towards that divine partner not to be expected of one so perfect and exact in the discharge of every, the slightest, demand upon him as Christ always was? Can there be more than one satisfactory answer to these queries, viz., that Christ was *not* joined in his nature with any divinity, and that he knew of no divinity in the universe save the One God, his Father, alone?

Last scene of all, the dying Saviour cries, "Father, into Thy hands I commend my spirit," and gave up the ghost. He spoke of but *one* spirit; yet Nicenism tells us of *two* natures in him, each "whole and perfect," requiring a spirit to each, and therefore two spirits for both. This is a great discrepancy. Who is right—the Saviour or Athanasius?

Inasmuch as the true Christian faith comprises an acknowledgment of the origination of Christ's body through the influence of the Divine Spirit taking the place of a human father, we are the farthest possible from denying that a very great advantage to Jesus himself, and to mankind as his beneficiaries, accrued therefrom. Untainted by the contamination of a long line of more or less sinning progenitors—as he would have been with the honest Joseph for a father—Christ was thus the first and founder of a new creation, fresh and pure from the being of God himself. The Divine Spirit having assumed the relation of an earthly father, it follows that Jesus, his direct offspring, could be no other than a "begotten son;" and because he was the *only* such offspring, he was unavoidably the "only-begotten Son of God." Then, as the child of the Holy Ghost, Christ was the first of a spiritual creation, as Adam was the first of the material creation; whence the exact propriety of Paul's reference to Christ as the "last Adam, a quickening spirit."

Now, then, there are within the scope of our cognizance two conditions of being—a material, derived from the first Adam; a spiritual, of which, on earth, Jesus Christ was the fountain or head.

Moreover, the material race of beings, having sinned and come short of the glory of God by reason of their disobedience to His will and law, fell obnoxious to the sentence against such, and so subject unto death, the advertised penalty for sin. On the other hand, the spiritual creation, through the obedience of its founder and head under every circumstance of trial and temptation, did, in his person, win its way through sorrow, suffering, and temporal death to life everlasting in glory ineffable.

What, then, did God for the race of Adam in bringing into existence such a one as Jesus Christ? God thereby gave the race of Adam an opportunity of leaving a condition terminating in sin and death, and of becoming engrafted into a state the tendency and end of which are holiness and life eternal. "For as in Adam all die, even so in Christ shall all be made alive." And, not to forestall what may properly follow hereafter, the entirely simple and rational way to this is to turn the back upon Adam and his propensities, and to take upon us the ideas and principles of Christ, or, as the scripture expresses it, to have "repentance towards God and faith towards the Lord Jesus Christ."

This process of leaving Adam and enlisting under Christ

is suitably denominated by Christ a "new birth," for all who become subjects to it practically enter a new world, with new prospects, new aims, new hopes, new fears, new affections, new dislikes, new associates; in a word, there are to them a new heaven and a new earth. "If any man" says the Apostle "be in Christ, he is a new creature; old things are passed away; behold all things are become new." This change from the spiritual dominion of sin and Satan is also called a "deliverance from the power of darkness, and a translation into the kingdom of God's dear Son."

In John 3: 2 Nicodemus freely acknowledged the divinity of the source of Christ's wonder-working power, "for," said he to Christ, "no man can do these miracles that thou doest except God be with him." Jesus offered no objection to this admission, but indicated that there was something beyond miracle-working, namely, dwelling in the kingdom of God, to which access could be gained only by a new birth of the spiritual part of man. Jesus gave Nicodemus to understand that he, the Son of man, was not only "a teacher come from God," or heaven, but was a dweller "in heaven," or the kingdom of God.

The notion which mistakingly prevailed in the latter part of the second century and during the succeeding centuries down to the present moment, that because Christ was truly called the "begotten Son of God," he was, therefore, and necessarily, constituted of the same substance, essence, or material as God himself, arose from the measuring of heavenly things by earthly ideas. Reading in the Bible of Christ's great exaltation and glory, it has been assumed by hasty inference that his nature must be greatly superior to the nature of men in general; in fact, nothing inferior to the nature of God himself. But this is erroneous. In Christ we behold human nature elevated to its true, its best condition. And that is exceedingly high in the scale of the universe, for it is made in the image of God. That image Christ always retained unsullied and unimpaired. The Epistle to the Hebrews places this very important matter in a just light. Christ, the Son of God, is therein described as God's appointed heir of all things; the brightness of God's glory and the express image of his person; more distinguished than the angels proportionately to the higher name than theirs which he has inherited, for besides that God never called an angel "Son," as He did Christ; He commanded the angels, when He brought Christ into the world, to be prostrate as they should to a Son of the Most High. And that world to come God has not subjected to the rule of angels, but to Jesus, who, though temporarily inferior to the angels because of his death, is now crowned with glory and honor, and become the captain of the salvation of many sons, *also* brought to glory. These "sons" Christ is not ashamed to call his "brethren," being like him, men, partakers of human flesh and blood, and framed in the image of God. This consists with what the martyr Stephen saw in heaven, namely, "Jesus, the Son of *man*, standing on the right hand of God." At the very outset of Christ's career he told Nathanael and Philip that they should "see the angels of God ascending and descending upon the Son of *man*." Thus we may estimate the exceeding loftiness of a perfect manhood dwelling in the peace of God.

The physiological circumstances of the generation of Jesus Christ, about which the "early fathers," and a great many since them, have wonderfully busied themselves, God has never seen fit to reveal—not even, perhaps, to archangels; though he has graciously condescended to supply us in the gospels with a mass of very precise information about Christ's parentage on both sides, for the sufficient intelligence and satisfaction of honestly-inquiring minds. But the manner of the production of the soul and mind of any being whatever is a God-preserved secret. Nor will any difficulty here present itself to any right-thinking intellect, for such will always joyfully acknowledge the absolute omnipotence of God, in that God is "able, out of the bare stones of the field, to raise up children unto Abraham." There is therefore nothing about the revealed statement of the origination of Christ that ought to tempt us beyond the simple New Testament record, or lead to the invention or adoption of extravagant or mystical theories, so as to bring us under the just censure of striving to be wise above what is written. It is a subject revealed in so far as divine goodness has seen fit to reveal it. To seek to penetrate beyond that would be foolish as well as impious.

RECAPITULATION.

We have thus passed in survey and examination the leading doctrines inculcated in the Articles of Religion of the Protestant Episcopal Church—an undertaking, by the by, that if attempted in England, the country of their formation, would, not many years ago, have subjected us to ecclesiastical censure and criminal prosecution under law and canons enacted, and never since repealed, in the reigns of Queen Elizabeth and King James the First. The articles of the Episcopal Church have not been thus selected because of any special dissent from or disapproval of the doctrines of that church more than of the doctrines of the several other churches that gather under the Nicene banner, but for the reason, chiefly, that its articles, so far as we have been able to consider them, comprise the dogmas generally entertained; are open and above-board, and very accessible. As an ecclesiastical organization, the Episcopal Church here, in the mother country, and in her colonies, is second to none in point of respectability, moral, mental, and mundane; and is well entitled to the very high consideration in which it is held the world over. It has done noble work for mankind at large, and will do yet more if, hereafter, it shall cast off the testaceous Nicene integument in which a semi-reformed Christianity encased it in the twilight times of Henry, Edward, and Elizabeth, and stand forth in that only true liberty wherewith Christ maketh men free.

We have seen that the birth of Nicenism was not blessed, for there came along with it bigotry, intolerance, and persecution within the church itself. It proclaimed *not* "peace on earth, goodwill to men." The Emperor Constantine originally intended nothing of a violent kind, but his associations with Alexander, Athanasius, with the Spanish Hosius, and like-minded ecclesiastics, soon implanted roots of bitterness which have overspread the greater part of the earth, and may yet require ages to eradicate. Nor were the Athanasians alone to blame, for their Arian opponents, if a faint trace or two less remote from the truth of the scriptures, were but too ready, when opportunity offered, for reprisals and vengeance. The great mistake laid in bringing theological differences for settlement before a tribunal of state. The emperor's proper course was to insist on public order, and that if the contending sectarists could not agree in thought, they should agree to differ. They would thereby have learnt the lesson of toleration, at least.

If Constantine was harsh and severe, the performances of the Spaniard, Theodosius, who followed him in the empire about the year 379, were revolting. He quaffed full draughts of Nicene bigotry, though but for that he might have been a moderate and benignant ruler. In the case of a seditious outbreak at Antioch, he exhibited a forgiving disposition, but at Thessalonica, where he had often and long resided, he caused to be slaughtered many thousands of people who had been treacherously enticed to witness the games at the public circus. For three hours the bloody work went on by the hands of barbarian troops; no questions were asked as to who were citizens and who were strangers; old and young; male and female; guilty or innocent; all were subjected to the destroying sword. It is true that there were in Thessalonica those who merited the punishment due to the cruel murders of a favorite general and several officers of the emperor, and they should have suffered condignly, but the indiscriminate slaughter of guilty and innocent, with no previous effort to distinguish the one from the other, was wholly unjustifiable. The Archbishop of Milan, Ambrose, severely arraigned the emperor, and put him under eight months' penance for his sanguinary crime. But Ambrose himself showed how deeply sectarian malice had penetrated the hearts of the religionists of those days. The bigoted monks and people of a little town on the Euphrates, stirred up in part by their bishop, burnt a Jewish synagogue and a Valentinian meeting-house. The local authorities and even the emperor insisted on a fair reparation, but Ambrose resisted this just settlement and succeeded in protecting the incendiaries because they had victimized nobody better than Jews and heretics. In the city of Constantinople Theodosius gave vent to his vindictive fanaticism by the expulsion of the Arian bishop from the Cathedral of St. Sophia, with all his clergy, and the immediate transfer of all the Arian churches, a hundred in number, to the comparatively few Athanasians. The emperor's orders were enforced by a large body of the Imperial Guards. Six weeks afterwards Theodosius abolished all professions of religion throughout his empire, save that of Nice alone. Church anathema, excommunication, fines, confiscation, exile, ruin in every form awaited all who accepted not the Homo-ousian. It was this emperor who convened the synod of Constantinople in A. D. 381, known as the Second General Council, and who must be regarded as the final establisher of the Nicene faith. Under his rule it was death to keep Easter on any but the regulation day, and in his reign the office of Inquisitor of the Faith was first instituted, to be followed up and brought to an accursed consummation in poor priest-ridden Spain by a fellow-countryman of Theodosius, him of ever execrable name and memory, Thomas of Torquemada.

Our attention is now called to a subject of less general cognizance. Something of a spirit similar to what so unhappily prevailed in the post-apostolic age seems to have more or less pervaded Nicenist writers, preachers, and teachers in all the years since the Reformation. One of its symptoms is an overweening veneration for the "early fathers," as they are unctuously termed, by which it is meant to say that the Holy Scriptures are made to revolve like satellites round the "fathers" and their dogmas, instead of the fathers round them. Whether this is because the Bible is too plain, direct and matter of fact for the mystery-loving tastes of our theologians, who find more scope for their imaginations in the fancies of Justin Martyr, Origen, Cyprian and others than they do in the nobler and more serious teachings of scriptures, is a matter we shall not wait to determine.

But to such a pass does this extend that the direct agency of Him, the Creator, whom we have been in the habit of identifying with the Jehovah I AM of the Old Testament, is not only practically pushed aside in behalf of an imaginary Christ, but we are told that the chief processes of man's salvation were perfected long ages before the date of the world's creation, and even the creation of the angels, and all this by Christ alone! How does this remind one of the way in which in the far east among the Hindoo priesthood, Vishnu, the second in the Hindoo triad, with his avatars, or incarnations, has wellnigh totally obscured the two other co-divinities, Brahma and Siva, but Brahma especially? Not only is Christ alleged to have been the creator of man, but also the being who in an assumed body walked in the garden of Eden, gave the law from Sinai, and was the visible, embodied teacher of Adam, Noah, Abraham, Job, and Moses! Thus Christ is accounted to be the demiurge of the material, moral, and spiritual worlds, leaving to Him whom the New Testament never fails of denominating Christ's "God and Father" little other than the office of a sinecure. A remarkable idea of this character was hatched and fledged in a lecture before the English University of Oxford, in one of the early years of the present century, by the notable Dr. Reginald Heber, afterwards bishop of Calcutta. His fourth Bampton lecture has very much to say about the "Triune God;" the first person of which he probably assigns to God the Father, but the second and third places he allots to the Son and Holy Ghost, respectively, supposing the Son to be no other than the archangel Michael, and the Holy Ghost the archangel Gabriel. He undertakes to say that "Michael is one of the names ascribed to our Saviour in his pre-existent state;" that "Michael is the chief priest and expiator of heaven;" that his name "implies the image and likeness of God."

Of Gabriel, he says that his name "implies strength or active power;" that in him "we shall recognize a person in himself eternal and divine; that it was Gabriel who "rained fire on Sodom, and who is called the Son of God when he descended to protect the faithful worshippers of God in the Babylonian furnace," and more to the same purpose. It will be remembered that in his popular hymn, "From Greenland's Icy Mountains," Bishop Heber denominates Christ as "Creator." And all this in most pious oblivion of the Saviour's repeated admonitions of the sole godhead of the Father, and that "true worship" can be offered to no other than to Him. What a commentary is this on the perverse power of a false education!

Touching the dependence to be placed on the "early fathers," the learned and indefatigable John Milton says: "Whatever time or the heedless hand of blind chance hath drawn from old to this present, in her huge drag-net, whether fish or seaweed, shells or shrubs, unpicked, unchosen—those are the "fathers." And the justly-celebrated Jeremy Taylor, in his masterly book on toleration, entitled The Liberty of Prophesying, says: "There are some that think they can determine all questions in the world by two or three sayings of the fathers, or by the consent of so many as they will please to call a concurrent testimony; but this consideration will soon be at an end, for if the fathers, when they are witnesses of tradition, do not always speak the truth, as it has happened in the case of Papias and his numerous followers for almost three ages together, then is their testimony more improbable when they dispute or write commentaries." And another of the same name, a bright light of the English church of the present century, Isaac Taylor, though of the Nicene persuasion, writes as follows: "By steps too insensible and easy to admit of their being now distinctly traced, the religious system professed in the Christian church had, in the course of two hundred years, reckoning from the death of the last of the Apostles, become capitally distinguished from the Christianity of the Apostles; and from that time onward continued to move, with a steady and uniform progress, and always straightforward, until it presents itself to view in the terrible sublimity of a monstrous tyranny unmatched in cruelty, perfidy, and profligacy. And, assuredly, we are far from having as yet thrown off all those superstitions that sprang up in the second and third centuries, and which the Romish church inherited and expanded. The Lutheran reformation was a glorious beginning that waits for its consummation. Had it, indeed, been complete and consistent in principle and in practice, it would have been universal in its actual spread. The Papacy still lives, and it must live *until Protestantism shall be reformed.* We are still entangled in the snares woven in the age of Irenæus, Justin Martyr, and Cyprian."

Augustine, bishop of Hippo, in Numidia, was born near the middle of the fourth century, and consequently had a good opportunity for knowing the writings of the earlier fathers. He says, "Compositions of this kind have not canonical authority. Readers of the fathers are not to suppose that the testimonies produced from their works are unexceptionable, for their opinions may in particular cases be untrue. Truly catholic and praiseworthy as they were, we are not to esteem their writings on a level with holy scripture. On the contrary, we may, with all the honor and deference due them, blame whatever in them, by divine assistance and sound reasoning, we discover to be unfounded."

The Rev. John Collinson, of the English Church, in his lectures on the Ancient Fathers, remarks, "Whatever were the causes of religious degeneracy, it is certain that by imperceptible degrees the doctrines of men superseded the letter of scripture and became the acknowledged standard of religious truth." To such a length, says Mr. Collinson, did this infatuation extend, that "to propose doubts, to weigh opinions, was declared contumacy and presumption, and to differ, heresy. The authority of the fathers was exaggerated beyond all bounds. It is granted that the fathers were men fallible and infirm; they committed mistakes; neither did they write in the style of elegant scholars; they have incautiously advanced some things of which the church of Rome has taken advantage as a foundation for superstition."

From the foregoing authorities something near the just value of the writings of the early fathers—though many of these have been in more recent times sadly interpolated and corrupted—might be estimated. They are useful as testimonies to what happened in their days respectively, but are to be held in no lofty account as standards of religious opinion or authority. But another lesson might be learnt, and one that will be of immediate application to our own times and our own people. I refer to the propensity among those not braced up by a well-grounded and firm reliance upon teachings purely divine and the unimpassioned dictates of right reason, to accept the often crude judgments of professional teachers of religion as final and conclusive. This works badly for both teachers and taught. It encourages carelessness and superficiality in the one, and becomes the fertile source of ignorance, indifference and practical irreligion in the other. It is a virtual non-compliance with that special command of the Saviour, "Call no man upon the earth your master, for one is your Master, namely, Christ, and all ye are brethren."

The excursion we have made through the early centuries of our era has sufficed to show how little real submission has been yielded to the authoritative truth delivered by Moses (Deut., 6: 3 to 9), and very pointedly reannounced by the greater than Moses in Mark, chap. 12, verses 28 to 34. Christ's orthodoxy in respect to Mosaic or true Jewish doctrine was tested on this occasion as it had been on others, and proved to be beyond the ability of his bitterest enemies to impugn as heretical. They ceased, therefore, to interrogate him. Had Christ made reply conformably to what passes for "orthodoxy" in these present days, he would have been most promptly convicted and condemned, and, quite likely, stoned to death upon the spot. That authoritative truth, leading all the other truths of the Bible, and of the compendious Apostles' creed, was overset and obliterated, so far as they could do it, by Constantine's gathering in his palace at Nice, and a tinsel fabrication violently substituted for the old popular creed. Thenceforward "they taught for doctrines the commandments of men." But the "first commandment of all," binding Jew and Christian Gentile alike, can never be thrust quite out of sight. It will forever stand at the portal of the true religion to which finally all that love and seek salvation through the "door of the sheep" will come. The "first commandment of all," understood by Christ exactly as understood by the Jew, insists on the proper unity of GOD— He, and "none other but He"—having nothing to say about any evasive "unity of *godhead*," in which there might be a million separate and distinct individuals gods, as says St. Paul, " gods many." Trinity is not unity, but the negation of it, and a profession thereof shows a hankering after what both Old and New Testament interdict. Perhaps a general overthrow of affluent church establishments will be one of the agencies requisite to the purification of doctrine and worship, for so long as ministers of religion are rewarded with exuberant incomes for urging dogmas concocted at Nice, they will, as human nature is mostly constituted, be very apt to blink the pure and uncompromising teachings that emanated from Nazareth.

THE DISCIPLES OF CHRIST is a self-named religious organization which, according to the statements of its friends, sprung from a germ of sentiment in the mind of Thomas Campbell, a Presbyterian minister and a native of the north of Ireland, who, in the year 1809, deploring the differences and divisions among Protestant sects, and being dissatisfied with certain "human inventions" of bad portent that had sway among them, set about attempting a remedy. His aim was, if possible, to restore to the Christian world the faith and love of the primitive church, and, in seeking that end, to propose no "terms of union, communion or co-operation not as old as the New Testament." In 1823 a periodical was started in Bethany, Virginia, called "*The Christian Baptist*, under the charge of Alexander Campbell, a son of the said Thomas, which continued seven years and was superseded by a monthly magazine, *The Millennial Harbinger*, which ran for forty years. The results of the labors of these men will appear truly great from the present, approximate, statistics of the denomination, which counts in the United States, in round numbers, 570,000 members, divided into 4900 congregations, supplied by 3700 ministers, mostly in the Western States.

The Church polity is mainly like the Baptist, but much less rigid and uncompromising, and they baptize by immersion. They regard baptism, if undertaken in the right repentant spirit, and with a sincere purpose of amended and obedient life, as assuring remission of past sins. They admit to the Lord's Supper all who have been baptized and lead Christian lives, and make the supper a part of the regular Lord's day worship.

They lay it down as an abiding maxim "To speak when the Bible speaks, and to be silent when the Bible is silent;" doubtless, an excellent maxim, if lived up to as well as professed. They are solicitous of being classed among the so-called "evangelical" denominations, and by way of proof of it insert among the foremost of their "items of doctrine" the following, viz.:

"The revelation of God, especially in the New Testament, in the tri-personality of Father, Son, and Holy Spirit."

Candor compels our expression of belief that in reaching back for the faith of the primitive church the Disciples found neither in the Bible nor in the age "as old as the New Testament" any such doctrine as the tri-personality of God. That doctrine, if such it must be called, was not broached in the first or New Testament century, but in the fourth century, which fact is incontrovertibly signalized by the substitution in the fourth century of the Nicene for the Apostles' creed, and the enforcement of the new dogmas by imperial decree and military subjugation.

In performing the rite of baptism the "Disciples" couple the usual *Apostolic* formula of baptizing "into the name of the Lord Jesus" with the supposed formula of "into the name of the Father and of the Son and of the Holy Ghost," as found at the close of Matthew's gospel; from which latter quotation it seems very probable that they acquire the confidence to allege that the New Testament reveals God as a "tripersonal" being. The almost numberless instances of the statement of the unity of God in both the Old and New Testaments—of statement in the most direct, didactic, and positive manner—put upon the devotees of "tripersonality" the necessity of making the very most of any crevice or interstice, no matter how minute, in the free, generous, and unsuspecting diction of the Bible, through which the glimpse of a possibility might be caught that tripersonality is even so much as hinted at. The verbal collocation of the names of the Father, of the Son, and of the Holy Ghost at the close of Matthew is thus very often made the occasion for an inference to which the whole tenor and drift of the Bible is a contradiction; yet it is upon just such an inference that the baseless fabric of tripersonality is fain to ground itself. There are numerous other places in the New Testament where the names of God and Christ and the Spirit of God are brought into propinquity, yet not one of these is ever referred to for tripersonal purposes, the reason being that the fuller matter of such texts forbids it.* In the text in question its very compendiousness and summary-like character are turned to an account which nothing suggested in it will justify; yet it is held to by not a few Nicenist writers as with almost a death-grip.

---

*Nicenists, in their penury of proof of the Trinity doctrine, do not hesitate to substitute inference for evidence, and so to leap at their desired conclusion. This is eminently what they do in taking the bare mention of the names of Father, Son and Holy Ghost in Matt., 28:19, as proof of the Trinity. There is no lack of passages of scripture wherein the three are mentioned, not barely by name as in the said text, but in connexion with what they vouchsafe in behalf of man's salvation. Let Nicenists give just heed to these instructive texts, and they will not fail to acquire genuinely scriptural ideas upon the great subject. Among these texts are Matt., 3:16; 12:28; Acts, 2:32 and 33; 5:30 to 32; 7:55; 10:38; Romans, 8:9 and 11; 15:16 and 30; 1st Cor., 6:11; 12:3 to 6; 2d Cor., 1:21 and 22; 3:3; 13:14; Gal., 4:6; Eph., 1:17; 2:18; 4:4 to 6; Philipp., 3:3; Heb., 2:3 and 4; 1st Peter, 1:2, &c.

The justly-respected Whately, late Episcopal Archbishop of Dublin, is one of the writers who places exceeding reliance on the verse, Matt., 28: 19, as a proof text for the Trinity. One would think his quality and quantity of brain and candor of spirit should have led him to an opposite conclusion. See his "Logic" under the note Person. After stating, truly enough, the difficulties encountered by many conscientious persons on the subject of the Trinity and the danger they apprehend from dwelling upon it, he says, "Though it is, in fact, the very faith into which, by our Lord's appointment, we are baptized." Could a much blinder leap at an erroneous conclusion be made? If Dr. Whately and people of this day are so baptized, the converts under the Apostles were *not*. Are we to conclude that the whole company of the Apostles, without a known exception, so blundered about the purpose and duty of baptism as to mistake concerning the faith with which it was connected, or to ignore the authority that appointed it? Such must be the conclusion if Dr. Whately's notion is correct. Who, then, is in the wrong, *all* the Apostles or Dr. Whately? We must go with the majority, and vote against the excellent and learned Doctor. What then? The conclusion follows that the text Matt., 28: 19 does not teach the Trinity, and that Christ had no intention that it should. Undoubtedly Father, Son and Holy Ghost are representative names for the whole Christian religion. The Father is God; the Son is the Son of God; and the Holy Ghost is the Spirit of God. Rightly to know each of these is life eternal, and a prayerful resort to God's Word will furnish that knowledge.

The occasion on which Christ gave the injunction in Matt. 28:19 was one of unexceeded interest and importance. Having been before his crucifixion Messiah to the Jews only, Jesus was now under divine appointment the universal Messiah, and with the universal Father and His universal Spirit, a principal agent in the regeneration and salvation of the whole human race. Consult on this, Hebrews, 5: 5, 6, 10 and adjacent verses; also, Hebrews, 7: 20 to 25. A respectable authority (International Cyclopædia, under Creeds and Confessions,) states that "What has been called the Apostles' creed is the earliest form of the Christian creed that exists, unless we give precedence to the baptismal formula at the close of St. Matthew's gospel, out of which many suppose the Apostles' creed to have grown." These remarks tend to confirm the view we have taken relative to the summary-like character of

Christ's parting instructions. If the Apostles' creed grew out of this text it was for the reason we have given, viz., that to be serviceably understood the text required a proper expansion. And if such expansion is made in the Apostles' creed, in which mention is made of but One God, the Almighty Father, no Trinity is taught. Lastly, they evince but little respect for the fearless and truth-speaking quality of the Lord Jesus who suggest the thought that (having taught the opposite of the Trinity all his previous life) he waited till near the moment of his departure to break to his Apostles, in brief and obscure words, the inscrutable "mystery." Anyway, the Apostles saw no Trinity in Christ's parting commands, for they never taught or recognized it.

If we take for a foundation-fact of our creed the saying of the Lord Jesus that the Holy Spirit "proceedeth from the Father," then we must regard the Father and the Holy Ghost as much one and the same entity, or being, as a man and the spirit of that man are one being. God and the Holy Ghost have therefore really one and the same personality, the Holy Ghost being a spiritual emanation or procession from God Himself.

Now, we learn from the scriptures, and our own observation is confirmatory, that the Infinite Supreme does not communicate to or with His creatures in His immediate personality—they could not survive it—but by His Spirit; by the communicative power of which Spirit it was that the Saviour himself was originated almost 1890 years ago; was anointed for his messiahship; led into the wilderness to undergo his temptation by Satan; returned after his temptation to his country of Galilee; was inspired to preach the gospel and the acceptable year of the Lord; was enabled to perform a numberless series of miraculous works throughout his most faithful ministry, and by which he gave commandment to his Apostles shortly before his ascension; which same Spirit, promised to him by the Father, with whom it originates and from whom it proceedeth, he shed forth in profusion upon his disciples on the day of Pentecost; and by which, lastly, after having received from the Father the grand revelation of things which must sooner or later "come to pass," Jesus admonished, threatened, and encouraged the churches of Asia Minor and closed the sacred record of the Word of God.

It was because the miracles that came from the mouth and hands of Christ were really executed by the Spirit of

God, that the sin of certain Jewish scribes, who sacrilegiously attributed those miracles to diabolical agency, was condemned as absolutely and for ever unpardonable. That was a deliberate and designed insult, and no mere misapprehension or mistake, upon the goodness and honor of the Most High God, that not even the benign forbearance of Heaven, which worked miracles for man's convincement and salvation, could forgive. A word spoken against Christ (it is not said against the Father, as some Nicenists pretend) would be forgiven, "but whosoever speaketh against the Holy Ghost, it shall not be forgiven him, neither in this world nor in the world that is to come." The blasphemy against the Holy Ghost was a giving to the devils the glory that belonged to God alone, for who save God could perform the signs and wonders that were displayed? It was a crime of the most reeking flagrancy; an alliance with Pandemonium.

In endeavoring to explain the creed of the "Disciples," that "Jesus of Nazareth is the Christ, the Son of the living God," their books and pamphlets seem to lack entire candor and straightforwardness. They appear to seek to identify the scriptural phrase "Son of God" with the unscriptural Nicenism "God-the-Son," so as to get out of the former the illegitimate meaning conveyed in the latter, which latter, being a human invention and having no status in the Bible, they do not commit to print. Perhaps it would have been better and safer in the long run, if, in starting a new society, the Disciples had gone for their foundation down to hardpan (such, for instance, as 1st Timothy, 2: 5), and so have patiently worked a "return to the simple faith and practice of the uncorrupted church"—a consummation they have not yet achieved. They could then have more consistently enlarged "about obeying the Saviour's commandments," particularly the first-of-all of them, as he defined it in Mark 12: 29. That might have been a considerable step towards a restoration of the "simple religion of Jesus as he gave it to the world in the beginning,"—in saying which, and other things like it, the Disciples proclaim their belief that the religion of Jesus, as now mostly professed, is *not* "the simple religion he gave the world in the beginning." In which, quite likely, they are more than half right.

THE CONGREGATIONALIST body is divided into Trinitarian and Unitarian congregationalists. The former class will now engage our attention. It is Nicenist, while the latter is not.

The Trinitarian congregationalists constitute a numerous and highly respectable branch of the church of our day, and are especially strong in the Eastern States of the Union. The following is believed to be pretty nearly their present strength: congregations, 3700; ministers, 3600; communicants, 385,000.

Their church polity is less absolutely individual, independent, and self-controlling than the Baptist, but free from such government as that by presbyteries, synods, and general assemblies, as with the Presbyterians. Congregationalism is less self-governed than the Baptist, in that each society acknowledges a connexion or relationship with other similar societies for the purposes, when necessary, of mutual counsel and help; yet, if need be, in the last resort, it falls back upon itself alone. Of course, nothing like Episcopalianism, even in the form adopted by the Methodist Episcopal church, has any allowance whatever in this church.

The Congregationalists, whilst acknowledging the form of baptism by immersion to be good, regard other methods by aspersion as equally so, and administer the rite to persons of all ages, from the youngest to the oldest.

That the Congregationalists are Nicenist, might be inferred from their being Trinitarian. No portion of the great Nicenist mass is, in fact, more doctrinally thoroughgoing than they. They also adopt to the fullest extent the opinions first brought clearly out by Anselm, on the subject of the atonement. Anselm was by birth a Piedmontese, but Romish archbishop of Canterbury in England during the reigns of William Rufus and Henry the First. As just stated, the Congregationalists are thoroughgoing in their doctrinal views. As for our humble self we feel towards them as it seems the Apostle Paul might feel if he were now among us, and for about the same reason; almost provokingly so. At all events, as we read, lying open before us, the pleasantly written and, in a literary aspect, the able discourse of a Congregationalist doctor of divinity, specially preached and printed in one of our foremost cities, we are unavoidably reminded of how Paul felt whilst taking his tour through the city of Athens and beholding that city wholly given to idolatry.

The learned doctor remarks that "if a man wishes to know what he must do to be saved, and goes to a Baptist, Methodist, Episcopalian, or Congregationalist minister or Christian, they will each tell him, for substance, that which will lead him to pay *divine honors* to Jesus Christ. If he kneels in prayer with them, they will *pray to Jesus Christ* as the Saviour of the world. Let him sing with them, and they will sing hymns in accordance with that new song which is sung before the throne. This is what we believe to be meant by calling on the name of the Lord Jesus Christ, both theirs and ours. It is rendering *divine worship to Jesus Christ* as the redeemer of men."

There was an occasion in the course of the Apostle Paul's extended ministry when the same question as the foregoing was asked of him and his prison companion Silas:—"What must I do to be saved?" Paul's answer was: "Believe on the Lord (not God) Jesus Christ, and thou shalt be saved and thy house." The questioner, it was Paul's jailer, after having performed fitting acts of personal respect and kindness, showed his ready faith in Christ by being "baptized and all his straightway," and then " rejoiced " at the blessed change that had been wrought upon him, "believing in God with all his house." Previous to this the Apostle Peter, with the eleven other Apostles around him, answered a similar question put to them by the heart-stricken thousands to whom they had been preaching, "Repent and be baptized, every one of you, upon the name of Jesus Christ for the remission of sins, and ye shall receive the gift of the Holy Ghost. For the promise is unto you and to your children and to all that are afar off, as many as the Lord our God shall call." It is not necessary to cite other like instances. These are enough to show that the Apostles did nothing whatever that would lead the converts, Jews, as most of them were, to "pay divine honors to Jesus Christ," "to pray to Christ," or "render to Jesus Christ divine worship." When Jesus Christ was preached by the Apostles he was not preached as a God to be worshipped with divine honors, but as a master and teacher and an opener of the pathway to heaven, to be obeyed and imitated. He was preached not as the object of prayer but as "Jesus of Nazareth, a *man* approved of God by miracles, wonders, and signs which (Christ did not perform of his own ability but which) *God did* by him"; and then afterwards by the same power of God was himself raised from the dead. In like manner Paul, when speaking at Athens of Christ as the medium through whose visible instrumentality the invisible God will judge the world, denominated him a "man" whom God "had raised from the dead." Besides these two apostles there is the clear, unmistakable testimony of Christ himself that he was a "man who told the truth which (was not original with him but which) he had heard of God." Most certainly then there is no good reason for supposing that to be a safe path to salvation which worships with "divine honors" a man, or any other but God, as those must worship who worship Christ in the supreme degree of paying him "divine honors." Christ, who refused even to be called "good," never claimed such; he would not have such; he would have been shocked at and repelled such had they been offered him, for none knew better than he that he was not entitled to them. What his own duty was and the duty of all men (Congregationalists included) he showed by quoting, in answer to Satan's enticement, from Deuteronomy, "Thou shalt worship the Lord thy God, and *him only* shalt thou serve." Christ taught his disciples to pray to the Father alone, as he prayed himself; and one of the last commands of the closing book of Revelation, as uttered by Christ's representative angel to the Apostle John, was "Worship God."

Nor let any lay the flattering unction to their conceits that because men are baptized into the name of Christ that Christ is thereby deified. The very reverse is the case. We are baptized into Christ not because he is God but for the very reason that he is man like unto those who are baptized into him, and who thereupon and thereby enter into his name and "put on" Christ. When Paul sharply censured the Corinthians for their schisms and contentions he put them the questions, "Is Christ divided? Was Paul crucified for you? Or were you baptized into the name of Paul?" They indeed were not, but were baptized into Christ who had died for them, and thereby became partakers in his death and what followed it. We are baptized into Christ because Christ was crucified, died, was buried, rose again from the dead, and finally ascended on high. Our baptism puts us into union, or, rather let us say, unity with Christ. "For we are members of his body, of his flesh, and of his bones," (Eph., 5: 30.) After having received a true baptism we are regarded and should regard ourselves as being dead to this present world; our true and hopeful life being hid with Christ in God. But to so much as think a thought which in any way connects the idea of death with the personality of God is most dishonoring to

Him who "alone hath immortality," and certainly indicates a low religious tone which no amount or degree of mere "evangelical" pretension can successfully conceal, whether taken on by doctor of divinity, priest, pope, or other mortal.

After several pages of matter of comparative indifference, our learned doctor proceeds to speak of Trinitarianism, as if he had not already asseverated almost the gravest point under that head. He quotes expressions of the Saviour in order to show Christ's testimony to the permanent validity of the Old Testament, and repeats the words "the law and the prophets," which might have had the effect of inducing more or fewer of his hearers to suppose him a very decided "law and prophet" man.

It cannot, however, escape notice that instead of bringing forward his proofs that the "law and the prophets" are on the Trinitarian side, he furnishes no testimony whatever. Now without going back to God's first announcement, through Moses to the Israelites, of His name I AM, we may remark that "the law" properly begins with the ten commandments, the first of which enjoins One God, in the singular number, and subsequently "Thou shalt worship *no other* God, for the Lord, whose name is jealous, is a jealous God;" and again, "Hear, O Israel, the Lord our God is one Lord;" whereas, according to the Trinitarian theory, it should have been "The Lord our God is *three* Lords. And in the notable song of Moses, God is quoted as saying "See now that I, even I, am he and there is *no* God with me." Would the Deity, if consisting of three equal, co-ordinate members, speak to His listening and dependent creatures concerning Himself or Themselves in language like that, every way calculated to produce a wrong impression? Is God to be thought of like that? And who are they that are bold to suggest such an imputation?

Was it not, then, considerably too daring a thing to say in the face of a congregation of people that the "law" favored Trinitarianism? With respect to the "prophets," will our doctor fare any better? The prophet David says in his Psalms, "Sing unto God, sing praises to His name; extol Him that rideth upon the heavens by His name Jah (I am), and rejoice before Him." Unto Thee," says David, "will I sing with the harp, O thou Holy *One* of Israel." "Thou art my Father (not Fathers), my God (not Gods), and the rock of my salvation."

That mighty prophet, the rapt Isaiah, speaks forth, "Thus saith the Lord the king of Israel and his redeemer the Lord of hosts, I am the first and I am the last, and besides me there is no God. Is there a God beside me? Yea, there is no God: I know not any." Yet for all this and greatly more that might be adduced, our doctor declares that there are "proofs that demonstrate the equal deity of three, and that there is a threefold distinction in God's nature." But his alleged demonstrations fail to appear and can be traced to nothing more substantial than dogmatic assertion. It goes to his credit, however, that he acknowledges the Trinity theory to be a "mystery," an "inexplicable enigma," somewhat inducing the idea that he advocates it upon the old monkish principle, "I believe, because it is impossible."

Pursuing his career of "mystery" and "inexplicable enigma," he sets forth the proposition that Christ has "two distinct natures in one person;" that is to say, that Christ is two distinct and diametrically different kinds of beings at one and the same time, though he was only one kind of being from all eternity down to a comparatively very late period,—in a manner, yesterday,—since, in fact, the time of Julius Cæsar. How so great a change as is involved in becoming partly some one else could occur to an unchangeable deity, our learned doctor does not explain, or even notice; perhaps because that, too, is an "inexplicable enigma." He cites no text from either the Old or New Testament wherein this amazing two-nature dogma is disclosed; whereas, were it an article of faith divinely imparted, we might rest assured that even miracles would be wrought, if necessary, to sustain it.

Adopting a kind of logic much of the inexplicable order, he asks: Why, if we deny Christ's deity, do we not "doubt and deny his *human* nature"? Because Christ said "Before Abraham was, I am." It is evident from this query that our doctor is one of the strangely numerous class even among learned professors of theology who suppose this text in John's gospel, 8:58, to teach Christ's pre-existence, or existence before his generation and birth as narrated for us in the gospels. Whether by honest inadvertence, or a less honest design of putting the scripture into the false position of a witness for pre-existence, we will not undertake to decide, yet so it is that the Trinitarian translators, by their inconsistency of translation, laid a trap in this text into which not a few have carelessly fallen. In the 24th and 28th verses of the same 8th chapter of John, the English pronoun *he* is placed after the words "I am." It is printed in italics to show that it is not in the original Greek, but is required by the sense. The same thing is done in the 9th verse of the next chapter; in the 5th, 6th, and 8th verses of the 18th chapter; in the 25th verse of the 13th of Acts, and elsewhere. The English pronoun *he* in the 8th chapter of John is put for the noun *Christ*, and had it been placed after "I am" in the 58th verse, as it is in the 24th and 28th verses, the translators would have been both consistent and right, and the meaning of Jesus that even before Abraham was born he (Jesus) was predestined to be the *Christ*, could not have been easily misunderstood. The wrongful omission of *he* in the said 58th verse is in marked contrast with what the same translators did in Mark, 13:6, and Luke, 21:8, where they were not satisfied with supplying the mere pronoun *he* after "I am," but put the indicated noun, *Christ*, itself. The late Revisers did little for truth and nothing for their own praise when they left the 58th verse as they found it in the older translation.

Other texts are quoted by our reverend friend which he believes to support his views touching the deity of Christ; in most of which, and we say it with no purpose of disparagement, he appears to be a novice in hermeneutics or scriptural interpretation. He is as literal as a child, or as were those dissatisfied followers of Christ who could not digest his figurative and picturesque expressions relative to divine things, and therefore "walked no more with him;" or, again, those malignant rulers and scribes who wilfully misinterpreted his teachings. It is undoubtedly true that, at the first blush, many, perhaps most, of Christ's profoundest lessons (which he designated "mysteries of the kingdom," Matt., 13:10 and 11) were given in parables or figurative speech; yet, it so providentially happens, or rather, we may believe, Christ distinctly intended, that his every dark saying should contain a key to its own solution, to be found by them who seek for it.

Thus in the next quoted text, John, 3:13: "And no man hath ascended up to heaven but he that came down from heaven, namely, the Son of man who is in heaven," the apparent difficulty of understanding how the Son of man came down from heaven, when the scripture itself testifies that the Son of man was born and reared upon the earth, is removed by the concluding sentence, which says "who is *in* heaven." To have "come down from heaven," and at the same time to be "*in* heaven," plainly points to what Christ meant by "heaven," viz., that it is not a place so much as a state of the soul, in which Christ always dwelt; the same state which is elsewhere described as "in the bosom of the Father," a state wherein God was continually present by the indwelling of His Spirit, which in Christ was measureless. The lesson taught by this text is that the presence of God's Holy Spirit in the soul is heavenly, and that to have it in the fulness possessed by Christ is *heaven;* for wherever God is, heaven goes with Him—a truth which all might experience would they drop their worldliness and give place to the celestial visitant. Christ points to his own experience in this matter, when, with the utmost emphasis, he said to Nicodemus, "We speak that we do *know* and testify that we *have seen.*" It was no visionary hallucination.

The next text is the third verse of the first chapter of John's gospel, where the allusion is not to Christ. To insist that Christ is the Creator, when he unequivocally said that of himself he could "do nothing;" and, again, that the Son can do nothing of himself," and did only that which was shown him by the Father, is at least to disregard, if not to contradict him. Our friend thinks to prove Christ's pre-existence by the text in John 17:5, where Christ prays for "the glory which he had with the Father before the world was." Now, this glory for which Christ prayed was prospective, not retrospective; it was a glory (verse 22) which his disciples "may behold," and was due to that love which in the far back ages the Father had entertained by anticipation for His obedient Son. God loved Christ "before the foundation of the world" just as he had prepared the kingdom for the righteous "from the foundation of the world," but which they were not to inherit till after the Son of man shall come in his glory. Paul tells the Ephesian saints that they were chosen in Christ "before the foundation of the world," and Peter says that Christ "was verily foreordained before the foundation of the world." In the Revelations, the Lamb is said to be slain "from the foundation of the world," all which plainly means in the anticipation, irreversible purpose, or foreordination of the Most High. The glory and the joy Christ prayed for had been "set *before* him," therefore it was future, for the sake of which he "endured the cross, despised its shame and was set down at the right hand of the throne of God," where personally he had never been before. To this effect is Luke 24:26.

Our Congregationalist friend makes a reference to the benediction in the last verse of the 2d Corinthians, expressing his unbelief that the "name of a created being and of an attribute should be associated with the name of

God," for he acknowledges the Father to be uniformly called God in the Bible and was the Jehovah of the Jews. Now the verse in question needs to be no other than it is to bear the severest criticism and yet not be subject to the conditions the doctor would impose. "The grace of our Lord Jesus Christ." Here is invoked on the Corinthians the personal favor of the Lord and Master of Christians, divinely so appointed. Of him who said to his disciples, "Ye call me Master and Lord, and ye say well, for so I am." He did not assume to be their God. Next is invoked "the love of God." As the God and Father of the Corinthian saints, what so natural and desirable as His love? And lastly it is implored that "the communion of the Holy Ghost be" likewise "with them all." That is, the common participation in the outpouring of the Divine Spirit. What, then, is there to cavil at? Christ tells the angel of the church of Sardis that he will confess the name of him that overcometh "before his Father and before his angels." Here the names of created angels are associated with the name of God, and if so, why not the names of the Son of God and of the Spirit of God with the name of God most high, who is "all in all"? Surely our friend is the most hypercritical of mankind and yet gains nothing by it. Not the faintest trace of a Trinity can be descried in 2d Cor. 13:14.

In calling attention to John 17:5 it is strange that our preacher had not got a sight of the preceding third verse, where he could have learnt who is "the *only* true God" to the exclusion of every other being. Was his vision controlled by his sectarianism?

He insists on Christ's native omnipotence in the face of Christ's most positive disclaimers :—John, 5:19 and 30; John, 14:10; John, 10:25 and 37. Also Acts, 2:22; Matt., 28:18; Matt., 20:23; Acts, 1:17. So with the divine attribute of omniscience which our doctor ascribes to Christ, though Christ himself pronounced to the contrary. Matt., 24:36; Mark, 13:32; Rev., 1:1.

It is objected by our reverend friend that if the word Trinity is not in the Bible neither is omniscience, or unity of God, or sacrament, or other much needed words. True, but the verbal equivalents of all these words are found there, as "God only wise;" "God is One," &c., but nowhere in the Bible is it said that Father, Son and Holy Ghost are one entity, except in the interpolated or spurious verse in 1st John, 5:7. The word Trinity has no equivalent in the Bible, consequently it is expressive of nothing in the scripture, and the scripture has no use for it. It is a word invented by Theophilus of Antioch towards the end of the second century, about the year 180, when the "perverse things" predicted by Paul to the elders of the church gathered at Miletus doubtless began to be agitated. (Acts, 20: 30.)

The preacher whose criticisms we are considering, sarcastically refers to what some have said concerning the Holy Ghost, that it is "divine influence." That might, indeed, be a narrow and unsatisfactory statement, yet words are used in scripture indicating its manner of operation as proceeding, anointing, filling, falling, shed forth, poured out, &c. Thus Christ breathed on his disciples the Holy Ghost, which we may be sure was a breath divinely influential on the recipients, though nothing was ever hinted about the disciples worshipping the breath as a personal being distinct from the personality of God the Father from whom it originally proceeds. So true is it that "the Lord is that Spirit." (2d Cor., 3: 17.) The Holy Ghost was dispensed not only by Christ himself, but by his Apostles in answer to prayer. (See Acts, 8: 15 to 18; also Acts, 19: 6.) A *person* could not be "shed forth" or "poured out," and especially not a divine personality by human hands!

Our critical friend is dissatisfied with the Lord Jesus himself when the latter speaks discordantly with his cherished ideas. When Christ says, "My Father is greater than I," the doctor fails to see in it "even a common reverence for God and an ordinary sense of propriety." It would have suited him much better had Christ said "My Father is *no* greater than I." He thinks it almost "no wonder that some call Christ fallible."

The doctor refers to the mistranslated text in Philipp., chap. 2d, that "Christ thought it not robbery to be equal with God." St. Paul did not say that. The Revised version, though of Nicenist preferences, gives it thus: Christ "counted it not a prize to be on an equality with God." A better interpretation will be that though Christ stood before the eyes of men endued with the divine faculty of performing miracles, and so was like to God, he made no personally advantageous use of that distinction, but took upon him the character of a servant, for which self-humiliation he was rewarded by God and given a name before which all men must bow and every tongue confess (what?) that Jesus Christ is (not God but) Lord, and all finally to the glory of God the Father. Whoever imbibes error from the gross mistranslation in verse 6, may find an antidote in verse 11.

As to Christ being "a mere man," that is all that by the constitution of his nature Moses and the prophets, Christ and his Apostles, ever claimed him to be. But that did not make him any the less the Son of God and Saviour of the world. (Acts, 3: 22 to 26th ; Acts, 5: 29 to 32.) His true distinction arose out of his sinless obedience, the matter concerning his nature being comparatively an inferior consideration. The more that in idea he is removed from being in nature a man, the further he is off from being for us a suitable earthly exemplar and heavenly mediator.

Our Congregationalist teacher is sometimes so captivated with one part of a text, that he overlooks the corrective to his ideas to be found in another part. He quotes, "No man knoweth who the Son is but the Father, and who the Father is but the Son, and he to whom the Son will reveal him." From this he argues that there are mysteries in Christ's nature which are not fathomed except by the Father; they are compared to the mysteries in the nature of the Father. Equally astonishing, Christ represents himself as *alone* capable of knowing the Father." Now, the doctor's word "alone" flatly contradicts the Saviour's concluding clause, which declares the possibility of the Son's revealing the knowledge spoken of to men of women born. The knowl- is therefore not of that inscrutably mysterious character the doctor supposes, and may have nothing in connection with those Athanasian "mysteries" which were set up at the Council of Nice, and which have kept mankind so many dreary centuries entwined, like Laocoon and his sons, with hateful and pestilent superstitions. Having superseded the the Apostles' creed with their new fabrication, free scope was given to the most extravagant fancies, which were nailed down upon the acceptance of mankind by ruthless penalties and persecutions.

So far we go with a comparison of Nicenist theology with the Word of God. We propose to give some attention to the soteriology, or salvation doctrines presented in the Nicenist system. The Bible leaves us in no doubt about the fall of our first parents, from a state of innocence and friendship with heaven, to one of disobedience and disloyalty towards their Maker. They distrusted His words and believed the falsehoods of another. This was their fall, and the cause of their losing God's approving favor. It was the fruitful cause of the wanderings, the sins, and sufferings of countless millions to-day and in all time. Can a return to the favor of God be retraced, if the forgiving mercy and Spirit of God will permit it? Blessed be God, such a return is even invited; God, the offended One, proffering the invitation and indicating the way of restoration.

In speaking on the subject of salvation, it will not be amiss to inquire, first, From what do men hope to be saved? Is it from natural death, that is to say, the death of the body? No man expects this. All men are sure that, sooner or later, and at no very distant day at the farthest, physical death will strike every one of us. It is plain, then, that though we may lawfully strive to protract the hour of our departure to the latest possible moment, the last moment cannot be evaded. Sin entered into the world and death by sin. All have sinned, and come short of that perfect obedience which is the glory of God. All, therefore, must die and give their bodies back to the dust. Christ, then, did not come to shield man from natural death, which is the penalty appended to the breach of the divine law. Even Christ's meritorious self-surrender and sacrifice, perfect as it was, could not do that. The divine fiat must have its way, and is utterly inevitable. Our first parents ate, indeed, the fruit of the forbidden tree of good and evil, but they failed of tasting the fruit of the tree of life. This brought down upon them the unrelieved weight of the dread penalty, "in the day that thou eatest thereof thou shalt surely die." Still, man is a duplex being. His mortal body envelops an immortal soul. Created originally in the image of God, man's spiritual part will inherit the divine immortality; or, at all events, the book of God gives no intimation that after the general resurrection the human soul will ever cease to be self-conscious. How, then, shall it survive? In the divine favor, or out of it? This is a tremendous inquiry, the very greatest of all questions to every soul of man. After the failure of the first denizens of the earth to obey the dictates of their better conscience they fell down to depths of corruption, violence, and wickedness, no longer tolerable even to the forbearing patience of heaven; that is to say, after 1650 years of such abandonment, all living creatures, with very minute exceptions, were swept out of existence by a universal watery deluge. On the renewal of the earth under better auspices, God set on foot a scheme of mercy for the benefit of the souls he had interposed to save.

Before we go farther it might not be inopportune to remark that in the world before the flood there does not appear to have been any organized system of moral and spiritual education for mankind. They seem to have been left to their native instincts, and the ever-available opportunities of assistance from God's Holy Spirit, for we see that Enoch found means to reach a degree of excellence so high that God released him from the penalty of temporal death, whereby Enoch gave evidence to his cotemporaries that there is another world than the material one.

It would not do, then, to leave mankind any longer to the mercy of their merely natural instincts. There must be a system of moral and spiritual instruction, and for this God laid a foundation in the call of Abraham out of the Ur of the Chaldees. In Abraham all the families of the earth were to be blessed, for he was a man whose loving trust in God had been tested in a severe and remarkable manner. His progeny, through his more immediate offspring, Isaac and Jacob, or Israel, were gathered into a choice portion of the fertile land of Egypt where they had an opportunity of becoming in the course of more than four hundred years a numerous people. Whilst the mass of mankind were steeped in heathen ignorance and corruption, means were adopted by which this Abrahamic or Hebrew family should become a receptacle of the knowledge of the One True God and of His will, making them the salt, or saving element, of the whole earth. Moses, raised up by God in due time to be their leader and champion, demanded, under the divine authority supported by a series of signal miracles, the release of the Hebrew people from Egyptian servitude and their departure to a land where they might uninterruptedly serve God. Numerous were the promises of the Egyptian king to comply with the demand of the Israelitish leader and just as numerous were Pharaoh's refusals to fulfil his engagements. The last great pressure brought to bear against Pharaoh's stubborn reluctance was the simultaneous privation of life in the case of every individual first-born of the families of Egypt and of the first-born of their cattle; the families of the Israelites quite escaping. This escape was obtained through obedience to God's premonitory command, by his servant Moses, that on an appointed evening each Hebrew family should kill a lamb or kid of a year old, without blemish, saving the blood, with which by the dipping into it of a bush of the plant called in our language hyssop, (in Hebrew *êzob*,) the two side-posts and the lintel overhead of the door of every dwelling should be stricken. Also it was commanded that no one should leave a dwelling till morning. "When," says the sacred record, "the Lord, in passing through Egypt, saw the blood upon the lintel and side-posts, He *passed over* the door and suffered not his destroying angel to enter and smite the occupants." Hence this great occasion of Egyptian punishishment and Israelitish deliverance is called the *Passover*, and has been annually commemorated by the Hebrew people from that day to this, or more than three thousand three hundred and seventy years. It will be impossible to overlook the peculiar provision of divine wisdom and goodness in ordaining this deliverance of the Israelites. They were to use the occasion to prepare themselves food for a sudden journey; they were to eat it as in haste and to be personally girded around, with staff in hand, ready for the start. There were wisdom and goodness in this; and in the premonition to strike the side-posts and lintels of each doorway with blood, there was a signification to the people of all nations and times that man's deliverance from the destroyer must be by the shedding of blood, typical of the surrender of life. For that is the only acceptable equivalent, reparation, or atonement for sin, according to the irreversible law delivered in Leviticus 17: 11—"it is the blood that maketh atonement for the soul." The Israelites were saved from destruction by the Egyptians by no severe personal task, no painful exertion of their own, but by a simple and easy compliance with the ordination of God. They had faith in the divine command.

When the Lord Jesus Christ was keeping, in pursuance of what became him as a faithful Jew, his last passover on earth, he took bread and gave thanks, and breaking the bread, distributed to his disciples and said, Take, eat; this is my body. And he took the cup, and gave thanks, and gave it to them, saying, Drink ye all of it; for this is my blood of the new testament, or covenant, which is shed for many for the remission of sins. As their bodies absorbed and appropriated the blood and the wine in the way of bodily sustenance, so were the souls of the disciples to be nourished and their spiritual life sustained by feeding on the body of truth he represented. Christ was the antitype or reality of which the paschal lamb was the type or shadow. He was slain to furnish spiritual aliment for the journey from this world to the Canaan above, and to yield the preservative blood for the remission of sins, and consequent protection from the destroying agencies that await on rebellion against God. He was and is the Christian's passover. The bread, representing Christ's body, was broken, the wine, representing Christ's blood, was shed, not for himself, but for his people—for his church. His death, followed by his resurrection, carried him into heaven, where he stands in the holy of holies before the mercy seat, in the very presence of the majesty of God, to act as mediating high priest to intercede with the Father for the frailties and pardonable transgressions of his people. Not the blood of bulls and of goats, as under the provision of the Levitical institution, was what he offered, but it was his own precious blood, or life, freely surrendered to the will of God. And this offering God can freely accept in the post-resurrection time, whilst the humble follower of Christ will faithfully use on earth every means, and become continually more and more like his glorified Master. We perceive in this that the original law of God is fully vindicated in the bodily death of every man, whilst under the new covenant sealed by Christ's blood in behalf of his brethren of the human race, of whom he is the representative, God's promise of salvation to all who will comply with the requirements of Christ's laws can have full effect. God's mercy, let it be repeated, is free to act in behalf of the souls of men, the honor of His law being amply vindicated by the infliction of the penalty of death upon their bodies. Yet this is not without terms, those terms being the true acceptance of Christ as master, legislator, exemplar, and Lord of the life and conduct. This is just what the Bible means by believing in Christ and seeking salvation through him. It is thus that Christ becomes the Saviour of the world. Death could not hold Christ in its benumbing grasp, since Christ's righteous obedience opened for himself and the race in which he held brotherhood an entrance into the kingdom of God. He regained Paradise for mankind.

Such, then, appears to be the soteriology of the New Testament, viz., repentance towards a justly-offended yet forgiving and gracious God our Creator, and faith in Christ's once effectual reconciling, or atoning, sacrifice on the cross, and present continuous intercessory work. This was the sum, the compendium, of Paul's teaching for three years to his beloved flocks in the churches of Ephesus and regions of Asia Minor.

In his tenth chapter to the Romans Paul indicates the nature of the faith preached by himself and the other Apostles, namely, That whosoever openly acknowledges in the world's face the lordship or legislative authority of Jesus of Nazareth over the life and conduct, and unfeignedly believes that God raised him from the dead, shall be saved. In this our day these are easy terms. In the day of St.

Paul the same terms must have been often accompanied with very considerable peril not only to personal liberty, but to life itself. The Apostle Peter, with equal succinctness, placed the conditions of salvation in repentance and baptism into the name of Jesus Christ for the remission of sins, with that comforting benefit to follow as a seal of the divine acceptance, the gift of the Holy Ghost. And lastly, Christ himself, more briefly, but not less comprehensively than his Apostles, said, as a part of his last communication with his disciples, "He that believeth the gospel and is baptized, shall be saved; and he that believeth not shall be damned." In all these cases it must, of course, be understood that both the repentance and the faith are to be heartfelt and sincere. Neither God nor Christ can be deceived a hair's breath.

It is not to be doubted that declarations such as the foregoing from the lips of Christ himself and of his two great Apostles are conclusive as to the terms and conditions of human salvation for every soul of man. The mental constitutions of many of the race are not suited to abstract investigations, for which reason the foregoing practical directions comprise the substance of what is necessary in every case. Wayfaring men, though worldly unwise, need not err therein. Others of the race, differently constituted, instinctively crave the reasons why the methods of salvation are what they are. They want the philosophy of salvation. Nor is it very hard to find, seeing we have before us the free and open Word of God. If, in our endeavor to state this there be some repetition of previous ideas and texts of scripture, we entreat forbearance.

The philosophy of salvation, or of soteriology, may perhaps be most readily reached by a preliminary reference to the great statute book and history of the ways of God with man. When man, a moral and responsible being, was put upon the earth he was placed under law, or a line of limitation. Breach of this law, trespass beyond this line, was disobedience or sin, to be followed by the inevitable penalty of a forfeiture of life. God did not create man and surround him with the choicest blessings to be repaid with ingratitude and rebellion. Man was tempted by a deficient trust in God's word to break the law, and thenceforth became obnoxious to the penalty of death.

This brought forward a new question, What shall become of the two sinning beings? Shall they be immediately cut off, or permitted to stock the earth with their offspring under an opportunity of learning obedience and regaining the favor of heaven? The latter alternative was adopted by the God of mercy, but after between 1600 and 1700 years of trial, so exceedingly few were the instances of obedience, and so numerous the transgressions, that it is written, "God repented that He had made man, and it grieved Him at His heart." One single human being, Noah, found favor with God, on which account God resolved on saving him and his, but abolishing all the rest. Then came the punishment of the flood, annihilating, save Noah and his family, the whole race of man.

Though Noah and his family were preserved, sin had not been entirely dislodged from the world. As before, sin was always followed by its penalty, though that had been so terribly evidenced in the flood. Then arose the further question, Shall death be perpetual and God's high purpose in creating man be frustrated? God had determined otherwise. After the reintroduction of mankind upon the earth there were doubtless here and there centres of devotion and service acceptable to the Most High; but it was the wise and gracious purpose of God to constitute a system or order by which the duties of man to God should be made matter of instruction and iteration. Hence the call of Abraham, the trial of his faith, the sojourn of his progeny in Egypt till they had grown to the proportions of a nation; their establishment in Canaan, the delivery to them of a body of laws suitable for their personal and national guidance, their wanderings and punishments for infidelity to the wise and holy laws that had been delivered to them. Among those laws there was announced one involving a principle of the most important character and of very far-reaching effect. It is that we have mentioned in Leviticus 17:11, in the few but commanding words, "It is the blood that maketh atonement for the soul," that sacred element because it is the only commodity accepted in the exchange for sin, for it is authoritively written, "Without shedding of blood there is no remission" of sin. Blood is the symbol or representative of life, which God alone can originate and which alone will He accept in acquittance for the debt of sin.

During the existence of the Hebrew commonwealth, of which God was the Supreme Head, transgressions and sins were atoned for by the sacrifice of various animals, whose blood was poured out. But the system proved not to be perfect in its effects, and could not have an influence in any state of being beyond this world. In due course of time, therefore, there was one born of the stock of Abraham;

"born of a woman, born under the Levitical law," and therefore subject to its obligations. This was Jesus of Nazareth. Now, the Lord God had said, "All souls are mine; as the soul of the father, so also the soul of the son is mine; the soul that sinneth it shall die." Contrariwise, the soul that hath not sinned is under no obligation to die. Now, as a matter of fact, the life and conduct of Jesus were sinless. His bitterest enemies, with all their arts and efforts, totally failed to convict him of any transgression. An impartial witness, Pontius Pilate, the Roman procurator, said to Christ's accusers, "Ye have brought this man unto me as one that perverteth the people, and behold I, having examined him before you, have found no fault in this man touching those things whereof they accuse him; no, nor yet Herod, for I sent you to him; and lo, nothing worthy of death is done unto him." And in the like manner was the testimony to his innocency everywhere. "He went about doing good to the bodies and souls of men." Now, here we have a man, free from sin himself, and therefore not obnoxious to death for any wrong of his own. If he were willing to die for others, and God were willing to accept his life's blood in "atonement for the souls" of others who had sinned, who could object to the legitimacy of the transaction, especially when we bear in mind that every sinner thus redeemed will have paid, or must hereafter pay, the additional penalty of his own physical death according to the terms of the inexorable law? For Christ's blood makes no pretension to being shed to save from the death of the body, but only that of the soul.

That Christ was willing to die to save his people from the penal consequences of their sins is evident from his picturing the impending torture of his body and shedding of his blood by the breaking the bread and dividing the wine at the last supper. Had he been disinclined to yield his life, all the legions of heaven would have been ready to sustain his refusal. Then, on the other side, the resurrection of Christ marked the divine acceptance of Christ's oblation, so that nothing is lacking to the entire completeness of the salvation by him so far as God and Christ are concerned. Christ can save unto the uttermost all that come unto God by him. Let, then, none of his people be deficient on their part in that faith and those works proper to a Christian.

The scriptures make us assured that Jesus Christ will be mankind's final judge. Could there be one so fit? Himself man, knowing what was in man, and having been touched with the feeling of our infirmities, and in all points tempted as we are, how just and proper the selection! Whether as high priest for intercession, or a righteous judge to determine degrees of guilt, none so suitable as Jesus Christ.

But there is yet another aspect in which this subject might be viewed. Christ was a born Jew; a member of the Israelitish system and an element of its polity, and as it pleased God that all salvation should be through Jewish forms, Christ was still all appropriate. On earth Christ was not a priest to exercise a merely typical priesthood, but was called to heaven to be a priest most real and effectual after the pre-Levitical and high order of Melchisedec, king of peace. Christ was thus in every point of view before the mercy-seat in right of a divine vocation; of his perfect offering of his own precious blood and life; of himself.

On the whole, then, we perceive that God can be just to his own honor and dignity and a justifier of him who trusts in the acceptableness of Christ's atonement. The spirit of Christ's life and priesthood is a thoroughly hearty and loving concurrence in the law and will of God. "Sacrifice and offering," said he, "Thou would'st not; then said I, Lo, I come to do Thy will, O God."

The scripture testimonies to Christ are numberless. He paid the ransom of his blood to rescue his people from their dread responsibility to the divine law, blood being the only commodity exchangeable in the case. Christ only had the blood for the purpose. Of all the millions upon the earth Christ was the single being that could rightfully call his soul his own. Every other soul was forfeit; mortgaged beyond its owner's redemption. His only was free to be disposed of as he would. His people are thus said to have been redeemed, bought back, released from the bonds of sin and sin's penalties. Thus they are doubly his debtors; debtors by the beneficence and example of his life; debtors even yet more heavily by his most generous and self-sacrificing death. Christ is also the propitiation for our sins, and, by God's acceptance, for the sins (if repudiated) of the whole world. His people's robes are washed white and clean from the stains of sin in the Saviour's blood. Thus purified, Christ's people become conditioned to receive their crowns of righteousness, and with them an entrance upon life eternal.

After this digression we return to our reverend Congregationalist doctor, and gather the views of his church on soteriology. In two separate places, at the distance of fourteen pages apart, he lays down the principle that Christ's atonement derives "its infinite worth and efficacy from the presence of the divine nature in his person," a presence which he has quite failed in his attempt to prove. Complementary to this he also remarks, following Anselm's lead, "how impossible it is, in the nature of things, for a creature to atone for sin." On this point between us let appeal be made not to some indefinable "nature of things," but to the last arbiter, the Word of God. The earliest intimation, according to the general belief, is that in Genesis, 3: 15, where the sin-dispelling power of Christ is referred to in the saying that "the seed of the *woman* shall bruise the serpent's head." Is not the "seed of the woman" indisputably human? Again, when Moses, in Deut. 18: 15, foretold that the Lord God would raise up unto the children of Israel a prophet from the midst of them, of their brethren, like unto himself, "into whose mouth God would put his words," it would not be easy to define a being more decidedly human than the promised prophet, which is Christ. In the 53d chapter of Isaiah, which is wholly devoted to a prophecy concerning Christ, the future Saviour is portrayed as "a *man* of sorrows and acquainted with grief;" also, as one who "had done no violence, neither was any deceit in his mouth. Yet it pleased the Lord to bruise him; He hath put him to grief; when thou shalt make his *soul an offering for sin*." In the 32d chapter of the same prophet it is said that "a *man* shall be as a hiding place from the wind and a covert from the tempest." "By his knowledge," saith God, "shall my *righteous servant* justify many, *for he shall bear their iniquities*."

In all these testimonies and allusions no hint of deity is given; no "divine nature" intimated; but all is human. So in the New Testament the Apostle Peter teaches that the only name given among men whereby they can be saved is the name of the *man* Jesus whose domicile was at Nazareth. Paul, at Antioch, in Pisidia, taught his hearers that Jesus was of the seed or family of David, and that through him, thus humanly defined, come remission of sins and justification from all things from which mankind cannot be justified by the Mosaic law, which demands to be kept intact. Paul kept back from his hearers nothing that was profitable to them, and shunned not to declare the whole counsel of God. In his great Epistle to the Romans Paul shows how by "one man sin entered into the world, and death by sin," and how by "the righteousness of one came the free gift upon all men unto justification of life ; for if through the offence of one many be dead, much more the grace of God, and the gift by grace which is by one *man*, Jesus Christ, hath abounded unto many." So that Paul was wholly ignorant concerning that "infinite worth and efficacy" arising from the "divine nature and supreme deity of the Son," taught by old Anselm and our Congregationalist, for he described all the "abounding grace and gift of righteousness" which come to the people of God to the "obedience and righteousness" of the "one *man*," Jesus Christ. In that most striking chapter, the 15th of the 1st Corinthians, Paul states that "since by man came death, by *man* came also the resurrection of the dead; Christ, as the first fruits," rising first, and then afterwards, at Christ's second coming, Christ's true followers will rise. Not a hint does Paul furnish about any "divine nature" or "supreme deity" in Christ as having any office, operation, or function whatsoever. The Apostles never taught as does our Congregationalist, that one part of God required to be sacrificed to another part of God, or that God had to be sacrificed to himself. Scripture has no tendency that way, and puts no strain upon human reason or common sense.

Paul elsewhere teaches that there is "one mediator between God and man, the *man* Christ Jesus, who gave himself a ransom for all," yet the Congregationalist says it is "impossible in the nature of things for a creature, a man, to be a ransom or to atone for sin," in which the Congregationalist coincides with Anselm but disagrees with Paul. The reverse is the case with our humble selves, who differ with Anselm but coincide with Paul.

It will be observed that the scripture doctrine of salvation does not suppose that Christ's sufferings and death constituted an amount of punishment inflicted upon him equal to the quantity of punishment which the redeemed would otherwise unitedly endure to all eternity. They do not say, as some Nicenists do, that Christ suffered a penalty equivalent to the sum of the penalties that, but for him, would be suffered by the multitude of the redeemed. Nothing so gross as that, which shuts out all idea of forgiveness on God's part. On this theory there is no meaning in that petition of the Lord's prayer " Forgive us our trespasses," or in the language of the Apostle John that, in case of our sincere confession, "God is faithful and just to *forgive* us our sins and to cleanse us from all unrighteousness." Christ intimates that forgiveness may take place both in this world and in that which is to come, and upon the cross he cried aloud for his torturers, "Father, *forgive* them, for they know not what they do."

Now, the scriptural system of salvation supposes that God is continually exercising the merciful quality of forgiveness towards the members of Christ's church through the intercession of the Saviour in His immediate presence. It is against God that sin is committed, and God only can forgive so as to cancel the wrong. Of course he may delegate that power. God cancels sin, and "justly," as St. John remarks, when the penitent sinner, lamenting his past infidelity, sues for pardon with the earnest purpose in his heart to cease to do evil and learn to do well. Heaven takes due account of our frailty, and well knows that we were born under many a tendency to be and to do wrong. If, then, a new and right purpose has providentially sprung up within us; if we are humbly willing to accept the gracious plan of redemption and recovery which the New Testament holds forth; if we are baptized into Christ and to the best of our ability with prayer and supplication live after his laws and commands; then will God send down His Holy Spirit into our hearts, writing His will in our minds, and greatly aid our path to eternal peace. Thus by his life of pure precept and holy example, followed by a death exhibiting a perfect trust in God and assurance of a blissful immortality; by an ascension into heaven itself and the exercise of mediatorship and intercession there on our behalf, Jesus is entitled to be regarded, obeyed, honored and loved as a Saviour indeed. And, let it not be forgotten, these inestimable services, all performed without trenching upon the supreme sovereignty of the Infinite I AM, Jehovah, the LORD. All took and takes place to the "glory of God, the Father."

If there is no scriptural basis for the notion that the "efficacy and infinite worth" of Christ's "sufferings and death" must be referred "to a divine nature in Christ," neither is it rational. For what is there in deity that can suffer, or become the victim in a sacrifice? How can a Divine Being shed his blood, seeing he is pure spirit and without flesh and blood? Can deity be bruised? Can the soul of deity be made an offering for sin? Can the soul of deity be poured out unto death so that deity may die? But one answer and that a negative can be made to these queries. Atonement, or reconciliation, can be made by man only, and by man only was it made in the person of Jesus Christ of Nazareth. He stood as the head and representative of our human race, the "captain of our salvation made perfect through sufferings," and who "by the grace of God tasted death for every man" that wills to be represented by him, has been baptized into him, and lived consistently since. Besides all which, when did deity sin that it should be required to make atonement? When one was required to open the great book and loosen its seals, who responded but "the Lion of the tribe of Judah, who was slain and hath redeemed *his* people to God by his blood out of every kindred and tongue, and people and nation"? None of this can be predicated of any but a member of the human race.

Notwithstanding that the teachings of Christ and his Apostles leave no doubt as to that from which mankind require to be ransomed or rescued, namely, from the mastery of sin, alienation of heart from God, ruin and death eternal,—the ancient professors and writers on Christianity, who are called the "Fathers," seem to have been no little befogged and puzzled about it. Failure to study the scriptures in a proper spirit and temper must have been the cause of this obscurity, which was to a considerable extent its own punishment. But upon this subject we prefer adopting the statements of others, and copy from the article on Atonement in the International Cyclopædia, as follows, viz. : "In accordance with the full and explicit teaching of holy scripture, we find the sufferings and death of Christ were ever regarded as of primary and essential importance in his work of redemption, but notwitstanding this, we look in vain throughout the early centuries of the Christian church for anything like a systematic development of the doctrine of the Atonement. The germs of the doctrine existed, but without any logical connexion or clearness. The early church of fathers dwell with a sort of inspired devotion upon those facts of the gospel which represent Christ as the sacrifice for our sins ; as the ransom paid for our redemption ; as our deliverance from the power of Satan ; as the restorer to mankind of whatever was lost by the fall of Adam, but they seldom attempt to show how those blessed results connect themselves with the sufferings and death of Christ ; neither do they show in what manner the atonement has objectively been made, nor how it is brought to the experience of its individual subjects.

During the first four centuries there appeared no certainty of opinion as to whether those sufferings and death of Christ were a ransom paid to God or the devil! The latter supposition is the more prevalent, and is shared by Origen and Augustine. Gregory of Nyssa explains this opinion by saying that the devil consented to receive Jesus as a ransom because he regarded him as more than an equivalent for all those under his (Satan's) power; but that, notwithstanding his subtilty, he was outwitted, for, owing to the humiliation in which Christ was veiled, Satan did not fully recognize him as the Son of God, and, consequently, was himself deceived. But, having consented to receive him as a ransom for mankind, he was righteously deprived of his dominion over man, whilst he could not retain Jesus when he discovered him to be the Holy One of God, being horrified and tormented by his holiness.

Athanasius first of all successfully controverted this notion, and maintained that the ransom was paid to God. He argued that as God had threatened to punish transgressors with death, he could but execute his threat. But then it was not becoming the character of God to allow his purpose in the creation of man to be frustrated by an imposition practised upon Him by the devil. The only expedient, therefore, which remained for man's deliverance from death was the incarnation and sacrifice of the Logos in his stead, by which the justice and veracity of God would be maintained, man delivered, the law fulfilled, and the power of the devil broken. Tertullian never uses the term "satisfaction" with respect to Christ's atonement for sin in the sense of vicarious satisfaction, but only in the sense of making amends for our sins by confession and repentance.

But these ideas remained in a most imperfect and altogether undeveloped condition till Anselm of Canterbury reduced them to order and presented them in logical consistency. We must regard Anselm, therefore, as the author, at least as to its form, of the doctrine of vicarious satisfaction, which, under various modifications, has ever since been held as the orthodox doctrine of the church. The infinite guilt which man had contracted, by the dishonor of his sin, against the infinite great God, could be atoned for by no mere creature. Only the God-man, Christ Jesus, could render to God the infinite satisfaction required. God only can satisfy Himself. The human nature of Christ enables him to incur, the infinity of his divine nature to pay, this debt. But it was incumbent on Christ, as man, to order his life according to the law of God. The obedience of his life, therefore, was not able to render satisfaction for our guilt. But although he was under obligation to live in obedience to the law, as the holy one he was under no obligation to die. Seeing, then, that he, nevertheless, voluntarily surrendered his infinitely precious life to the honor of God, a recompense from God became his due, and his recompense consists in the forgiveness of the sins of his brethren. In this form of the doctrine we are taught the necessity of an active vicarious satisfaction. But Anselm nowhere teaches the passive satisfaction; he nowhere says that Christ endured the punishment of men. Nor do we find in his writings the development of the subjective side of the doctrine—namely, how the satisfaction rendered to God mediates the atonement in the experience of the believer.

According to Anselm, the satisfaction rendered by Christ was greater than the guilt for which he atoned; and it needed to be greater, for the payment of the debt due to God gave men no claim to the favor of God. Thomas Aquinas and his followers maintained Augustine's opinion of the infinite value of the blood of Christ, rendering it more than sufficient; whilst the Scotists maintained that it was sufficient only because God was pleased to regard it as sufficient.

Luther's opinion is that man's righteousness is the "imputed righteousness" of Christ. Dr. Trench's idea is that "Christ's sacrifice was vicarious. He died not merely for the good of, but in the room of and in the stead of, others. He tasted death for them. He did this of his own free will. He saw that nothing else would overcome their sinful perversity and wilful obduracy, and that this would be effectual to do so."

A review of this statement will disclose most of the disagreements it exhibits with the letter and spirit of the Bible. If the early centuries of the Christian church were without a "systematic development of the doctrine of the atonement" it was because they had turned their backs upon the ample teachings of the Bible, and were casting about to patch out their other inventions and so get a complete system which they could feel was all their own, and to which they could invite the submission of mankind. It seems they did not find this so easy as it was to bedizen and furbish out the good old Apostles' creed in their Nicene fabric; to dogmatize about the person of Christ, and lay down novelties to be forced, on pain of banishment or other severer penalties, upon popular acceptance. The uncertainty of the "Fathers" "during the first four centuries" whether the "ransom" residing in the sufferings and death of Christ was paid to God or the devil, verges on the ludicrous. That men of the reputations of Origen. Augustine, bishop of Hippo, and Gregory of Nyssa, with an alleged majority of their cotemporaries, should have supposed the ransom to be the devil's right, must let in no inconsiderable light upon the degenerate ideas then prevailing. The notion of Athanasius that the ransom was paid to God (he got near but did not distinctly see that it was paid to the authority and dignity of the divine law) is extremely little in accordance with what the Bible inculcates relative to the character and ways of God, for God does not desire to cause pain, privation and suffering for their own sake, or because He is irresistibly sovereign, but for the best good of those who are to be educated and improved by those expedients. God is the infinitely wise and beneficent Father of His rational offspring. The spirit of Athanasius has been reproduced in the ideas of John Calvin and President Edwards, who appear to have thought it a safe thing to urge the divine character as rather that of a stern ruler than of a beneficent Father. Athanasius's assumption that the "only remaining expedient for man's deliverance was the incarnation and sacrifice of the Logos," is an assumption more conformable with his own inventions and dogmas than with the truth of God and the doctrines of the Bible. If the vindication of the divine authority consists in the due and universal execution of the primal sentence pronounced against sin, viz., that death is its sure requital, then the divine benevolence is left open to operate on the conditions of the new covenant, which conditions are a cordial belief in the life, death, resurrection, ascension, and mediatorship of Christ, with a steady obedience to the institutions and moral and spiritual precepts of his Gospel. No man is authorized to demand for the "maintenance of the justice and veracity" of God more than God himself demands. "Blessed," said Christ, "are they that hunger and thirst after righteousness, for they shall be filled." A hearty desire engages the favor of heaven, which here or hereafter, and quite possibly in both states, will reward the desire with the object it sincerely craves. The principle of pardon, forgiveness, mercy to the genuinely penitent and meek, has vastly too little consideration and weight in the systems of Athanasius and his followers, yet the scriptures abound with that blessed mercy which "endureth forever." As to Anselm's doctrines, they are but natural offshoots from the Nicene basis, which is self-complimented with the title of "orthodoxy." We have seen that the "man," Christ Jesus, and not the imaginary and unscriptural "God-man," is competent to supply all the "ransom" that is called for by the law of that God, who will have all men to be saved and to come to the knowledge of the truth. The fond notion or analogy about an "infinite" satisfaction being called for by God because He is an infinite being, finds no encouragement from the Bible. God knoweth our frame and remembereth that we are dust. He proportions the burden to the back that is to carry it; besides all which God gave us the constitution and nature we possess. That other notion that Christ, as finite man, incurred a debt which he alone as infinite God could pay, (*i. e.*, pay in part to himself,) may have captivating features for some minds, but it is thoroughly alien to the Word of God. Whilst it is undoubtedly and absolutely true that Jesus had done nothing to subject him to the common sentence of death, and his death took place by his own consent, still, had he not died he could not have been Christ, and his refusal to die would have been contrary to the will and purpose of his Heavenly Father. And although Jesus had all along contemplated and spoken of his death, yet, when the trying moment actually arrived, his human nature thrice spoke distinctly forth in deprecation of the bitter cup presented to his taste, though concurrently therewith his soul displayed from its inmost depths the presence of a principle stronger than the love of life and dread of agony and death, that is to say, the principle of immovable rest and trust in the will and love of God. He said to his recalcitrant disciple Peter: "The cup which my Father hath given me, shall I not drink it?" He might indeed, without then dying, have continued to be the good-man Jesus, but in order to be Christ, God's anointed and Saviour of the World, every way perfect in precept and example, Jesus was under high obligation to die. God had determined on the death of His Son, and that made his death quite obligatory. Can any doubt this? What was Christ's own testimony on this head? In reasoning with those disciples on their way to Emmaus he said, "Ought not Christ to have suffered these things and to enter into his glory?"—into which he could not have entered but for the antecedent sufferings. Again, "Thus it is written and thus it behooved Christ to suffer and to rise from the dead the third day, and that repentance and remission of sins should be preached in his name among all nations, beginning at Jerusalem." Christ needed to die for every man, that every man may be baptized into his death, and so to die to the present world and rise again in and with Christ to a life immortal. Now, he that thus died and rose again was the man Jesus of Nazareth; the resurrected man, with hands and feet and a complete bodily organization, and not a spirit, much less, a deity. Through this man, with whom his Apostles "ate and drank after he rose from the dead," "repentance and remission of sins were to be preached among all nations," no matter what Athanasius and Anselm, and similar self-appointed creed-makers, might say or think.

Anselm's idea that Christ's satisfaction can be measured by the side "of the guilt for which he atoned" and is found to exceed it by a necessary overplus, suggests that he must have had a table of weights and measures by which to estimate guilt and righteousness. It is the said overplus only, according to Anselm, which entitles us to a "claim to the favor of God." Thus God is inferentially regarded as a stringent creditor and stern taskmaster, who demands to the uttermost, and whose unrelenting severity is mitigated only by the abounding virtue and excellence of Christ's satisfaction; from which there follows an inevitable contrast between the characters of God and of Christ, to the advantage of the latter. Were this as thus represented, the testimony of the scriptures to the forbearing mercy of God, to his loving-kindness, pity, and compassion, would be inaccurate and futile. With almost no doubt it may be concluded that to these teachings should be referred that noticeable preponderance of praise and thanksgiving offered to Christ in hymn books and poetical compositions over what is rendered to God. Christ is glorified as the practical benefactor. God's own declaration is virtually forgotten that "the Lord God is merciful and gracious, long-suffering and abundant in goodness and truth, keeping mercy for thousands, forgiving iniquity, transgression, and sin; but that will by no means clear the guilty"— meaning, we dare suppose, the incorrigibly, incurably guilty. Here is forgiveness for the penitent and not a thought of a satisfying equivalent. David prayed to God to "remember His tender mercies and loving-kindnesses, for they have been ever of old." "Remember not," said he, "the sins of my youth, nor my transgressions; according to thy mercy, remember thou me for thy goodness' sake, O Lord." "Good and upright is the Lord; therefore will he teach sinners in the way. Look upon my affliction and my pain, and forgive all my sins." What is the meaning of the word "forgive," but to treat the wrongdoer as if he were innocent? What is the meaning of the word "mercy," but the pardon and sparing of such as are obnoxious to punishment? The 103d Psalm and the 15th chapter of Luke's gospel justly describe these blessed elements of the divine character. And Isaiah, "The sacrifices of God are a broken spirit; a broken and a contrite heart, O God, thou wilt not despise." But above everything, let us call to mind the Saviour's assurance that "God so loved the world, that he gave his only begotten Son, that whosoever believeth in him should not perish, but have everlasting life." The Saviour's great excellence and glory consisted in his perfect concurrence with the will of God, cost him what of labor, endurance, agony, and suffering it might; but the benignity of the divine character was the originating and sustaining agency in the salvation of man. "Why," asked the Saviour, "callest thou me good? There is none good but one, that is, God."

In saying that Christ's sacrifice was vicarious, and that he tasted death instead of, or in the place of, every man, Dr. Trench appears to indicate that Christ's temporal death was a substitute for the eternal death of which his people were in peril. But this has nothing scriptural to sustain it. Doubtless Christ's sacrificial offering was essential to his becoming an intercessory mediator before the mercy seat in heaven. In that way the death on the cross becomes largely a preventive of his people's eternal death. For, says St. John, "If any man sin, we have an advocate with the Father, Jesus Christ, the righteous." Not "an advocate with the Father," because—as our Congregationalist would say—of "a divine nature in Christ giving infinite worth and efficacy to his sufferings and death," but because he is "Jesus Christ, *the righteous.*" Christ's spotless character, and not a superhuman nature, constitutes him the world's great advocate before the court of heaven.

A thought will possibly occur to some minds—If Christ be our advocate before the Father, then he is not the judge on the throne; that highest dignity God retains, as He does the disposal of other dignities, and the knowledge of the day of judgment and certain other times and seasons, in His own power. Hence, when Christ told the people that he had power *on earth* to forgive sins (a power that was also extended to his apostles), he meant to restrict the power to the "earth," and not to claim it as his universally. We see, hence, how appropriately he is called our prophet, priest, and king. Prophet, while conducting his ministry on earth; priest, now in heaven to appear in the presence of God for us; and king, subsequently to the great judgment-day, when "the restitution of all things" shall have taken place and his kingdom be without end.

THE PRESBYTERIAN CHURCH, comprising numerous subdivisions, is a large and respectable branch of the great Nicene profession. Statistics report that there are a few thousands less than a million members of the Church in the United States, with a ministry of almost nine thousand individuals and twelve thousand church edifices. It is claimed by Presbyterians that their denomination owns thirty thousand church buildings over the entire world, with a membership of thirty millions.

In respect to moral character, intellectual attainments, and all those qualities deemed creditable among men, the Presbyterians rank with the foremost. None are firmer in their attachment to their church, its doctrines and polity, and none more decidedly Protestant or reliable in their support of existing civil and religious liberty. Holding principles Calvinistic in the main, the tenacious and sturdy spirit and temper of their chief founders, John Calvin and John Knox, seem diffused throughout the mass, and impart a characteristic sternness and rigidity. A Presbyterian writer, referring to somebody's complaint that "Calvinism plies men with hammer and chisel,"—admits it with exultation. "It does," he says, "and the result is monumental marble. Other systems leave men soft and dirty; Calvinism makes them of white marble to endure for ever." Would it could be said that Calvinism or something else had not endowed many of the name with marble hearts which could endure the infliction of terrible yet unmerited miseries and sufferings upon others who differed with them upon topics of a religious nature. It is written with an indelible pen on the pages of history that though Calvinists have invariably antagonized the Church of Rome, they have not, on occasion, refused to join Catholic persecutors in hunting down to ruin and destruction innocent men whose only crime has been an open and consistent advocacy of the pure and unsophisticated teachings of God's Word. Switzerland, Italy, Holland, and Poland in particular, testify to the persecutions perpetrated by and with the advice and consent of John Calvin himself, of Theodore Beza, of Farel, of Bullinger, and others of that ilk, too numerous to mention. Happily for the world at large the unwisdom, as well as the wickedness, of despotic cruelty has come to be clearly seen, especially when directed against the exercise of sincere and conscientious investigation of religious subjects. The most and worst done in the persecuting line in these days is the occasional characterization of an opponent's ideas as coming from a rationalist, a sceptic, unbeliever, or, with somewhat of special vigor, from a Socinian. Hard names have kindly taken the place of hard blows.

With all their inveteracy against the Roman Church the Calvinists did not probe down in the days of the Reformation, neither have they since gone deeper for and with reform than to make changes in church polity, ecclesiastical usages and the externals of public worship. They have accepted and become exceedingly sturdy sticklers for the innovating enactments of the synod of Nice and those other pompously styled "ecumenical" synods, or councils, which make notorious the fourth and fifth centuries of our era.

The written standard of faith of the Presbyterian Church everywhere is the Confession of the Westminster Assembly of Divines, which was drawn up in the year 1643 and made national in Scotland by act of Parliament in 1690. It consists of thirty-three divisions or chapters, very much more minute and voluminous than the Articles of the Protestant Episcopal Church. In the chapter on the being of God it is said, "There is but one only living and true God, who is infinite in being and perfection, a most pure spirit, without body, parts or passions, immaterial, immense, &c., &c., &c., hating all sin, and who will by no means clear the guilty." Passing by the inconsistency of describing the deity as "without passions," yet exercising the passion of hatred towards sin, the great similarity or rather identity of the leading article of the Episcopal Church with this chapter becomes evident, and particularly in the section which says, "In the unity of the, or *this*, godhead (though no godhead had been mentioned) there be three persons of one substance, power and eternity—God the Father, God the Son and God the Holy Ghost."

There must have been an unusually cogent reason for this close verbal coincidence of the two churches at this particular point, which reason probably consists in the fact that neither church could devise any other way that looked like getting out of the insurmountable difficulty of reconciling the statement of God's strict oneness with the statement of his triplicity; or, that the three severally coequal beings—God the Father, God the Son, and God the Holy Ghost—incontestably *three* parts—are contained in the "One only God" who is "*without* parts."

It was therefore not a real but only a seeming solution of the difficulty; in fact, an evasion; yet such as might escape popular detection. "God" and "godhead" are not synonymous or convertible terms, as the chapter covertly intimates, because "God" is a masculine noun, implying individuality and uniqueness, whilst "godhead" is a neuter noun of multitude, capable of containing an unlimited plurality. When, therefore, the words "the" or "this godhead" were written down as if synonymous with the word "God," which had preceded, an artifice was practiced quite out of place in a solemn declaration purporting to teach millions the truth on the most sublime of all subjects, the being of the Supreme. The inconvertibility of the two words "God" and "godhead" may be further illustrated by putting the word "godhead" into the first definition, and the word "God" into the second. Both words will then be seen unsuitably placed, which would not be if they were equivalent and convertible.

In a further description of the three persons of the Trinity, the Westminster Confession practically nullifies the deity of the Son and Holy Ghost, and also their co-equality with the Father. It says, "the Father is of none, neither begotten nor proceeding; the Son is eternally begotten of the Father; the Holy Ghost eternally proceeding from the Father and the Son." Now, it is characteristic of true deity that it is underived and self-existent. These points are fully admitted by the Confession relative to the Father, but denied to the Son and Holy Ghost, for the Son is "begotten" and the Holy Ghost "proceeding." There is, however, a very great obscurity in describing the Son as "eternally begotten," which may very well mean *continuously* "begotten," especially as we learn from scripture, and it is the general judgment and belief, that the Holy Ghost is continuously "proceeding." The Father, then, is by the very showing of this Confession itself, the only underived, self-existent God; the fountain of being; of whom the Son is "eternally" (whatever that might mean) begotten, and the Holy Ghost "eternally" proceeding; no self-derivation or self-existence in either.

As an additional evidence of the unsound foundation of the Nicene and Calvinistic doctrine, it is not unworthy of note that the Westminster Confession rests its grand dogma of "God the Father, God the Son and God the Holy Ghost" on the once assumed scriptural—but now well known and universally acknowledged spurious—text, 1st John, 5: 7, as read in the King James translation. So, as time goes on, falls or rots away prop after prop of the Nicene edifice.

In a later chapter the Confession enjoins that "Religious worship is to be given to God the Father, Son and Holy

Ghost, and to *him* alone," using the singular pronoun "him" as if the human mind, when it has three distinct objects placed before it, could regard the three as but a single object "alone." Those who may happen to prefer giving "true" religious worship to "Him alone" to whom it is due, will do well to consult Christ's conversation with the woman of Samaria, as found in the 4th chapter of John's gospel. Compared with this the Westminster formulary exhibits a great deal of surplusage.*

---

*The Presbyterian or Westminster Confession is as follows on the subjects of the Divine nature and of the generation of Christ:

Chapter 2, section 3.

"In the unity of the godhead there be three persons of one substance, power and eternity; God the Father, God the Son and God the Holy Ghost.—1st John, 5: 7—(*Spurious.*)

"The Father is of none, neither begotten nor proceeding; the Son is eternally begotten of the Father, the Holy Ghost eternally proceeding from the Father and the Son."

Chapter 8, section 2.

"The Son of God, the second person in the Trinity, being very and eternal God, of one substance and equal with the Father, did, when the fulness of time was come, take upon him man's nature with all the essential properties and common infirmities thereof, yet without sin, being conceived by the power of the Holy Ghost in the womb of the Virgin Mary, of her substance. So that two whole, perfect and distinct natures, the godhead and the manhood, were inseparably joined together in one person, without conversion, composition or confusion; which person is very God and very man, yet One Christ, the only mediator between God and man."

Section 3.

"The Lord Jesus, in his human nature thus united to the divine, was sanctified and anointed with the Holy Ghost above measure," &c., &c.

On the subject of the generation of Christ the Presbyterian symbol is ungrammatically expressed, and is so entangled and intervolved as to require considerable pains to unravel it. The Episcopal article, though not free from difficulty, is comparatively plain and intelligible. The Presbyterian declaration, when straightened out, states that the second person in the Trinity took upon him man's nature of or from the substance of the Virgin Mary, being, viz., *which had been*, conceived by the power of the Holy Ghost, because the symbol cannot mean, though it verbally says, that very and eternal God, the second person in the Trinity, of one substance with the Father, was conceived in the womb of the Virgin Mary. It is to be understood, then, that according to the Presbyterian Confession, the "One Christ" is the result of an annexation of the second person of the Trinity to the human fruit of the conception by the Holy Ghost; that is to say, the human child Jesus, produced from the influence of the Holy Ghost upon Mary, received by annexation to its person (presumably at the instant of the aforesaid conception) the "whole, perfect, and distinct nature" of the second person in the Trinity. Annexation, it will be perceived, escapes "conversion, composition and confusion," and remains the only conceivable interpretation of the alleged "taking upon him" mentioned in section 2. Christ is, therefore, according to this symbol, a duplex being, part God and part man, both parts being "inseparably joined together." It must hence follow that there is a manifest difference

It is not our purpose to make any extended review of so great an aggregation as the Westminster Confession, which—whilst interspersed with numerous points both true and good—looks mainly like a magisterial dictation of what every one on earth, and perhaps out of it, ought to believe about divine things, but, after a passing remark on a single sentence, to present the Presbyterian doctrine on the important subject of Baptism, and close with a rapid sketch of Calvin and Knox, the veritable rocks whence this system was hewn and the pits from which it was digged.

The single sentence of the Confession referred to is that which declares that "the sin of our first parents God was pleased to permit, having purposed to order it to His own glory," which teaches to the ordinary apprehension that God permitted sin, if he did not ordain it, because it furnished him an opportunity whereby better to enhance His own glory than Adam and Eve's sinlessness would have done. This, however, seems to involve the consequence that God's interest in man's sin was greater than in his righteousness, for which reason God permitted the

---

between the Episcopal article and the Presbyterian dictum, for whilst the latter (therein agreeing with scripture) shows the Holy Ghost to have been the actual genitor of Jesus, the former ascribes his paternity to the God-the-Son, saying nothing at all in that connexion about the Holy Ghost or God the Father. Yet both churches claim to be orthodox.

One or two notes and queries step in here. Note 1st, that whilst both Episcopals and Presbyterians mention God-the-Son, the second person in the Trinity, as a principal party to the generation of Jesus, neither Matthew nor Luke, nor the Apostles' creed, in their accounts of Christ's origin, seem to know anything whatever about it. The earliest statement of the doctrine is in the Nicene creed, and to this our orthodox friends adhere in preference to the unvarnished testimony of the New Testament. Note 2d, that if at the instant of conception the "two whole, perfect and distinct natures" of the second person of the Trinity and of the human child Jesus "were inseparably joined together," "never to be divided," it must follow that they continued in the same "inseparable" state of junction during the virgin's whole gestatory period; and further, that she was delivered of the second person of the Trinity and of the human babe at the same time. Such must have been the result of the alleged "inseparable" junction. Note 3d. It is said in one of the gospels that Gabriel's visit "troubled" Mary; what might have been her trouble if Gabriel had told her that she should bring forth not only a human son, Jesus, but "very and eternal God, of one substance and equal with the Father!" Gabriel spared her such astounding intelligence, not, most likely, out of any special kindness, but because, like Matthew, Luke, and the authors of the Apostles' creed, he was himself quite uninformed upon the subject. Note 4. Protestant Episcopalians and Presbyterians have been known to reproach Roman Catholics for designating the Virgin Mary "Mother of God." Now, reflecting on their own articles and Confession, can it be said that they do not furnish the Catholics with a good excuse for so doing? More than that, do they not furnish the Catholics with a justification? And no wonder, when, on a cardinal doctrine, both parties are inspired from the same source.

sin. Not only does this appear to reverse all our best ideas of the perfect rectitude and holiness of the Divine will and government, but to contradict the Apostles' doctrine that by sinning men have not furthered, but "come short of the glory of God." Calvinistic doctrine is pervaded with the notion that the interior compelling force of the Divine Mind is the desire to manifest forth the Divine power and glory, and in the pursuit of this end to be willing to overlook every other consideration and every other being in the universe. Instead of a righteous father ruling with a father's just authority Calvinism regards God as a stern and jealous monarch, ever intent simply on Himself. It seems to have missed appreciation of the Saviour's assurances of the Divine relation and the Divine love at the time he announced his own personal departure to Mary Magdalene at the sepulchre, and said, "Go to my *brethren* and say unto them, I ascend unto *my* Father and *your* Father, and to *my* God and *your* God."

The Westminster Confession is Pædobaptist, and teaches that "dipping the person is not necessary, but that baptism is rightly administered by pouring or sprinkling water on the person." Not wishing very much to antagonize the Confession on this head in our own person, we will let John Milton mainly represent the views we hold, taking Milton to be at least equal, head and shoulders, to Calvin or Knox, or any of their associates.

Under the gospel, the first of the two great sacraments, or sealings of the covenant of grace, whereby men testify their faith and obedience to God with a sincere heart and grateful remembrance, is Christian Baptism. The form of this sealing, or sacrament, is an immersion into water, (Milton preferred *running* water,) signifying their regeneration by the Holy Spirit and their union with Christ in his death, burial, and resurrection. The going down into the water represents *death and descent* into *the grave;* the temporary concealment under the water represents *burial*, which is a temporary withdrawal from the world's ken; and the rising again out of the water represents *resurrection.* Thus the rite of baptism by immersion symbolizes the great distinguishing and central truth of the Christian religion which it was so hard to get the world in the days of Christ and the Apostles to believe, as we may note in Paul's plaintive interrogatory before Agrippa, "Why should it be thought a thing incredible with you that God should raise the dead?" The entire suitableness, therefore, of baptism by immersion—for baptism by simple pouring or sprinkling is meaningless—must be evident to every mind, and all the rather when we recollect it was the form adopted by John the Baptist; was accepted by Christ in his own case; practiced by Christ's Apostles, and was prevalent throughout the Christian world in the early ages and centuries of Christian history, and as continued down thence is the only form in use at the present day in the Eastern or Greek church, and wherever, as in Russia, that church holds sway.

Milton quotes Christ's command to baptize at the close of the gospels of Matthew and Mark, showing the indispensable necessity of baptism. "He that believeth and is baptized shall be saved, and he that believeth not shall be damned," and by the text, observing the order, first, belief, conviction, and conversion; then corporal baptism, followed by a newness of life, even "as Christ was raised from the dead by the glory of the Father." See also the first few verses of the sixth chapter of Paul to the Romans, and likewise the twelfth verse of his second chapter to the Colossians. Baptism represents—as by dramatic rehearsal—the death and burial of the "old man," with the rising again, whereby he has become altogether new.

Milton goes on to say that, in contemplation of baptism, rightly understood, "infants are not to be baptized, inasmuch as they are incompetent to receive instruction as a believer, or to enter into a covenant, or to promise or answer for themselves, or even to hear the word. For how can infants, who understand not the word, be purified thereby, any more than adults can receive edification by hearing an unknown language? For it is not that outward baptism which purifies only the filth of the flesh, that saves us, but "the answer of a good conscience," as Peter testifies, of which infants are incapable. Besides, baptism is not merely a covenant, containing a certain stipulation on one side with a corresponding engagement on the other, which in the case of an infant is impossible, but it is also a vow— of the nature of an oath of allegiance—and as such can neither be pronounced by infants nor required of them. "It is remarkable," says Milton, "to what futile arguments those divines have recourse who maintain the contrary opinion." They allege the text in Matthew 19: 14, "suffer little children to come unto me, for of such is the kingdom of heaven." It appears, however, that children were not brought to Christ to be baptized, but "that he might put his hands upon them and pray. And Christ laid his hands upon them and departed thence," with no mention of baptism. Mark says Christ blessed the children, which he no doubt did. From which Milton concludes: "Let the church therefore receive infants which come unto her, after the example of Christ, with imposition of hands and benediction, but not with baptism." As to Christ's saying "of such are the kingdom of heaven," he had respect to their simplicity and innocence, which cannot be said of infants who have not as yet the faculty of reason.

As touching Acts, 2: 39, whence Pædobaptists argue that the "promise is to children as well as to others," if they will only read two verses further on they will find it written "they that gladly received the Apostle's word were baptized," showing that understanding and will were necessary qualifications for baptism, neither of which is possessed by infants. In respect to the supposed parallel between Jewish circumcision and Christian baptism, no such analogy exists, for females do not have part in the first, while baptism is for all people and nations without distinction in the second, for the remission of sins and sanctification, a sign of our death and resurrection with Christ. For baptism there must be previous knowledge and faith; of which infants and young children are incapable.

Infants were not fit for the baptism of John, who required repentance and confession of sin; still less fit are they for the baptism of Christ, which demands knowledge, repentance and faith.

Referring to the appropriateness of immersion, Milton continues: "It is in vain alleged by those who, on the authority of Mark, 7:4, and Luke, 11:38, (where the practice of frequent washings of cups and of the hands by the Jews is alluded to,) have introduced the practice of affusion, or sprinkling, instead of immersion, that to dip and sprinkle mean the same thing, since in washing we do not sprinkle the hands, but immerse them."

With respect to what is often called the "baptismal formula," in Matt., 28:19, "go ye therefore and teach all nations, baptizing them into (not in) the name of the Father and of the Son and of the Holy Ghost," Milton rightly alludes to the total omission in the New Testament of all record that the Apostles ever used this so-called formula, the circumstance of which omission makes it far from improbable that the baptism indicated by Christ in this text was not the bodily baptism in water—which would follow in due order and sequence—but the preliminary spiritual baptism or indoctrination into the mind and heart of the convert, well defined by a baptism into the name (that is, the knowledge) of the Father, Son, and Spirit, which will comprise the whole Gospel. A baptism *into* a name or names is surely not the same thing as a baptism in water, nor can a mere immersion of the body in water be a substitute for it, though the latter may well symbolize the reception of it, and be a public testimony thereto.

The indication that the supposed formula in Matt., 28: 19, was not intended by Christ as an indispensable feature in the ceremony of water-baptism, has this to prove it, viz., that nothing of the kind anywhere else appears, unless it is to be understood that the mention of "the Son" in the text would naturally suggest that water-baptism had special reference to him, and to him only, because he only died and rose again, which the Father and the Holy Ghost assuredly did not. Baptism into their name must, therefore, be a totally different thing from the baptism into Christ as understood and practiced by the Apostles. Paul indignantly inquires of the Corinthians if "Paul was crucified for them? or were they baptized into the name of Paul"? He does not ask if they were baptized into the Father and the Holy Ghost. From all which it may be concluded that the baptism alluded to in Matt., 28: 19, was an indoctrination into the gospel in its every branch, each respectively presided over by Father, Son and Holy Ghost, so that to mention those names separately was to comprise in an impressive manner the whole body of divine truth—the whole gospel. This conclusion is borne out by the parallel texts in Mark, 16: 15 and 16, and Luke, 24: 47. It cannot be doubted that if Matt. 28: 19 was intended to be as now commonly supposed, the other three gospels would have similarly enforced that meaning, whereas not one of them nor the whole book of the Acts, with its numerous instances of baptisms, has a syllable or hint that way, but altogether in the direction we have indicated.

Since baptism symbolizes "buried into death" and "being planted together in the likeness of Christ's death," and the baptized Christian is regarded as "dead, and his life *hid* with Christ in God," it inevitably follows that baptism cannot be effected by any representative ceremonial which does not carry the subject of it temporarily out of sight. This excludes affusion and sprinkling, which are performed with the subject in full sight during the whole of the ceremony.

Voluminous have been the discussions touching the scriptural meaning of the word "baptize," originally Greek. We will simply state what seems to be indisputable, that it is a compound word, consisting of the two parts "bapt" and "ize," whereof the former means *dip* or *immerse*, the latter thoroughly or with effect. The whole, therefore, to *dip thoroughly;* that is, out of sight.

Lastly, if, in the judgment of Christ and his Apostles, pouring or sprinkling was as good as full baptizing, why did they subject their converts to the more difficult and unpleasant ceremonial when the simple and easy one would answer just as well? It is hard to think from their known benevolence they would do anything of the kind.

Of the general purport of Christian baptism, though it may seem tautological, let us briefly remark that it indicates an entrance into the Church of Christ, which is the kingdom of God. The baptism by water signifies the subject's spiritual disconnection with this world and his coascension with Christ: the baptism into the Spirit cements the believer's union with the pervading power of the world to come. How palpable, then, the verity of Christ's words, "Ye must be born from above."

When Peter, on the day of Pentecost, preached that opening address of the Apostolic band, and 3,000 far from tractable Jewish people were converted, Peter prefixed the indispensable prerequisite of repentance to the rite of baptism, to which succeeded the gift of the Holy Ghost. So when Peter and John found that the converts in Samaria had simply been baptized into the name of the Lord Jesus, they petitioned that the complemental blessing of the Holy Spirit might be granted them also. It was granted, for it had been probably kept back that the gift might authenticate those two Apostles to the Samaritan people. Such are the wisdom and goodness of God and of His Son. Again, at Cesarea in the house of the Centurion Cornelius, baptism and the gift of the Holy Ghost were imparted; though in this case the order was changed, the gift came before the baptism, very likely to provide that Peter should be admonished that God's purpose was to confer on Gentiles as well as Jews, repentance unto life. The circumstances of the baptism of Cornelius and his household forcibly teach the indispensableness of the act of outward baptism. Though the Holy Ghost had been imparted, the necessity for baptism had not been superseded, because visible baptism signalizes visible entrance into the church or body of Christ, which is the kingdom of God. One more instance will suffice to show that baptism is the prescribed method of entrance into the Christian church. When the twelve disciples at Ephesus, who had been baptized only by John's baptism and did not know whether there were any Holy Ghost, were more thoroughly instructed, Paul counselled their baptism into the name of the Lord Jesus. This being accomplished, the Holy Ghost was communicated to the whole party, with miraculous gifts superadded. It may not be inopportune to remark at this point, that if the modernly supposed "baptismal formula" is indispensably necessary to the right celebration of Christian baptism, then the Apostle Paul, on this occasion alone, caused twelve baptisms to be wrongly conducted, to say nothing of the multitude of cases elsewhere of the same erroneous character. The Protestant Episcopal Church would not admit to its communion such as these twelve Ephesian converts, because the aforesaid "formula," which that church regards as the "essential part of baptism," was not complied with when they were only "baptized into the name of the Lord Jesus." The Presbyterian Church coincides with the Episcopal in its views concerning baptism, except only as to sponsors, and translates Matt. 28: 19 with the same misleading inaccuracy. It would also refuse communion with persons baptized as were those twelve Ephesian converts, and for the same reason—that baptism merely into the name of the Lord Jesus is informal and insufficient. No candid Episcopalian or Presbyterian will deny that the motive behind the exclusive devotion shown by their churches to the mistranslated text in Matt. 28: 19 and their consequent disparagement of the apostolic practice, is the support presumed to be furnished by the said text to the Athanasian Trinity. But that support is the slenderest imaginable.

JOHN, the second son of Gerard Cauvin, or CALVIN, was born in July, 1509, at the diocesan city of Noyon, in the north of France. Gerard was secretary to the bishop, notary apostolic and procurator fiscal, a man of ability and in excellent repute. His wish was to give his children the best attainable education, and circumstances being favorable, his son John profited thereby to an uncommon degree. He was educated partly at Noyon under his father's strict eye and jealous care, with a view to entering the Catholic Church, and at the early age of twelve was made chaplain. Thus early in life he exhibited many of the traits that marked his career throughout; laborious, faithful to his duties, silent and grave in demeanor, he took no part in the sports and diversions of his fellow-students, but often severely censured what he deemed to be their shortcomings "with a measure, even," says one of his admirers, "of acrimony." Indeed, it is said, that his companions fixed upon him the epithet or nickname of "accusative." Soon after his induction to the chaplaincy of La Gesine he received the tonsure at the hands of Bishop Hangest, which made him capable of becoming a priest. In 1523 the plague struck Noyon, and many of its people were cut off. Calvin's father was much exercised for the safety of his son, and procured for him permission to remove temporarily to Paris without the loss of his incomes. He went there in company of some youths of the noble Mommor family, with whom he had been long associated, and took up his studies in the college of La Marche under the charge of Maturin Cordier, famous for his scholarship and skill in teaching. Calvin's progress in his studies was rapid, and the proficiency he attained in the knowledge and use of the Latin language remarkable. At this time the Roman priesthood and the bigoted Francis 1st, King of France, caused Protestant blood to flow in streams. Calvin fell in with one Olivetan, who had translated the Bible into French, which Calvin read, and his faith in the popular Catholic religion became so much shaken that he rejoiced in never having become a Catholic priest. His father, being dissatisfied that one so competent as John was making so little money, advised him to abandon the church and take up the civil law, which, agreeing with Calvin's own feelings at the time, he left Paris and went to Orleans, commencing there the study of the law, and with such devotion that his health suffered. He then went to the city of Bourges, finding there Melchior Volmar, a German Lutheran, from whom he learnt Greek and the reformed religion. When at Bourges he was advised of his father's death, which took him back to Noyon, where he remained till the year 1532. Abandoning now the study of law he resumed theology, but according to the principles of the new faith. Persecution for religion's sake was terribly rife, and the king's heart obdurate, which Calvin hoped to soften by publishing an edition of Seneca's treatise on Clemency, with a commentary, which he dedicated to his friend, the Abbot Claude Mommor. No such good effect followed, but a heavy expense devolved on Calvin, which he honestly discharged by the sacrifice of a part of the property he had received from his father. About this time, say 1533, Calvin was an advocate for making the pure Bible the basis of church doctrine. Nicholas Cop, regent of the Sorbonne, delivered before that college an address which had been written for him by Calvin; but it was so full of the reformed ideas, and particularly of the doctrine of justification by faith, that it produced an explosion in the college, and Cop had to flee from Paris. He betook himself to Basil, in Switzerland, a retreat for refugees from Romish persecution. Calvin was compelled to take care of himself by concealment, and, flitting from place to place, found temporary safety at Nerac, where Margaret, queen of Navarre, a sister of the king, though of the new faith, had her court. Thence Calvin returned to Noyon and to Paris, where he had to keep retired. About this time Michael Servetus, a Spanish physician, and a decided reformer, crossed Calvin's path. Servetus went further than Calvin, in that he, resting on the Bible pure and simple, denied the doctrine of the Trinity, and a day for debate on the subject was agreed upon between them, though Servetus did not appear at the appointed time, either from fear of his opponent's arguments or the minions of Rome. At this period, too, Calvin encountered some Anabaptists, with whom he contended about their belief that the soul continues dormant between the period of death and resurrection. He wrote a book to refute this view. On leaving Paris he went to Angouleme and taught Greek. His next travel was once more to the city of Orleans, and thence to Poictiers, where he preached and organized a ministry. But he was compelled to flee from France, and he bent his steps towards Basil, the house of refuge. One of his servants cruelly robbed him on the way, so that he had to borrow some money wherewith to get to Strasburgh. At length he arrived in Basil, and was welcomed by the numerous refugees gathered there. Here he went on with his Institutes of the Christian Religion, which he had already commenced. He wrote the dedication to Francis the First in such choice Latin as almost to constitute the wonder of the age. To some editions is prefixed the device of a flaming sword, with a motto in Latin, signifying "I came not to send peace, but a sword." His next movement was to Italy, on a visit to Reneè de France, Duchess of Ferrara, who, like Queen Margaret, entertained the reformed ideas. Calvin now designed seeking a place of permanent residence at Basil, and set out for that city; but finding the usual route obstructed, was obliged to take Geneva by the way. Here, casually meeting with the two French refugees, William Farel and John Viret, he was prevailed on to remain, and was forthwith elected by the magistrates and people professor of theology and preacher. His age at this time was about twenty-seven. One of the first acts of Calvin and Farel was to draw up a system of reformed religious doctrine whereby the distracted notions of the people might be brought into a reasonable uniformity. To this the people were required to swear fealty. Calvin also prepared a catechism for children at school. He complained of certain irregularities, and declared his refusal to celebrate the Lord's Supper till they were removed. He also refused to submit to some regulations lately adopted by the canton of Berne, which included the use of unleavened bread at the Lord's Supper; that the baptismal fonts, which had been removed from the churches, should be restored, and the old customary feasts be reintroduced. This brought on a conflict, the result of which was that a vote was taken, and Calvin and Farel were ordered out of Geneva within two days. They submitted. Calvin went to Berne and Zurich, and then to Strasburgh, where he was allowed to start a church on his own model. He married in Strasburgh one Idelette Van Buren, a widow, and remained there till 1541, keeping up a correspondence with his friends at Geneva, where disorder reigned and efforts were on foot to restore the papal power. All this only tended to open the way to Calvin's return to Geneva, whither his friends invited him and whereat he arrived in September, 1541, the decree of banishment having been duly revoked. He soon became master of the situation, and found himself immersed in a multitude of duties and services of various kinds. He had for antagonists, political and otherwise, two men, Pighius and Jerome Bolsec, the latter of whom was originally a Carmelite friar at Paris, but becoming attached to the reformed doctrines went to Ferrara, and there probably met with Calvin. He assumed the profession of a physician and made his way to Geneva, but in 1551 he allowed his disapproval of Calvin's doctrine of absolute decrees so to affect him, that one day after the close of public worship, but while the congregation was still full, he lifted up his voice and denounced said doctrine in a loud and indecorous manner. For this he was imprisoned, and finally banished. "He then," says Mosheim, "returned to the place of his nativity and to the communion of Rome, and published the most bitter and scandalous libels, in which the reputation, conduct, and morals of Calvin and Beza were cruelly attacked."

Another of the somewhat numerous persons with whom Calvin fell into conflict was Sebastian Castalio, about six years younger than Calvin and a native of France. He met Calvin at Strasburgh in 1540, and subsequently went to Geneva, where, by reason of his extensive learning and fine taste, he became master of the public school, which position he might have retained indefinitely but for Calvin's vengeful spirit and unbounded worship of his own dogmas. As it was, Castalio was head of the Genevan school only three years. It so happened that Castalio could not approve of punishing what Calvin and company were pleased to call *heresy* by inflictions as if for crimes; neither could he bow down to their notions about predestination; he did not also share Calvin's ideas about the Song of Solomon; thought what seemed to him right concerning Christ's descent into hell, and was supposed to hold some views in common with the Anabaptists. Therefore Calvin and Beza persecuted him, and drove him with his large family to look for a living elsewhere than in Geneva. He went to Basil and taught Greek in the university, but his circumstances were so narrow as on one occasion to suggest to him to catch some driftwood that was running during a freshet in the river Rhine. Calvin, however, charged him with *stealing* the wood; to which Castalio firmly but meekly replied, claiming the right to catch for himself what belonged to nobody in particular, and appealing to the people of Basil in defense of his moral character. It is evident from what is recorded that Calvin and Beza essayed some efforts to get their victim driven from Basil, but he was too good and learned a man for the people to treat in that way. He translated the Bible into Latin and French, and wrote other works, dying in poverty at the age of forty-eight.

The historian Mosheim gives other instances of Calvin's indulgence in tyranny and personal hate, to wit, Calvin's "intimate friend and patron, Jaques de Bourgogne, a man illustrious by his descent from the dukes of Burgundy, who had settled at Geneva with no other view than to enjoy the pleasure of conversing with him." This gentleman had employed Jerome Bolsec as his physician, and was "so well satisfied with his services that he endeavored to support him and to prevent his being ruined by the enmity and authority of Calvin. This incensed Calvin to such a degree that he turned the force of his resentment against this illustrious nobleman, who, to avoid his vengeance, removed from Geneva and passed the remainder of his days in a rural retreat."

Another instance was George Blandrata, an Italian physician and divine, who after practicing medicine in Poland and Transylvania, returned to Italy, but was compelled by the Inquisition there to fly. He went to Geneva, calling himself a Catholic, but as Calvin suspected he was an Arian, Blandrata had to flee Geneva likewise. He became physician to Sigismund and Stephen, emperors of Poland.

Bernardino Ochino, an Italian, was also made to feel the bigotry and intolerance of the same parties. He had been a general in the order of Capuchins, but after his conversion became pastor of a reformed church at Zurich; yet not sufficiently curbing his intellectual forces so as to suit the scale of opinion established by Calvin, he had to betake himself to Poland. Theodore Beza is supposed to have done himself no credit in pretending to justify the treatment visited upon Ochino.

Some estimate might be formed of the style of government set on foot in Geneva by Calvin after his final return thither. It could inflict all kinds of censures and punishments as far as excommunication. Many disliked this as endangering a return to papal tyranny, but Calvin maintained his ground and upheld the Consistory, of which he was perpetual president. He was also president of the Assembly of the clergy. He would never allow any change or modification of his system, which looked to making Geneva to the Protestant world what Rome was and is to the Papal. As a sample of the interference of his laws and regulations with the social and personal rights and liberty of the citizen, we have an account amusing enough to read about when applied to others, but which must have been vexatiously bitter to actual experience. A bride on her way to church was arrested for having her hair too much decorated, and was kept under arrest for three days. Two ladies who attended her shared the same fate, as did the serving woman that bedecked the offending head. This was done by the power of the Consistory under the influence of Calvin's church.

But of the enormities whose number was doubtless legion, there is one which stands forth never to be forgotten—the cold-blooded destruction at Calvin's instance of the honest but indiscreet Servetus, of about the same age as himself, and whom he had met many years before. Servetus had been wandering about Europe, a firm believer, if sometimes an injudicious proclaimer, of the unity of God in one person, and was on his way to Zurich by the route of Geneva. He arrived at the last-named city in the middle of July, 1553, a refugee from Papal persecution on account of his creed. He remained in Geneva almost a month and was to leave for Zurich on the 14th of August. The day before his intended departure he went to church, where the keen vision of Calvin descried him. More than seven years before this, viz., on the 13th February, 1546, Calvin had written to Farel telling him that in case of the entrance of Servetus into Geneva, "I shall never permit him to depart alive if my authority be great enough." Servetus had written a book designed to disprove the doctrine of the Trinity. He had also verbally uttered the same sentiments. At Calvin's instance Servetus was arrested (for no present crime, legal, social, moral, or ecclesiastical, in Geneva) on a charge of heresy and blasphemy, Calvin appearing as accuser, reminding us of the sobriquet "accusative" which his fellow students had put upon him in his younger days. It was said, too, that at some time and somewhere, Servetus had put grit between Calvin's teeth by making the declaration "that neither the Bible nor the Ante-Nicene fathers knew anything of the Trinity, and that the doctrine stands as the great obstacle to keep Jews and Mohammedans from becoming Christians."

After a protracted trial, in which accuser and accused displayed much dialectic skill, Servetus was condemned and sentenced to die by burning at the stake, which was carried into effect without delay on the 27th October, 1553. Farel was Calvin's tool to superintend the execution, and stolidly expressed surprise that Servetus did not enter upon a discussion and defense of his doctrine while the flames were wrapping themselves around him! Servetus cried out again and again, "Mercy," "Mercy." His cry was not, however, to the marble hearts around him, but to the Saviour above him, for he said, "Jesus, thou Son of God, have mercy on me." We know from Calvin's own expressed purpose to Farel, written more than seven years and a half before, that he kept the homicidal intent in his heart all that time at least. How many prayers did he offer up within that interval; how many homilies; how many sermons did he preach; how many sinners did he exhort with the spirit, not of Christ, but of one far nearer the beginning of human history and with a name not much unlike his own—lying undetected in his heart?

Servetus left behind him in Geneva some fellow-believers, who were banished, a punishment that might have been ample enough for Servetus himself, but which would have been still unnecessary had the vengeance of Calvin been able to keep quiet perhaps less than twenty-four hours.

Of such things was John Calvin capable in his older and, what ought to have been, his better days. John Calvin, once the advocate for making the Bible, and the

Bible only, the ground-work of the faith of the church; John Calvin, the fugitive from popish persecution and cruelty; hiding, flying, changing his name, and expending his noble powers in the vain endeavor to bring the bloodthirsty bigot, King Francis, to clemency. A writer in Dr. Philip Schaff's Encyclopædia tells us that Calvin's conversion, when he was about twenty-two or twenty-three years of age, was like the Apostle Paul's, "radical and permanent." There was probably no very great difference between the age of Paul and of Calvin when they were converted, taking the Encyclopædia at its word. Calvin was in his forty-fifth year when he caused the burning of Servetus, and had been "converted" more than twenty years. What was Paul's condition of soul at more than twenty years after his conversion? Could he have permitted himself to waylay, arrest in a church, and cause to be horribly murdered, a man who had committed no crime, and who was on the point of quietly leaving the vicinity of which he was not a citizen, and but a transient visitor? Sectarian bigotry must have overturned the judgment before the conclusion was arrived at that the latter half of Calvin's life furnished any really satisfactory proof that Calvin was ever converted at all; or, at any rate, that he was fit to go into the same scales with the merciful, magnanimous, and Christ-like Paul.

There was a time in Paul's life when he and Calvin bore spiritually a close resemblance, but that was before Paul's mission to Damascus. Paul's life and character improved with his age; for anything that appears, Calvin's grew worse and worse. Some are eager to mitigate Calvin's inhumanity by remarking that bitter prejudice and intolerance were the faults of the age in which he lived, but they were not more prevalent and powerful than in the days of Paul. A great professor and paragon of Christian excellence; a mighty theologue and master of all divine wisdom and knowledge; the author of the famous Institutes, ought to have more benefitted by his own doctrine than to exhibit such a practice as his. Besides which, could he learn nothing from the cruelty of the king; nothing from his own writings in aid of Seneca's appeal for clemency; nothing from his own sufferings and the miseries of others, of which he must have known so much? Was all as nothing before the seductions of place and power? Suppose the plea of extenuation is put in that Farel, and Beza, and Bullinger, and the mild Melancthon, and no matter how many more, gave their countenance to

Calvin's transgression, what does that show but that their reformation was no more than a halfway affair, needing a better and higher advance than anything to which they had attained. Calvin had, in his day, been vouchsafed heart-cravings for a full return upon the pure and simple truths of the Bible, but he permitted them to fade out and vanish away. Samuel Taylor Coleridge is quoted as saying that the cruel burning of Servetus was not "Calvin's guilt especially, but the common opprobrium of all European Christendom;" of which the real meaning is that Christendom, including Calvin, was little more Christian than in name, and that the Reformation and reformers were not by any means so perfect as they took themselves to be. Blessed be the God of all grace that He has in this western land, free from the dust and cobwebs that begrimed the churches of the old world, given the first complete opportunity for the free seeding, cultivation, and harvest of His heavenly truth, which furnishes a better safeguard for liberty and prosperity of soul and body than all the forces, treasuries, and hierarchies on the face of the earth.

This sketch of the life and deeds of John Calvin terminates with recording that on his death-bed he admonished Beza and his other friends and co-workers against repeating the combination, in any one individual, of the chief civil and ecclesiastical authority of the little Genevan Republic. He breathed his last on the 27th May, 1564.

The other great Presbyterian and Calvinistic champion was John Knox, born at Haddington, in East Lothian, in the kingdom of Scotland, in 1505. His education commenced in his native town and was completed at the University of Glasgow. He took orders about 1530 and continued in the Catholic church as secular priest and apostolic notary till 1543. The reformed religion had by this time considerably extended itself in Scotland and attracted Knox's attention. He formed an acquaintance with George Wishart, a fervent preacher of the doctrine of justification by faith. The treacherous inveiglement of Wishart into the hands of the Catholic cardinal primate Beaton, followed by Beaton's trial, conviction and execution of Wishart for heresy by burning at the stake, fixed Knox's sentiments in favor of the Reformation. These sentiments becoming generally and rather dangerously known, Knox conceived the design of visiting Germany, but was prevailed upon by two gentlemen, who had placed their sons under Knox's tuition, to retire for protection into the castle of St. Andrews, which had been wrested from Catholic possession by less than a score of reformers who, by the thrust of a sword in the hand of James Melville, reciprocated on Beaton's person the violent death of Wishart. Knox was now advised to become a preacher, and with diffidence complied, commencing to preach in 1547. He vehemently assailed popery and made many converts. A party of Catholics, mixed Scotch and French, assisted by French ships in the harbor, attacked and gained possession of the castle of St. Andrews, and Knox, with a number of the Protestant garrison was, by the terms of the capitulation, transported to France. He was sent to the galleys and suffered much rough usage for about a year and a half, when by the probable interposition of the young English king, Edward the Sixth, he was restored to liberty and went to England. There he met Archbishop Cranmer, through whom he got a licence to preach, and occupied pulpits at Berwick on Tweed, Newcastle on Tyne, London, and some places in the south of England. On the accession of "Bloody" Mary to the English throne, Knox left Britain for the continent, and going to Frankfort-on-the-Main preached there to a band of British refugees. Differences having broken out amongst them as to some church ceremonials, Knox went to Geneva, and, of course, made Calvin's personal acquaintance. But an invitation to return to Scotland having been extended to him, he accepted and arrived back in 1557. Then he married. He next went to Geneva with his family. He preached in Geneva till 1559 to the English congregation. He wrote a book entitled "The first blast of the trumpet against the monstrous regiment of women," which brought down upon him the resentment of two queens, Elizabeth of England and Mary of Scots. From Geneva he returned to Scotland, in 1559, arriving at Leith the 2d May. Knox was proclaimed an outlaw and a rebel, but continued firm, preaching at Dundee and Perth, where a great riot took place, which ended in the destruction of much Catholic Church paraphernalia and the laying the houses of the grey and black friars in ruins. He travelled thence to St. Andrews, where he preached four days, with the result of changing Romish to Protestant worship, and after that made a circuit over a large part of Scotland, continually preaching. On the 7th July he was elected minister of Edinburgh. Queen Mary arrived in Scotland from France in August, 1561, and sent for Knox, who is said by some to have behaved discourteously towards her, but which by others is denied. He was tried for treason and acquitted. A controversy was started between him and a Catholic abbot, named Quinton Kennedy, forty persons being appointed on each side as judges. Each side claimed the victory. Having been some time a widower, he married a second wife in 1564. He preached before Darnley, the Queen's husband, and offended him. In October, 1570, Knox was stricken with a fit of apoplexy, and left Edinburgh for St. Andrews, remaining there fifteen months. News having arrived of the horrible massacre in Paris on St. Bartholomew's day and for six days after, viz., from August 24th to 31st, 1572, Knox preached a sermon denouncing the French king, Charles the Ninth, as "a cruel murderer and false traitor." The same year, on the 24th November, John Knox bade adieu to all earthly things, dying in the presence of his wife, family, and friends. At his funeral the Earl of Morton said, "Here lieth a man who in his life never feared the face of man; who hath been often threatened with dagge and dagger, but yet hath ended his days in peace and honor." Knox left two sons and three daughters, and the reputation of an exemplary private life. His maxims of conduct were regarded as too severe, and his manners sometimes too stern and harsh, which strongly suggests his archetype John Calvin, for him he followed in every important particular, as hath the Presbyterian Church of Scotland likewise, in doctrine, rites, and form of ecclesiastical government. When a writer in Dr. Schaff's Encyclopædia asserts that "Calvin based his system (of doctrine) upon the Apostles' Creed, and followed its lines," plain truth demands the comment that, if he did, it was only as the Council of Nice based their system on the same model, using it as simply a skeleton to be fitted in with matter conflicting with and even contradictory to it. The axioms and principles out of which Calvin and his disciple Knox wove the texture of their system are declared to have been that "the authority of the church is supreme"; "the church is our mother"; "outside the church there is no salvation"; "her ministry is divinely constituted, and to it believers are bound to pay deference"; "her authority is absolute in matters of doctrine, but when civil cases arise she hands the offenders over to the state for punishment." Calvin "aimed at theocracy," wherefore he naturally fell into the same lines of thought and resorted to the same modes of expression as the Romish doctors and dogmas he so much denounced, the difference being that with them the sacred church was Papal, with him Presbyterian, according with the judgment of the poet that "old Presbyter is but Pope writ large." One can hardly mistake the source of those Blue Laws of some of our Eastern States, as well as of other bluish notions supposed to be domiciled there.

In the way to ascertain the existing doctrines of the LUTHERAN CHURCH it will not be necessary to do more than indicate the principal causes that led to the Lutheran Reformation.

In the popedom of Julius the Second and on the 18th April, 1506, was commenced the great cathedral church of St. Peter's at Rome, with Bramante d'Urbino for architect. To Julius succeeded John de Medicis as Leo the Tenth, a man of bright parts and a promoter of learning, though of no special devotion to holiness, albeit an archbishop at eleven years of age. Leo surrounded himself with a brilliant but luxurious and expensive court. Under color of requiring large funds to prosecute the building of St. Peter's and to unite Christendom against the Turks, he was induced to institute markets for the sale of indulgences in Switzerland and Germany, which indulgences were declared to have the effect not only of a remission of temporal pains and penalties annexed by the church to certain transgressions, but of the punishments reserved in a future state to sin and impenitence. Thus the spiritual concerns of the present and future worlds were assumed to be under the dominion of the pope. Reasonably enough, these indulgences had a tendency the very contrary of the promotion of virtue and holiness. In order to quiet the natural remonstrances of the intellects and consciences of mankind, the doctrine was promulgated that there actually existed an immense treasure of merit, composed of the pious deeds and virtuous actions which the saints had performed beyond what was necessary for their own salvation, called Works of Supererogation, additional to the infinite merits of Christ. That this excess of merit (which they looked at as an affair of avoirdupois, like any other market commodity) was applicable to the deficiencies of others, and was placed within the control and dispensing power of the pope, so that he could assign to such as he saw fit portions of this inexhaustible merit suitable to their respective degrees of guilt, and sufficient to deliver them from the present and future penalties due to their sins.

To manage the matter of the sale of these commodities it was requisite to have an agent on the spot. For this, in Germany, Albert, the young archbishop of Mentz and Magdeburg, offered himself and was accepted. As with Leo himself, Albert was not well in funds, so it was agreed that the profits of the traffic should be equally divided between the pope and the archbishop. But a sub-agent was also wanted to execute the actual sales, and for this one John Diezel or Tetzel, a Dominican monk, was chosen. He had an approved experience in this kind of business.

Just at this time, A. D. 1516, there was at the University of Wittemberg, in the county of Mansfeld, in Lower Saxony, a young monk of the Augustine order, *Martin Luther* by name. He was professor of theology in the university. A number of people one day applied to him to hear their confessions. Their transgressions and sins had been bad enough, but after confession they refused to abandon their sins and commence reformation. Why so strange a refusal? They informed Luther that they had bought indulgences which would protect them from punishment, do what they would. But Luther would not absolve them, and held their indulgences worthless. The disappointed people reported this to Tetzel, whereupon a conflict broke forth between him and Luther. Tetzel loudly denounced all that should question the validity of the indulgences, and even threatened to burn them as heretics. Luther, on the other hand, taught that true repentance, a change of heart, a willingness to bear the cross, and a doing of good works was the true way to Divine absolution, the only absolution of any value. To explain and enforce his views Luther drew up ninety-five reasons, or " theses " as he called them, and fixed them against the church door at Wittemberg. He also wrote to his archbishop, Albert, humbly asking that prelate to withdraw a book he had written to help forward the sale of the indulgences. But neither Albert nor any of the great clergy sided with Luther, who thereupon went to Rome.

Every passing day's experience and observation tended to confirm Luther in the opinions and course he was pursuing, so that standing upon the firm ground of scripture, and steadily relying upon the Divine protection, he went bravely but meekly forward, until indulgences, the pope, and doctrines of Rome lost their hold over the judgments and consciences of an important section of the Christian world. The conquering principle in Luther's hand was the substitution of a Divine free gift for a remission purchased from man; it was a mighty step in the right direction, yet it rested considerably short of where it should have reached.

The present principal doctrines of the Lutheran Church appear to be, 1st, the Athanasian Trinity, with the adoption of the first four ecumenical councils and their doctrines; 2d, justification of the sinner before God by faith and not by works; 3d, infant baptism; and 4th, consubstantiation. Now, what is consubstantiation? This is answered by a Nicenist authority of acknowledged respectability, in these words: "Consubstantiation is the term by which Luther expressed the opinion which he held upon the nature of the elements in the Eucharist, as distinguished from transubstantiation, the doctrine of the Romanists. The Romanists assert, as the word they use implies, that the bread and wine are changed into the body and blood of Christ, and lose their former substance, although they retain the appearance, miraculously, to the senses. The Lutherans deny this change, but affirm that while the bread and wine do still remain in their natural substance, the body and blood are at the same time transfused into them, and thus that both are actually partaken of together."

This Lutheran opinion incontestably shows that neither Luther nor his followers were more than partially rid of Romish influences, whereby they left their reformation in conspicuous need of further reform. Indeed, as to consubstantiation, it looks much as if Luther hit upon it more for the sake of appearing to differ from Rome than of really differing, for as between it and transubstantiation, the latter is a shade the less unacceptable. Boldly to assert that the bread and wine are changed into Christ's body and blood is to rest the monstrous dogma on bare faith in the church; that is, "What were bread and wine have now become body and blood." There is the end of it and the mental exertion stops; but to declare that the still sensibly bread and wine have had transfused into them Christ's body and blood so that communicants get the bread and wine and Christ's body and blood together, sets the mind upon the unsatisfied inquiry, "Whence have come the body and blood, where do they reside, and what is the manner of their connexion with the material substances? Luther's dogmatism surpasses Rome's. Calvin's notion on this subject was thus: "I assert that the body of Christ is actually given to us in the sacrament to be the saving food of our souls; the Son of God offers daily to us in the holy sacrament the same body that he once offered in sacrifice to his Father, that it may be our spiritual food. If any one ask me concerning the manner, I will not be ashamed to confess that it is a secret too high for my reason to comprehend, or my tongue to express." And thus it is that the shrewdest followers in the wake of the councils of the fourth and fifth centuries, after accepting or propounding to themselves insoluble enigmas, (where the scriptures furnish spiritual truths perfectly intelligible and convertible to the Christian's use,) have at last to acknowledge that they are unable to explain or even to understand them.

The Augsburg Confession, the oldest of all the formularies of modern Christendom, was drawn up in the year 1530 by Philip Melancthon and approved by Luther. There are other such documents by Luther and others, but the Augsburg Confession contains the great magazine of Lutheran doctrines and dogmas. The Lutherans in Europe count fifty-five millions to eight hundred thousand in the United States.

Before proceeding further, the remark presents itself that it is strange, almost to unaccountableness, that Calvin and Luther and their able and learned coadjutors should have given countenance to such a doctrine as consubstantiation, or, as it was sometimes called, impanation, so near to transubstantiation that the distinction between them is almost without a difference. The knowledge of Luther, Calvin, &c., of the history of the middle ages could not but have taught them that the *canon of the mass* was started by Pope Gregory First towards the close of the sixth century. Notwithstanding this, everybody enjoyed the right of interpreting the manner of Christ's presence in the elements of the eucharist according to his own judgment, until Pope Innocent Third at the fourth Lateran council, in the year 1215, arrogantly decreed how that presence should thereafter be universally understood. This manner he described by the then newly-coined word transubstantiation, implying a perfect conversion of the bread and wine from being bread and wine into the actual body and blood of Christ that hung upon the cross. This pope, to whom the Roman Catholic Church is indebted for the introduction of transubstantiation, was the same lamblike innocent that put King John's kingdom of England under interdict, and organized in France and regions adjacent the *inquisition*, for the suppression of every man and woman's bounden and sacred right and duty of learning the truth concerning God and Christ, and their own preparation for an eternal world to come. The question recurs, what could have induced the so-called reformers of the sixteenth and seventeenth centuries to track after steps first imprinted by one pope of the sixth and deepened by another pope of the thirteenth century,—steps which by their own showing those reformers could neither explain nor understand? Can there be a better demonstration of the shortcomings of the alleged reformers as such, or of the incompleteness of their reformation?

Of the reformers who were upon the field of action three hundred years ago no one is more worthy of mention than Ulric Zwingli, who was born at the hamlet of Wildhaus, in the Tockenburg mountains, Swiss canton of St. Gall, on the first day of the year 1484, exactly seven weeks after the birth of Martin Luther. Ulric early developed a good capacity, and was sent to school successively at Basil, Berne, and Vienna, in Austria. He was ordained priest at twenty-two, and read his first mass at Wildhaus, his moral character being no worse than the generality of his cloth at that time, which is not saying very much. As early as 1517 he conceived the possibility of abolishing the papacy. About this time he was transferred to Einsidlen, where there was an abbey, over a gate of which was inscribed, "Full forgiveness of all sins can be had here." The abbey had in it an image of the Virgin Mary, believed to be capable of working miracles, to which crowds of pilgrims resorted. A Franciscan monk from Milan, in Italy, named Bernardine Samson, had come to Switzerland under patronage of the pope for the purpose of selling indulgences, and had amassed a good deal of money. Samson was titular chaplain to the pope. On going through the cantons he announced that he was "empowered to remit all sins"; "that he could dispose of Christ's merits to whoever would purchase them and bring their money for their indulgence." This aroused Zwingli, who had been elected preacher to the cathedral at Zurich, and who spared neither Samson nor his indulgences. At first the authorities of Zurich were indisposed to allow Samson to enter their city. But on his pretending to have some communication to make to the diet in the name of the pope, he was admitted, yet as his communication amounted to nothing more than matter relative to his indulgences, he was dismissed. He is reported to have carried back with him over the Swiss mountains three horse-cartloads of money.

The bishop of Constance, not relishing Zwingli's bearing towards indulgences and the like, sent a deputation to Zurich to put him down. One Hoffmann was at its head. He assailed Zwingli and his doctrines, to which the latter triumphantly replied that it was his right and duty to preach the Word of God, and not the teachings of Thomas Aquinas, or the Fathers, and that as bishop and pastor of Zurich he should insist on doing so. The Zurich city council sustained Zwingli, and the bishop's party were discomfited.

But a change came over several of the Swiss states. They sided with the Pope and his friends, and Zurich was substantially alone in the defence of the principles of the Reformation; but at a discussion of some chief points before the Great Council, Zwingli was victorious, and the preaching of the gospel was made free. Zwingli was married in April, 1524, to a widow named Reinhardt. Yet trouble was brewing outside the canton. Those cantons which remained attached to Rome found it impossible to form a close union with the Protestant or Reformed cantons, of which Zurich was a principal one. They were on the point of a struggle in 1529, but a temporary peace was patched up. In 1531 the Catholic cantons provoked an outbreak, and their forces being much the more numerous, the Zurichers were defeated at the battle of Cappel, and Zwingli, who was present as a chaplain, was killed October 11, 1531. The fanatic soldiers of the victorious foe wreaked their vengeance by dismembering and burning the dead patriot's body.

Zwingli's memory should suffer no reproach from his appearing with his countrymen in arms. No one, no matter what his profession in life, was exempt from military service in time of domestic war. On the subject of the Lord's supper the firmly-held opinions of Zwingli favorably contrasted with the extravagant ideas of Luther and Calvin. Zwingli's views were rational and consistent with an intelligent and practical interpretation of the Saviour's purpose and language, which were, that the breaking and offering to the disciples of the bread served at the supper-table indicated Christ's voluntary offering for their benefit of his body upon the cross, which was very soon to be but was not then yet erected. In like manner the free presentation of the cup of wine showed the equally voluntary shedding—to occur the next day—of his blood for them. The broken bread which Christ held (broken by himself) in his hand before dispensing it was not the body that was holding it, but was a figure or representation of that body the next day to be surrendered and sacrificed. So the common participation of the wine by the disciples was not a participation in Christ's actual blood then circling in full current through the vessels of his body, but a participation in that which represented the life's blood that on the morrow would be shed upon the cross. Christ's purpose in saying what he did at the supper was to furnish his disciples with an intelligent comprehension of the purport of the harrowing scenes upon which he and they were entering. To them it was given to *understand*—not to be puzzled with—the mysteries of the Kingdom. The same mysteries are presented to our intellectual apprehension, not to become objects of superstitious awe, but to feed our souls and to give us just conceptions of the principles that pervade the Divine government, and which encircle and bind our fate here and hereafter.

Christ's method of presenting to the minds of his hearers the truths of his sublime yet simple religion was by simile or parable. Some of his parables, if looked at superficially, were not only hard to be understood but impossible to be accepted as statements of fact and doctrine. When Christ told the Jewish congregation in the synagogue at Capernaum that he was "the living bread that came down from heaven," and that "except they ate the flesh of the Son of man and drank his blood they could have no life in them," they experienced a natural repulsion at language so preposterous, for they perfectly well knew that Christ's body commenced, grew, and was nurtured from the earth, and in their not distant neighborhood. Many of his disciples, therefore, regarded it as "a hard saying, who could hear it?" and "from that time went back and walked no more with him." Now, the trouble with them was that though disciples they were not discipled enough—not "disciples indeed." Their interest in Christ's religion was not deep enough to cause them to investigate and struggle for a due comprehension of it; to confer with Christ personally as they could easily do, and so have every difficulty completely solved. Christ did, indeed, on this occasion (as, in fact, was his custom) supply the displeased disciples with key enough to his seemingly dark saying to make all plain, for he gave them to understand that when he had been speaking of his body it was not the comparatively unprofitable body of flesh but the body of his doctrine to which he alluded, and the spirit that dwelt within it was the blood or life thereof. A single verse removes all difficulty, "It is the spirit that quickeneth; the flesh profiteth nothing; the words (or doctrine) that I speak unto you, they are spirit and they are life." The difficulty was not with the doctrine but with the hearers; their hearts were too hard and unbelieving.

When Christ, on another occasion, went out of the house and sat by the seaside, and then addressed the assembled multitudes from the little ship, he "spake in parables, and without a parable spake he not unto them." That is to say, he did not, as is the practice with ordinary preachers and teachers, talk on and on the sermon through, with the fate of having pretty much all that has been said forgotten within an hour or two, but he put something into the minds of his hearers that, like a hard-shelled fruit, requires to be much revolved and broken through, as to its hard and repellent exterior, before the precious kernel comes to view. His sermons were deposits in the minds of his hearers, to be turned over and over again and again, and thoroughly digested; among crowds; in solitude; by day and by night; at home and abroad; and at every turn discovering a new aspect and a new value. When, after teaching those multitudes from the seaside and they were sent away, Christ returned to the house, and when certain of his disciples, who were the subjects of a healthy anxiety, questioned him for an explanation of his parable of the tares, he immediately, and with the greatest lucidity, explained it all. "He that soweth the good seed," said Christ, "*is* the Son of man; the field *is* the world; the good seed *are* the children of the kingdom, but the tares *are* the children of the wicked one," &c., &c. Here the verb "is" or "are" stands equivalent to or substitute for the verb "mean," "represent," or "signify."

Whilst Luther, as Mosheim tells us, "maintained that the body and blood of Christ were really, though in a manner far beyond human comprehension, present in the Eucharist, and were exhibited together with the bread and wine," the "Swiss reformer looked upon the bread and wine in no other light than as the signs and symbols of the absent body and blood of Christ, and from the year 1524 propagated this doctrine in a public manner, and was subsequently followed by Ecolampadius, a divine of Basil, and one of the most learned men of that century." Martin Bucer thought the same way.

The opinion of Zwingli was that when Christ said, at the Paschal Supper, "Take, eat; this *is* my body," and "this *is* my blood of the New Testament," he made the same use of the word "*is*" that he did in explaining the parable of the tares, and in other like cases, namely, "Take, eat; this bread *represents* my body," and "this wine *represents* my blood of the New Testament, which is (will be to-morrow) shed for many." An effort was made by Philip, the protestant landgrave of Hesse Cassel, to procure an agreement between Zwingli and Luther as to the meaning of the Eucharistic feast, to which end a meeting of the two reformers, with their respective friends, took place at Marburg, the capital of Upper Hesse. The desired accordance was not achieved, each party continuing to think and teach as before.

On the subject of the Athanasian Trinity it is stated that Zwingli adopted that doctrine "mechanically."

THE BAPTIST COMMUNITY comprises churches of many names, representing just so many differences in doctrinal opinion or manner of worship, but the main branches are the Particular Baptists and the General Baptists; the former being Calvinistic and the latter Arminian in respect to doctrine. Our attention will be directed to the former, of whom there are said to be in the United States two and a quarter million of actual members, and five million who hold the principles. The churches a little exceed in number 24,800, with 15,500 ministers. In the whole world the churches are about 30,000, and seven millions of worshippers. That distinguished evangelist, C. H. Spurgeon, is a Baptist minister.

The Baptists, like the Presbyterians, are of the Nicene family, accepting as Christianity the dogmas that filtrated through the theological still set up by and worked under the direction of the Emperor Constantine in the year 325 after Christ, with infusions from John Calvin. Similarly to their near of kin, they are, denominationally speaking, an active, energetic, ambitious body, very zealous, and much attached to their church and its systems of doctrine and polity. They have done and are doing much good in the world, and are the peers of the people of any denomination in personal worth and general respectability. At the same time they are, perhaps, not quite perfect.

An elaborate work of somewhat recent publication, and manifestly accepted by the Baptist body, declares that "the Baptist denomination was founded by Jesus during his earthly ministry. Next to the great Teacher of Nazareth (says the book) our great leaders were the apostles and elders, bishops and evangelists, who preached Christ in their times. The instructions of our founder are contained in the four gospels; the heaven-given teachings of our earliest ministers are in the inspired epistles. The first Baptist missionary journal was the Acts of the Apostles." This, it must be allowed, is considerably elate and jubilant, and may be regarded by some other descriptions of religionists as a trifle more appropriative than appropriate. But let us apply the canon, or measuring rule, for all such pretensions and see whether this Baptist claim comes quite up to the mark and demand of Him who is so confidently alleged to be the "Founder of the denomination."

As to the one particular article of baptism, that is to say, baptism by immersion of the whole body, it can hardly be said that Christ was its founder or originator, for baptism was in most extensive practice by John, surnamed the Baptist, when Jesus journeyed a couple of scores of miles, or thereabouts, from Galilee to Jordan to be baptized of him. As a practical administrator of baptism John certainly preceded Jesus; Jesus, therefore, can with no propriety be denominated its founder; rather was he a partaker of it. That Christ confirmed the rite by his adoption of it in his own case is most certain; that he, or rather his attendant disciples, baptized converts, and that he enjoined it as a perpetual initiatory rite to his church, are facts which no Christian will hesitate about, or omit to comply with in his own person, though, most likely, baptism *after* Christ's death meant more than baptism *before* that event.*

Now, if Christ was the founder, and the apostles the leaders, and the gospels and epistles are the text books, of the Baptist denomination, will it not be reasonable to expect that the Baptists should be amongst the most pronounced of mankind in their "defence and confirmation of the gospel" in its fundamental and elementary principles? Ought any class of people on earth to be more resolute in rallying round, for instance, "the first commandment of all," elsewhere called "the first and great commandment?" But what *is* that preliminary, introductory, transcendent commandment of the religion of Christ? This is a very old question, and was directly put to Jesus Christ himself in his own proper person—say 1850 years ago. Is it not a little wonderful that the Baptists have never yet learned this prefatory command, but is it not a great deal more surprising that, for the most part, they resolutely refuse the right hand of fellowship to those that have learned to

---

* According to Dr. Thomas Armitage's sumptuous "History of the Baptists," at page 211, the opinions of Athanasius, Jerome of Dalmatia and Basil were substantially the doctrine we have proposed in these pages. They regarded Christ's injunction of "baptizing into the name of the Father, of the Son, and of the Holy Ghost," as primarily a matter of soul-instruction; if secondarily, of body-immersion. In like manner (if their practice is an exponent of their opinion) thought the whole apostolic band, for nowhere do we read of a corporeal baptism according to the modernly alleged "formula." It is stated in the "History" that Hippolytus, the Council of Nice, and even the golden-mouthed Chrysostom, with many others that ought to have known better, went sadly astray on this subject, preaching and teaching, in fact, "dangerous heresy."

strive to keep it? Said a listening and approving Jewish scribe to Jesus, "Which is the first commandment of all?" To which Jesus instantaneously answered, "The first of all the commandments is, Hear, O Israel, The Lord our God is One Lord; and thou shalt love the Lord thy God with all thy heart, and with all thy soul, and with all thy mind, and with all thy strength; this is the first commandment. And the second is like, namely, this, Thou shalt love thy neighbor as thyself. There is none other commandment greater than these." To which the scribe rejoined, "Well, Master, thou hast said the truth: for there is *One* God and there is none other but *He*." And when Jesus saw that he answered discreetly, he said unto the scribe, "Thou art not far from the kingdom of God." From this important passage of the gospel we are taught that a belief in the indivisible Oneness of God is the essential introductory part of the first commandment of all, to which the attention of Israel, and of all others who desire to believe aright, is most pointedly called. But in this prime and great injunction, taught first through the mouth of Moses, the predecessor and prototype of Christ, and then reaffirmed in the most public and positive manner by Jesus, our Baptist friends propose a change by way of amendment. They decline to hold to the idea common to the Messiah and the discreet scribe that God is One only. The *godhead*, say the Baptists, is indeed One, but there are contained in this One godhead three distinct persons, each severally God, viz., God the Father, God the Son, and God the Holy Ghost, and infer, what is quite remarkable, that the same Jesus who so emphatically announced the Divine Unity was himself all the while the second person of the aforesaid *three*, though for some unknown reason he concealed or omitted to mention it, and made use of language entirely inconsistent therewith. Any way, the Baptists reject the doctrine of Jesus and the Jewish scribe, and substitute for it a theory or doctrine that came originally out during the fourth century after Christ, from a collection of between three and four hundred men at an imperial city beyond the Bosphorus, whose angry disputes and tumultuary behavior for several weeks formed the strongest possible contrast to the peaceful unanimity of the Lord Jesus and the Jewish scribe. It is rather improbable that our Baptist friends often make the "first commandment of all" the subject of their pulpit meditations.

In addition to Christ's teaching that God is One, in the simple and proper acceptation of that Unity, he also taught that absolute goodness in its full and perfect extent is predicable only of this One God. Christ promptly repelled from himself the ascription of goodness, and said, "There is none good but One, that is, God," still indicating the strict unity of the Most High. To establish any doctrine inconsistent with this, it was indispensable to set up some authority other than Christ's. Nicene doctrine could flow only from a Nicene Council.

In the momentous matter of prayer, *to whom* and *how* it should be offered, Christ's instructions were neither obscure nor deficient. The Nicenist habit is to offer prayer to the Father, Son, and Spirit, but especially to the Son, to whom devotional hymns are far more numerously addressed than to either or both of the other participants in the Trinity. I find by actual count of the hymns in a small Baptist hymnal that 199 are addressed to the Son, 50 to the Father, 7 to the Holy Ghost and 5 to the Trinity, out of 426 hymns in all, the remainder being mostly of a general character.

But let us specifically betake ourselves to the Christian law and testimony, that is to say, to the precepts of the Lord and Master. As prayer is a matter of practical duty, Christ placed the subject before his disciples in the plainest and most practical way. "After this manner, therefore," he said, "pray ye, Our Father, who art in heaven, hallowed be thy name; may thy kingdom come and thy will be done," &c., &c. The command is to pray to the Father, and impliedly to the Father only, for the Father only is mentioned. All chance of ambiguity or mistake is thus anticipated; the one sole object of prayer is alone spoken of. All the nouns, pronouns and verbs throughout the prayer relating to the proper object of it are in the singular number. Not a word or hint is there about any two other beings, the Son and the Holy Ghost, as equally entitled with the Father to be invoked. No such thing in letter or spirit as, "O, Holy, blessed and glorious Trinity, three persons and One God,"—nothing so alien to Christ, to his apostles and to the whole Bible.

Further, Christ himself was eminently prayerful. His life was a life of prayer. It was because of their witnessing Christ's devotion to prayer that his disciples besought him to teach them to pray;—they did not mean to himself. To whom did Jesus Christ pray? To none other but that same Father he had indicated to them, for the simple and just reason that God was "*his* Father and *their* Father, *his* God and *their* God."

So jealous was Jesus of his Father's just rights and peerless glory that he deemed it necessary to warn his followers, before his final departure from the world, against a temptation that might assail them in the more or less distant future of tendering *him* Divine honors and invoking him in prayer. "In that day," said Christ, "*ye shall ask me nothing;* verily, verily, I say unto you, "Whatsoever ye shall ask the Father in my name (that is, as members of my body, the church) He will give it you"—teaching thereby that the proprietorship of all blessings and mercies resides in the Father only, who was and is accessible by prayer made in the name of His Son. How wide is this from the theory and practice of nearly the whole so-called Christian world!

In that memorable interview at Jacob's well in Sychar Christ announced to the Samaritans the same sublime truths he had proclaimed everywhere else. He apprized the Samaritans of the worthlessness of their superstitious worship as compared with the saving qualities of the worship which he himself and his fellow-countrymen, the Jews, offered to the Most High. Yet, after all, (he told them,) the true worship was not a worship of place or form, but the worship of the heart—a worship in spirit and in truth! About the association of any other being or name with the Father's as an object of worship Christ was profoundly silent; so that the many Samaritan believers who were converted under his instructions could have known nothing of those doctrines which in after and these present days are so unctuously styled "evangelical," and said to be indispensable to salvation.

Intermitting numberless, irresistible testimonies to the same great truths, we arrive in our way through the gospels, at that most impressive address of Jesus to his Heavenly Father, in which he declares it to be "life eternal" to know Him, the Father, as the "only *true* God," and Jesus Christ as the one whom the "only true God" hath "sent." Perhaps this is the greatest and sublimest text in either Old or New Testament. Being solemnly addressed by the Son of God to his Almighty and Gracious Father, it could scarcely escape this distinction. And to our human hearts, rightly attuned, what can address them like the hope of "life eternal"?—God's greatest of all gifts—beyond adequate contemplation! The whole seventeenth chapter of John's gospel is unique; it savors of the unity, the love, and bliss of heaven, where all shall be one in the indwelling, free Spirit of the Father, with the Redeemer and redeemed "made perfect in one."

The gospel of John terminates with a pointed notification of the purpose for which it was written. The opening chapter records the testimonies of John the Baptist, of Andrew, the brother of Peter, and of Nathanael, to the foundation fact that Jesus of Nazareth was the Christ, the Son of God and King of Israel. The twentieth chapter, after stating that many of the miraculous works which Jesus performed in the presence of his disciples were not described in that gospel, adds the testimony of John, the evangelist and apostle, to the same great fact which all men are called upon to believe, viz., that "Jesus is the Christ, the Son of God, and that believing, they might have life through his name." Nothing less does it say, nothing more, but *just* this, that Jesus is not God, not God the Son, but the Christ, "the Son of God that taketh away the sin of the world." Some have assumed for this particular composition of the beloved disciple the design of inculcating Nicenist ideas and principles. No greater misconception could be entertained, for the very contrary is true. The Bible contains no book which furnishes proportionally more testimonies to the sole godhead of the Father and the sonship, and subordination to him, of Jesus the Christ.

The first act of the apostles after Christ's ascension was the filling of the gap in their number caused by the treason and death of Judas Iscariot. They selected two, from whom they prayed to the Lord, their lately-risen master, to choose the one he might prefer. In this instance of prayer to Christ there was less of prayer in its ordinary nature and purpose than of direct personal reference to him of a question in which they knew his interest was paramount. There was, therefore, in it no infraction of the spirit, and scarcely of the letter, of his command to "ask him nothing" after his corporeal disappearance from the earth. It was entirely proper that the Master, who had originally chosen the twelve, should add whom he preferred to the remaining eleven. He chose Matthias, and this made up the complement. The only other instance in the book of the Acts where prayer was offered to Christ is that wherein Stephen the martyr cried aloud, "Lord Jesus, receive my spirit." But this, too, was a special personal occasion, a resignation into the hands of Christ, by which Stephen testified of his unseen, yet continued and immediate care of his people and of his headship over all things to the church, his body. When Michael Servetus was bound to the fiery stake at the instigation of John Calvin, he too cried aloud, "Jesus, thou Son of the Eternal God, have mercy upon me."

The book of the Acts, though not written by the Apostle John, follows John's gospel and the other gospels in testifying that "Truly, this man, Jesus, was the Son of God." It is scattered here and there throughout the whole book, about which it might be said with truth that if any man or woman as yet unacquainted with the foundation doctrines of the Christian religion desires to be informed in the surest and quickest way and upon the best authority, the single book of the Acts is to be recommended for the purpose. There is no church catechism to be compared to it. Let this book be first thoroughly and prayerfully perused and well understood, and a knowledge of the Christian faith in all its essential parts will be the happy result. We have in it the teaching and preaching of Peter, the first among the equal apostolic brethren, with his close companion, John, to all sorts of people, Jews and Gentiles, priesthood and laity, rich and poor, learned and ignorant. The preaching of Stephen, the first Christian martyr who was permitted to behold with his bodily eyes the secret interior of the court of heaven; of Philip the Evangelist, who baptized the eunuch; of that good man and full of the Holy Ghost, Barnabas; of James; of the prophets Judas and Silas; and last, though second to none, the celestially converted persecutor and admirable thirteenth Apostle, Paul. Now, all these were Jews and, until converted and at length fully taught, as thoroughly steeped in the prejudices peculiar to the Jewish nation as any people in it. If members of the Roman Catholic communion ever vindicated their rights as the freeborn offspring of the Lord Supreme, and conferred upon themselves the grace and mercy of exercising their faculties and reflecting on the contents of the Word of God—which it is to be feared they seldom or never dare to do—they would not open upon more than two chapters of the book of the Acts before being struck with the world-wide difference between the Peter who displays himself there, and the Saint Peter as he stands pictured before their own spellbound imaginations. Suppose they were to put themselves for a moment into the place of Peter's auditory and fancy themselves addressed by the apostle thus: "Ye men of the Roman Catholic persuasion, hear these words: Jesus of Nazareth, a man approved of God among you by miracles and wonders and signs which God did by him in the midst of you, as ye yourselves also know"—down to the end of Peter's address. The question is, Would such supposed Catholic hearers be "pricked in their heart" as those self-convicted Jews were, and ask, "*What* shall we *do?*" Would they not rather say, "Oh, that kind of preaching is too tame and lame for us—there is nothing at all in it about God-the-Son and God-the-Holy-Ghost, and the Trinity, and the Incarnation, and the Hypostatic Union, and Mary the mother of God, and the chair of Peter, and our Holy Father the pope, and the sacrifice of the mass, and purgatory, and holy water, and the sign of the cross, and saying prayers in Latin, and a great many other things that we have been accustomed to." Then, continuing onward, if examination were made of other sermons and speeches of Peter, they would all be found to the same effect, "How that God anointed Jesus of Nazareth with the Holy Ghost and with power; who went about doing good and healing all that were oppressed of the devil; for God was with him." There is mention here made of Father, Son and Holy Ghost, all very near together and luminously treated of, so that language could not pack more and more faithful doctrine into fewer words. Yet we have never seen this divinely-expressed text quoted in support of the Trinity. Can we conjecture why? Is it not because the text is too distinctly bright with truth and precision to admit of a shade of doubt about its meaning, not giving place to any uncertainty, as is somewhat the case with Matt. 28: 19, especially when mistranslated as in our common Bibles?

So in the case of Paul. When at Athens Paul felt impelled to address the polished but polytheistic Greeks, of which address on Mars Hill we have a very satisfactory compendium in the 17th chapter of the Acts. Here was an opportunity not to be surpassed for offering to an assembly tolerably fresh and unprepossessed the exact truth, whatever it might be, monotheistic or polytheistic. From their habits and general drift of thought, however, it does not seem extravagant to suppose that if monotheism and polytheism were evenly presented them for choice, they would have accepted the latter, since the subtleties of the Trinity might have been captivating to just that very style of people. What, however, does Paul really say in remarking on the altar inscribed "To the Unknown God"? Unity or Triplicity? But one answer can be made—Unity throughout. The One God "who made the world will judge it in righteousness by that *man* whom he hath ordained: whereof he hath given assurance unto all men in that He hath raised him from the dead." We shall leave it to Nicenists of all denominations to administer to the manes and memory of Paul the condign punishment he brought down upon himself for neglecting an opportunity at the heart of intellectual Greece, so excellent for inculcating doctrines which stand on the forefront of the now current creeds, confessions, decrees of councils, articles of religion, institutes, and what not. Even more than that; instead of teaching the Trinity he taught the simple Unity of God and the simple humanity of Christ—exactly the doctrine that burnt Servetus, Gentili, and others.

The voluminousness of the New Testament epistles will necessitate a mere passing recital of those leading texts which may be regarded as the great landmarks of Divine truth.

In Romans, 5:15, we learn that God's gracious gift of redemption comes through the intervention of "one man, Jesus Christ." In 1st Corinthians we find the people of God addressed and informed that the things "of the world, or life, or death, or things present, or things to come, all are yours, and ye are Christ's, and Christ is God's." This is the just order of gradation. So elsewhere; "the head of every man is Christ, and the head of the woman is the man, and the head of Christ is God." Speaking of objects of worship, Paul says there is "no other God but One." For "though" says he, "there be that are called gods and lords, and they are numerous," still "to us (professors of the Christian faith) there is but One God, (specifically,) the Father; and One Lord, Jesus Christ." In that incomparable chapter, the 15th of the 1st Corinthians, Paul gives us what is called the eschatology of our race. In the resurrection every *man* will rise in his own order, "Christ" (being man) "was the first fruits" from the grave; "afterwards they that are Christ's at his (second) coming." "Then cometh the end, when Christ shall have delivered up the kingdom to the God and Father; when he shall have put down all rule and all authority and power. For he must reign till he hath put all enemies under his feet. The last enemy that shall be destroyed is death, for he hath put all things under his feet. But when he saith all things are put under him (that is, under Christ) it is manifest that He (namely, God) is excepted who did put all things under Him. And when all things shall be subdued unto him (Christ) then shall the Son also himself (for the great mediatorial and recuperative achievement will have been worked through) be subject unto Him (God) that put all things under him (Christ), that God may be all in all." It can hardly be said that the Gloria Patri, &c., &c., so much repeated by our Episcopal friends in their services, is consistent either in letter or meaning with the foregoing teachings of the great Apostle. When God, the Father, shall thus be "all in all," then will have come that "restitution of all things" spoken of by the Apostle Peter in the book of the Acts; when, also, it shall be, as foretold by the prophet Zechariah, that "Jehovah shall be King over all the earth; in that day shall there be One Lord, and His name One." And so throughout eternity.

In Galatians, the Son of God is described as "made of a woman, made under the law," not a word appearing like what is contained in the Nicene creed, that he was "begotten of his Father before all worlds; came down from heaven and was incarnate by the Holy Ghost;"—about all of which, as it was not heard of till between two and three hundred years after Paul's death, Paul could, of course, know nothing.

In Ephesians, speaking of the unity of the Spirit and of the church, Paul shows how the idea of unity pervades every department of the Christian system; there being no hint, even, of triplicity, or trinity, anywhere. He says there is "One Lord; One faith; One baptism; One God and Father of all, who is above all, and through all, and in you all." Relative to the final object of human gratitude, Paul repeats in spirit and almost in letter the command of Christ to his disciples, "Giving thanks, *always*, for *all* things unto the God and Father, in the name of Jesus Christ our Lord." In Philippians Paul describes the self-humiliation and the incomparable exaltation of Christ, so "that every tongue should confess that Jesus Christ is Lord (he does not say God) to the glory of God the Father." The just distinction cannot be overlooked.

In Colossians, Paul gives thanks, always to God the Father, as the original source of every mercy and blessing, "who hath delivered us from the power of darkness and hath translated us into the kingdom of the Son of his love,"—of that Son who is *not* "the invisible God" and is *not* "the *Creator*," but who is the moral image or likeness of the God that is invisible, and the "first born of every *creature*." No one will suppose that an image, a likeness, a picture, is the original of which it is only a representation. Therefore Christ is not the God of whom he is the image. And, if a "creature," he is not the Creator. The teachings of Paul and the dictates of common sense coincide; the dogmas of Nicenism disagree with both.

In Thessalonians we find the same. "Thanks to God." Thanks to Him who is continually called "Our Father."

Christ's Father is called by Paul "the living and true God," reminding us of Christ's own similar language.

In the first epistle to Timothy, God is called "the only wise," "eternal king," "immortal," "invisible." And the "knowledge of the truth" Paul declares to be that "there is One God and one mediator between God and men, the *man* Christ Jesus." Unto this pure doctrine Paul declares he was "ordained to be a preacher and an Apostle," truthfully and without falsehood. Paul's ascription to God the Father is magnificent and sublime; the blessed and *only* Potentate; the King of Kings and Lord of Lords; who *only* hath immortality; dwelling in the light which no man can approach unto; whom no man hath seen or can see; to whom be honor and power everlasting. Amen."

Passing by the three briefer intervening epistles we come to that outpouring of Divine wisdom and goodness constituting the epistle to the Hebrews. By it we are taught not only the majesty and mercy of God, but the exceedingly high dignity in the scale of the universe accorded to the race of man. Man is the child of the All-supreme, whilst the angels are but His ministers. Man is the being to whom the Lord of the universe has "put in subjection the world to come," over which world, redeemed from all imperfection and become the Israel of God, Christ, the Son of man, and captain of man's salvation, will preside as God's vicegerent. The letter to the Hebrews points our "look unto Jesus, the author and finisher of our faith; who, for the joy that was set before him, endured the cross, despising the shame, and is set down at the right hand of the throne of God." So looking, and correspondingly acting, we shall "come unto Mount Sion and unto the city of the living God, the heavenly Jerusalem, and to an innumerable company of angels; to the general assembly and church of the first born who are written in heaven, and to God the judge of all, and to the spirits of just men made perfect, and to Jesus the mediator of the New Covenant, and to the blood of sprinkling, which speaketh better things than that of Abel." In all the richness of exposition with which this book abounds no trace can be detected of reference to Christ's pre-existent glory; nothing of his "leaving the starry crown," or "glory-circled throne," or "laying his robes aside" in some previous state of being before Gabriel announced to the virgin whose name was Mary that she had found favor with God and would be the mother of a successor to King David who would reign over the house of Jacob forever.

Christ's eye was not fixed upon anything that he had previously professed, but upon the "joy that was set *before* him," for the sake of which he "endured the cross, despising the shame," and was exalted to a place at God's right hand.

This epistle plainly evinces that Christ was not and is not God, because he was and is a high priest to God, a "high priest of good things to *come*," appearing in heaven itself as the forerunner and representative of all who believe in him as the Messiah. It ought to be needless to repeat that if Christ were "a high priest," and "a priest forever after the order of Melchisedec," he could not be the God to whom he was a priest. No such irrationality as that tarnishes the noble epistle to the Hebrews or any of the writings of its renowned author, nor, indeed, any part of the Old or New Testaments. The word of God throughout addresses itself to the healthy faculties and right reason of the family of man.

The epistle of the Apostle James, the brother, or rather, the cousin of the Lord Jesus, was directly addressed from the city of Jerusalem, where James continually dwelt, "to the twelve tribes of Israel that were scattered abroad." The epistle is fraught with the richest stores of heavenly wisdom for earthly use, chiefly of a practical character. If James's ideas were Nicenist, it cannot but be supposed that his epistle, having been addressed to Jews all over the ancient world, would be doctrinally controversial to no inconsiderable extent, for he would have written to a class of men always, then as now, extremely hostile to any idea that conflicted with their foundation-stone of faith in the strict unity of God. But there is very little reference throughout the epistle to mere doctrine, though in one place James says, "'Thou believest that there is One God; thou doest well; the devils also believe and tremble." James and his Jewish brethren were, therefore, on this point, entirely consentient; that is to say, no such dogma as the Trinity and no such notions as Nicenist or Athanasian notions had any lodgment in their minds.

It is held to be a sound maxim to explain scripture by scripture—the difficult by the plain, when that is happily possible. James, with a simple eloquence and beauty betokening the Divine, says, "Every good gift and every perfect gift is from above, and cometh down from the Father of lights, with whom there is no variableness, neither shadow of turning," or, as the Revised Version more accurately gives it in English, "With whom can be no variation, neither shadow that is cast by turning"; that is, with whom always and under all circumstances there is undoubted light. Now, to a childish or uninformed mind which had never become acquainted with scripture language, this phraseology of the Apostle might quite naturally at first sight appear strange, for the person would reasonably say "I do not comprehend how God's gifts should be said to fall down from the sky." Reflexion and attention would, however, in due time teach that the expressions "from above" and "cometh down" indicate that the gifts do not originate from an earthly source, but have their first impulse in the merciful purpose of God, who setteth and keepeth the thousand million-fold concerns of the earth—yes, and of the illimitable universe—in due succession and order. The same reflexion and attention would likewise suggest that the language of James supplies a key to the Saviour's meaning when he said, "I came down from heaven," and "I am the bread which came down from heaven," which so much confounded the Jews who heard them from the Saviour's mouth. Christ as little meant that he had personally descended or alighted upon the earth from the celestial realm, as James meant to say that the blessed munificence of the Divine Parent rolls down visibly in bales or packages upon the earth beneath. Yet the Saviour's language is equally as much misunderstood to-day by millions of minds who wait upon Christian—yes, upon Protestant—ministrations as they were misinterpreted by Christ's Jewish auditors. One of the purposes Christ had in view in the use of this language, which is by no means incorrect in itself, was to lift the minds of his hearers from a slavish subjection to merely local and temporal ideas up to a juster conception of the universality and spirituality in which they then and we now really dwell. In a very noteworthy text of scripture Jesus said, "If a man love me, he will keep my words; and my Father will love him, and we will come unto him and make our abode with him." And in Revelations, chapter 3d, Christ says, "If any man hear my voice and open the door to me, standing and knocking on the outside, I will come in to him and will sup with him and he with me." By such phraseology as this our good and gracious Master inculcates the nearness of God and Christ to every soul of us, and how practically we might, if we will, avail ourselves of their sacred society.

The two epistles of Peter, like that of James, are general letters, addressed to the Christian brethren scattered throughout Asia Minor. Like his preaching in the book of the Acts, they are consistent with his Jewish origin and education in divine things, to which had been superadded a rooted faith in Jesus the Messiah. Not a Nicene thought appears from beginning to end, but there are quite distinct intimations of the designs of the Most High as to the future destiny of the world which we inhabit, that there shall be "new heavens and a new earth, wherein dwelleth righteousness."

The general epistles of the Apostle John are specially impressive of the messiahship of Jesus and of the entire reality and genuineness of his bodily death and resurrection.

The epistle of Jude, the brother of James, exposes those who deny the *only* Lord God, and *our Lord* Jesus Christ.

We come at length to the concluding volume of the Sacred Record, the Revelation of St. John the divine, that is, the theologian. This revelation came to John through the intervention of Christ, but Christ was not its original author, for "God gave it unto him." It will be remembered the gospel speaks of Christ telling his disciples that the time of the coming of the great day of account no man knew, "no, not the angels which are in heaven, neither the Son, but the Father." Again, after his resurrection, he replied to the eager desire of his Apostles for information as to when Christ would "restore again the kingdom to Israel," that it was not for them "to know the times or the seasons which the Father hath put in His own power," or, as the Revised Version renders it, "which the Father hath set within his own authority." We perceive, then, that vast as was the scope of the authority and powers and knowledge delegated to Christ, it was not universal. There were limits which that blessed one freely acknowledged and declared, and showed thereby that great as was his own dominion it was circumscribed by the illimitable rule of his Father. Christ, therefore, was not the Father's equal, and was not, and is not, God. His Father was and is greater than he.

In speaking of the Most High, this last book of the scripture canon furnishes the same testimony as did one of the very earliest, sixteen hundred years before. Moses was commanded to give to the children of Israel then in Egypt the words "I AM," as the name of God, implying the Self-existent, Everlasting ONE. In announcing grace and peace to the seven churches of Asia, John speaks of God as He "who is, and who was, and who is to come"—and so on throughout—the Self-existent and Eternal.

Before passing forward from this cursory review of the several books of the New Testament, allusion might be made to the solemn warnings conveyed in the concluding chapter of the Revelations, of which the former is the succinct command to "Worship God," and therefore no other than God; and the latter is, to add nothing to nor diminish from the Word of God as written and delivered to mankind. The same solemn admonition was published, more·than once, under the old Jewish dispensation. Unhappily, our Bibles have been for ages and centuries disfigured by interpolated or added matter, which could have been placed there for no other purpose but to furnish evidence in behalf of human inventions which the pure scriptures did not teach, and thereby to pervert the faith of millions. The Revised Version it was well worth while to make, but when making it might have been more thoroughly and honestly done.

We are now in a somewhat better condition to determine with truth and fairness whether our exultant Baptist champion stands entirely justified in his appropriation of the Saviour and his Apostles as the very especial patrons and leaders of his church. There is nothing in the gospel account of the generation, gestation, birth, infancy, youth, manhood, and induction of Jesus into his supereminent office of Christ, or of his career therein, that will confirm the verity and propriety of those doctrines which the Baptists have adopted *en masse* from the councils of Nice and elsewhere, and which have flowed, along with other corruptions, through the polluted channels of the dark ages. Whilst Christ is claimed as *par eminence* the founder and exemplar of the Baptist denomination, they have not respected his judgment on so prime a matter as "the first commandment of all" sufficiently to make it their own, but—notwithstanding all we hear about their self-direction, democratic independence of thought, and the like—have permitted themselves to drift along, impelled by the force of the common current, and to feel pride in the association. Hence, notwithstanding the opportunities and advantages their position has afforded them, they are, except upon the single important point of baptism by immersion, undistinguishable from the general mass of Nicenists.

We cannot enter into argument specially to demonstrate in how many respects the Baptists are variant in their views from Christ and his Apostles; but having just mentioned one principal point as to Christ, will call attention to their comparative standing with one for whom they not unfrequently profess unbounded admiration—that is to say, the Apostle Paul.

If we turn to the twentieth chapter of what our champion calls "the first Baptist Missionary Journal, the Acts of the Apostles," we shall find that Paul, when at Miletus, sent for the elders of the Church of Ephesus, (from which city Miletus was distant about twenty-eight of our miles,) with whom he had a conference, expecting never again to visit that region. After reminding them of the apostolic devotion and disinterestedness of his life whilst among them, he calls them to witness that he had "kept back nothing that was profitable to them," but had testified to them, both Jews and Gentiles, publicly and privately, their solemn religious obligations of "repentance towards God and faith towards the Lord Jesus Christ." He took them then and there to "record that he was pure from the blood of all men, for that he had not shunned to declare unto them all the counsel of God." The people of his charge consisted of Jews and Gentiles. The Jews of that day, like their fathers before them and their descendants of this day, were immovable believers in the One Only God; to wit, the scribe who accosted Christ (Mark, 12: 28) respecting the first commandment of all. Now, if the Trinity and other associated dogmas were and are true, and a belief of them was and is indispensable to salvation, as Baptists and other Nicenists insist, why did not Paul teach those dogmas as "profitable" for belief and profession, because a part of the "counsel of God?" No such teaching, however, anywhere appears, for, had it appeared, it would have aroused a controversy between Paul and the Jewish converts earnest and emphatic beyond parallel, and not unlikely to prove the grave of Christianity everywhere. The Jews of our own day have no valid reason for refusing Christ as their Messiah, yet they point to the Trinity, a dogma Paul did *not* teach, as a justifying excuse for rejecting the doctrine Paul *did* teach, and that with all the solicitude his spiritual, mental, and physical organizations could exert. Such is the inconsequential status of Jewish argumentation at this day, but the bulk of those who account themselves Christians are about equal participants with the Jews in the logical and religious perversion.

The general conclusion is obvious; no such doctrines as the Trinity or the Incarnation and the rest were either "profitable" or any part of the "counsel of God." Paul did not teach them or know anything about them, except, perhaps, by prophetic foresight that they were amongst those "perverse things" to be thereafter spoken of by "men that should arise" within the Christian fold itself "to draw away disciples after them." That such false teachers did eventually arise and overwhelm the Christian world with their "perversities" the history of the post-apostolic ages but too abundantly and sorrowfully proves.

The Baptists firmly adhere to their specialty of immersion and adult baptism. They proclaim the rights of conscience, private judgment, and free expression in all properly religious matters, without interference from ecclesiastical or civil authority. They claim the independence of every individual church as to faith and worship, subject only to the law of Christ. They profess the Bible to be their only guide, source of knowledge, and standard of authority in religion, and that whatever is taught therein is to be believed, and what is ordained, to be obeyed. Christ, they say, is the only lawgiver to his church.

Notwithstanding all this brave profession, they practically acknowledge to reading their Bibles through Calvin's spectacles, and subject themselves to the consequent distortions;—a thing the more surprising since they assert Calvin to have been one of the very strongest of all foes to their baptismal system, for he abolished adult immersion wherever he could and put pædobaptism into its place. The Baptists declare their religious independence of all "princes and pontiffs, councils and conventions," yet where could they find a more thoroughgoing pontiff than Calvin, and, as such, one more inimical than he to the free exercise of thought, tongue, and pen? Touching their supposed freedom from allegiance to "councils and conventions," have they not quietly turned their backs upon the plain and positive teachings of Moses and the prophets, of Christ and his apostles, and gone after Nice and Constantinople, Constantine and Theodosius? If Cain, as the Apostle John says, "was of that wicked one and slew his brother," whence was the prompting in Calvin's heart to perpetrate, after years of deliberation, with equal opportunity for appeasement, an act of the same description as Cain's? Was it well and good to select such a one for a master and guide? Were the teachings and examples of Christ and his apostles so imperfect and unsatisfactory that their lack or demerit needed to be supplied from Calvin's fulness? And practically, as matter of fact, are not sincere and well-meaning applicants for baptism by immersion sometimes turned away because they find themselves unable to voice response to the Calvinistic shibboleth?

Furthermore: are the ideas entertained by Baptists touching the true honor and glory of the Most High always such as become His worshipping subjects? Is it ever heard among Baptists that God could die, could be subject to death? How scriptural and how right is the phrase, "Christ, the Mighty Maker, died, for man's, the creature's, sin;" or this other, "the death of Christ, my God"? Does the Bible furnish any pattern for or justification of such expressions? If not, may there not be a field for really Christian missionaries *to* Baptists as well as *from* them? And, altogether, is there not room and some little occasion for Baptists to abate somewhat of their stern and lofty tone, and candidly to acknowledge that, after all, they are neither so Reformed nor so scriptural as they might be? Especially might this happen after the exertion of a little modest and sincere introspection.

TO THE JEWS.

In any supposable controversy between a Jew and an Athanasian as to the Divine nature, common candor must admit that, taking the Old Testament for testimony in the case, the oneness or unity of God is abundantly proven, and the Jew must be adjudged the victor. The texts in Exodus, chapters 3d, 6th, and 20th; Deut., 5th and 6th, and the prophets at large, are conclusive that God is a single being.

This the Athanasian will not verbally disallow, but will nevertheless allege that in this One God, or rather godhead, there are included three distinct individualities, each equal to each of the others, and that when in the Old Testament God, Jehovah, or the Lord, is spoken of, it must be understood of this alleged composite and triple being.

All this might be disingenuous enough, and, in fact, a fetch, and a something wholly unsuspected and unthought of for more than a millenium and a half, yet such is the now prevailing Athanasian doctrine. Much and sufficiently subtle argument is advanced in behalf of it, which the Athanasians think ought to be regarded as convincing. Thus the Athanasian, Charles Leslie, in his "Short and Easy Method with the Jews," whilst warmly declaring that "we profess to worship none other but that one only God who spoke in Horeb out of the midst of the fire, and detest all thoughts of any other God," yet advocates "the Blessed Trinity," and asks "whether this one most simple and uncompounded nature of God may not be communicated to these eternal persons without either confusion of the persons or dividing of the substance, and does in no way interfere with the *unity of the nature*, because this very hypothesis supposes the *unity of the nature* in the strictest sense that is possible?"

Now, in this the old Homoousian leaven from Nice most prominently obtrudes itself, its idea being that the "unity of the nature" saves everything, because within that unity there may be included any number whatever of separate, individual, and mutually equal deities, and the whole be denominated in the aggregate, One God. On the other hand, the Jews of all time have believed, and do still believe, that the unity of God spoken of in the Old Testament means a unity or individuality *of person*, which comprehends a unity of nature, and that nature the sole property of the aforesaid one person without any participant in the whole universe. This undoubtedly correct view is sustained by the New Testament with a directness and particularity which will resist all Athanasian efforts to upset. If Moses drove the truth concerning the Divine unity into the minds and consciences of men, Christ clinched it fast forever.

Collate Deuteronomy 6: 4 to 9 with Mark's Gospel 12: 28 to 34, and see how powerfully Christ confirms and enforces the Divine unity and vindicates the Jewish conception of it. In John 17: 3 he particularizes the Father as "the only true God," (thus excluding himself from deity), and in his interview with the woman of Samaria, in John, chapter 4, confines "true worship" to the worship of the Father, a "worship which the Father seeks." In that true worship Christ comprehended his own. It was no blind and pointless service like that of the Samaritans, but an intelligent devotion. "*We* know" said Christ "what *we* worship, for salvation is of the Jews." Surely no testimony could be clearer, more definite or more conclusive. To his disciples a little before his departure from the earth he gave the information : "I ascend unto *my* Father and *your* Father, and to *my* God and *your* God." To the same effect his inspired Apostles spoke and wrote. The Acts of the Apostles is a strictly unitarian compilation throughout, and their epistles are all of the same tenor.

May we not, then, allowably ask if the New Testament is thus confirmatory of the great Jewish doctrine of the unity of God in one person, is not the New Testament entitled to Jewish goodwill and confidence? That book is no Trinitarian advocate, teaching for "doctrines the commandments of men," but a veritable continuation and completion as well as expositor of the Old Testament. It pointedly defines, and leaves no opportunity for sophisms and man-made mysteries. The Jew that turns his back upon that volume turns his back upon his inestimable friend.

After the glorious reigns of David and Solomon, the close of the latter of which was darkly clouded by the polygamous idolatry of one of the wisest of men, the Hebrew kingdom was divided. Ten tribes revolted and went off under Jeroboam the son of Nebat, with Samaria for their capital. The single tribe of Judah continued under the rule of Solomon; and, after him, his son Rehoboam, with Jerusalem for its capital. This split in the kingdom whose strength had consisted in its unity, inevitably led to the gradual decadence of the whole. Idolatry was the worm at the root. Severed into unfriendly fragments, the two peoples of Israel and Judah were successively carried away into captivity by Nineveh and Babylon. Seventy years of captivity in Babylon thoroughly cured the Jews of Jerusalem of their idolatry, and a number of them were allowed to return and rebuild their dismantled city. After numerous vicissitudes of fortune which it is not our purpose to enumerate, the whole country of Judea became, under the conquest of Cneius Pompey, a Roman province. Mark Antony, a member of the second Roman Triumvirate, granted to Herod of Idumea, or Southern Palestine, permission to assume the title of king of Judea. Herod, though naturally a tryant, repaired Jerusalem, partially rebuilt the temple, and was in other respects not unfriendly to the Jews. It was in his reign that Jesus of Nazareth, subsequently regarded as the Messiah, or Christ, was born. An expectation had been entertained and was about this time very rife in all the more civilized parts of the earth, that an extraordinary personage was about to appear, who should bring unwonted blessings to the human race. This personage seemed thus to be the "desire of all nations," of whom the prophet Haggai had said, more than five hundred years before, that he "should come." The remarkable predictive allusion of the Latin poet Virgil to such a visitant is also well known. Amongst the Jews this anticipation took the shape of a mighty deliverance from the galling Roman yoke, and so sanguine were the people, that, to use a modern term, they "discounted" their expected prosperity and became exceedingly elate and presumptuous, often going into sedition and revolts which the Romans invariably and sternly quelled.

On arriving at the age of mature manhood, Jesus of Nazareth proclaimed to the people of the district of Galilee, in which Nazareth was situated, that he had received a Divine commission, adopting as a text, on a leading occasion in the synagogue at Nazareth, a passage from the sixty-first chapter of the book of the prophet Isaiah, which well befitted the circumstances.

After his perusal of this passage of scripture, Jesus disclosed to his hearers, in language of his own, the gracious purposes of heaven in his mission. The record states that all who heard him "bare witness, and wondered at the gracious words which proceeded out of his mouth," thus closely agreeing with the testimony of another witness: " The law was given by Moses, but grace and truth came by Jesus Christ." The law, with its mandates and penalties, but Christ with a message of unpurchased mercy and spiritual enlightenment to the poor and the penitent. Yet how soon and how totally did those hearers forget his tender announcements, when, because he had simply reminded them of the ways of God in the times of Elijah and Elisha, they surged with animosity and took instant means to destroy him! How are grace and truth blended in this first introduction of Jesus to the world!—the kindest designs of heaven with faithful notice of duty to man. Could there be a surer token of a heavenly mission? And was not such a mission most loudly called for amongst a people who could rush from the worship of the synagogue to the sudden perpetration of atrocious murder?

Conformably to this beginning were Christ's life and conduct throughout his entire messiahship. He went about doing good to the bodies and souls of men. Can Judaism bear no cordially-approving testimony to such an example as this? And if not, why not? Where can Jews or anybody else find one so faultless and so gracious as this same Jesus of Nazareth—one, be it not forgotten, of their own people, and a descendant of their proudest prophet and king? Whence the silence of the Jews of modern times on this subject? Do they not *believe* the narrative? Then let them furnish some rational and intelligible account of the way in which such a fictitious history was invented, and whose were the more than wonderful yet fraudulent minds that devised so unbroken a stream of spotless goodness and truth. It is not a case for silence. Ignorement has no place here. Either acknowledge the superhuman excellence or give reasonable evidence that the whole Christian story is a cunningly-devised fable. The Jews lose no little by shutting out the light of Christ.

In the eighteenth chapter of Deuteronomy we find it written, " The Lord thy God will raise up unto thee a prophet from the midst of thee, of thy brethren, like unto me (that is, Moses); unto him shall ye hearken; according to all that thou desiredst of the Lord thy God in Horeb in the day of the assembly, saying, Let me not hear again the voice of the Lord my God, neither let me see this great fire any more, that I die not. And Jehovah said unto me, they have well spoken that which they have spoken. I will raise them up a Prophet from among their brethren like unto thee, and will put my words in his mouth, and he shall speak unto them all that I shall command him. And it shall come to pass that whosoever will not hearken unto my words, which he shall speak in my name, I will require it of him."

It is not to be supposed that any thoughtful and serious Jew, who wishes neither to deceive nor be deceived, will carelessly pass by this very important passage, or set lightly by its prophetic and admonitory instructions. None of us, Jew or Gentile, can afford to slight it. The motive to its promulgation was to supply a far milder method of communicating the Divine will than that which took place in Horeb on the day of the assembly—a method that would inspire less terror, yet not be a whit less obligatory. The words of God, spoken by the tongue of an authorized man, are fully as binding on the conscience and conduct as the Divine commands from the midst of blackness and darkness and tempest. The one only inquiry is, Are they commands of God?

When God approved the natural suggestion of the Israelitish people, as we see it in Exodus 20: 19, that not God in His own awful person, but that Moses should speak to them, then was instituted the Mediatorial system. Moses became—through the popular desire, confirmed by the Divine approval—the mediator between God and His chosen people. Such a mediator, also, was that future prophet to be—one that could hold communication with God and man. He must be a Hebrew by nation. Like Moses, he was to be a chief, a guide, a leader of his people. Like Moses, it was his great work to lead them out from the oppressions and corruptions of their previous condition and circumstances to the pure worship and service of God; and, like Moses, he was to conduct them through the waters of separation, by a life of faith, through a worldly wilderness to the promised Canaan of security, peace, and unassailable happiness.

Can we identify any personage in all history from Moses downward to the age of Herod that will fill the programme? As we have already intimated, no personage that could be acknowledged such had as yet appeared. Down to that the Desire-of-all-nations had not yet come. But in the reign of Herod an obscure and lowly birth took place in Bethlehem of Judea, from which in due time there matured a manhood wiser in words, greater in deeds and loftier in aspiration than had ever been seen before or since. The keen outlook of the expectant people was met by an object that fulfilled and more than fulfilled the popular hopes. How unspeakably joyous was that announcement by Philip to Nathanael, "We have found him of whom Moses in the law and the prophets did write, Jesus of Nazareth." That was a discovery indeed, filling their souls with unwonted views and anticipations. Then said the guileless Nathanael to Jesus in just acknowledgment, "Rabbi, thou art the Son of God; thou art the King of Israel." Thus early was Jesus announced Son of God and Son of man. He was Son of God far more truly than Adam, for Jesus was not formed out of the dust of the ground but was the immediate offspring of the Divine Spirit. He was also Son of man, being the seed of the woman. Thus Jesus was neither God on the one hand nor a common "mere man" on the other. He was the first and head of the new creation, always designed to be the future and final inheritors of this sublunary globe. Hence Jesus comes to be called the "last Adam;" the progenitor of a new race of men who arise by that second birth "of water and the Spirit." He will know and acknowledge those who are truly his children when they shall come forth from the dead, raised by him through the power lodged in his hands by the Everlasting Father. The regenerated earth will be the true Canaan; and Christ, under God, its perpetual king. How comes it that some, if not many, of the Nathanaels among the Jewish people of the present day do not have the moral intuitions and spiritual insight of the Nathanael of old? Their opportunities are and always have been superior to his. Christ's career had hardly then begun; the Jews of this age can know his whole existence. If Jesus Christ be not the prophet predicted in the 18th Deuteronomy, then God has delayed the blessed fulfilment considerably more than three thousand years. He has let pass not only that great extension of time without the expected fruitage, but has permitted the Hebrew state to melt away; its people to be driven from Palestine and scattered throughout the whole earth; their whole religious establishment of priesthood, sacrifices and temple worship to be obliterated, and all without giving the smallest indication that they will ever be restored. Has God failed of His purpose and His promise? Has His arm been shortened? Has He forgotten to be gracious? It might very well look so if the real Prophet has never been vouchsafed to us.

We now leave Deuteronomy and open the book of Psalms, the glorious contribution of the prophet-king David. Early in it, the 2d chapter, we read of the Lord Jehovah and His

Anointed, His Messiah. The Messiah, speaking by the pen of David, says, "I will declare the decree; Jehovah hath said unto me, Thou art my Son; this day have I begotten thee. Ask of me and I shall give thee the heathen for thine inheritance (mark that word 'inheritance') and the uttermost parts of the earth for thy possession. Kiss the Son, lest he be angry and ye perish from the way when his wrath is kindled but a little. Blessed are all they that put their trust in him."

Again, in the 45th Psalm, we read of a "King that is fairer than the children of men, whom God hath blessed forever." He is addressed as sitting upon a "throne which is for ever and ever; whose sceptre is a right sceptre, and who, because he loveth righteousness and hateth wickedness, hath been anointed by God, *his* God, above his fellows."

In the ninth chapter of the prophet Isaiah, which I shall take from the translation of the Episcopal Bishop Robert Lowth, we read, "For unto us a child is born; unto us a son is given; and the government shall be upon his shoulder, and his name shall be called Wonderful, Counsellor, the Mighty God, the Father of the everlasting age, the Prince of Peace. Of the increase of his government and peace there shall be no end. Upon the throne of David and upon his kingdom, to fix it and to establish it with judgment and with justice henceforth and forever; the zeal of Jehovah, God of Hosts, will do this."

The book of the prophet Isaiah is copiously supplied with chapters containing allusions of great significance. We would call particular attention to what is said in the 11th chapter relative to the stem of Jesse and the Branch out of his roots; to the 42d and 53d chapters, and to the 61st. The 13th of Zechariah is also very noteworthy as predictive of great events, and will repay serious and prayerful study. The last Old Testament allusion we shall refer to on this head is from the 5th chapter of the prophecy of Micah, but it is very pointed, and would seem little or nothing less than conclusive. In verse 2d we read: "But thou, Bethlehem Ephratah, though thou be little among the thousands of Judah, yet out of thee shall *he* come forth unto me that is to be ruler in Israel, whose goings forth have been from old, from everlasting." In the 4th verse: "And he shall stand and feed in the strength of the Lord, in the majesty of the name of the Lord, his God; and they shall abide, for now shall he be great unto the ends of the earth."

Who the learned Rabbi Isaac Leeser was is probably well known to many present. He was outspoken, and continued in the Jewish faith to the close of his days. In a statement of Jewish doctrine, which he caused to be published, he says: "The Messiah whom we expect is not to be a god, nor a part of the godhead, nor a Son of God in any sense of the word; but simply a man eminently endowed like Moses and the prophets in the days of the Bible, to work out the will of God *on earth* in all that the prophets have predicted of him. His coming, we believe, will be the signal for universal peace, universal freedom, universal knowledge, universal worship of the One Eternal; objects all of high import, and well worthy to be attested by the visible display of the Divine glory before the eyes of all flesh, just as was the presence of the Lord manifested at Sinai when the Israelites stood assembled to receive the law which was surrendered to their keeping. In the days of this august ruler the law, which was at first given as "an inheritance of the congregation of Jacob," will become the only standard of righteousness, of salvation for all mankind, when will be fulfilled to its fullest extent the blessings conferred upon Abraham, Isaac, and Jacob, that "in their seed all the families of the earth should be blessed."

Now, in this statement Mr. Leeser antagonizes the Sonship of Christ no less than his deity. That Christ is "not a Son of God in any sense of the word" is his plain, unmistakable declaration. This seems almost unaccountable when we reflect how distinct are the references to Christ, especially in the writings of David and Isaiah. In the 2d Psalm God is represented as saying, "Thou art my Son; this day have I begotten thee;" and by Isaiah in his 9th chapter, "Unto us a child is born, unto us a son is given," with numerous epithets and titles of extremely high distinction and glory, yet all due to the superintending "zeal of Jehovah, God of Hosts."

Elsewhere in his statement Mr. Leeser says, "We do indeed totally reject the idea of a Mediator either past or to come," yet that was precisely the office filled by Moses as between God and man, and it was for the exercise of his mediatorship, or interposition, that the terrified people of Israel so earnestly prayed. (Exod., 20: 19.)

Yet more painful is it to read Mr. Leeser when he says, "We reject him whom the Christians call their Messiah," as if the testimony to the anointing or messiahship of Jesus in the Old Testament were not to be accounted for. Again, we are the very reverse of agreeably surprised when Mr. Leeser declares his belief that "no mediator and no emanation from the Creator is conceivable." Here he excludes from the possibility of existence not only Christ but God's own Holy Spirit! Some mitigation of one's regret arises from his saying that neither a mediator nor a spirit proceeding from God the Father is "conceivable." This, then, is a matter for which Mr. Leeser's own mind, and not the Old Testament, is responsible. When Mr. Leeser, or any Jew, or Athanasian, or anybody else, takes to dogmatizing about the faculties in God, it is time to look out for mistakes and blunders. Very soon, indeed, in the book of Genesis do we meet with an announcement that there is a "Spirit of God," for it is no further on than in the 2d verse of the 1st chapter, where Moses tells us that in the creation "the Spirit of God moved upon the face of the waters." In the 6th chapter of Genesis, verse 3, Jehovah said, "My Spirit shall not always strive with man." And what was the prayer of Moses when, in Numbers, 11:29, he said to Joshua, "Would to God that all the Lord's people were prophets, and that the Lord would put His Spirit upon them." Would not this be an "emanation"? In Isaiah, 42:1, does not God say that He has put His Spirit upon His servant? In Isaiah, 43:8, God promises to "pour His Spirit upon the seed of Jacob and His blessing upon his offspring." See also Ezekiel, 36:27 and 37:14; but there is no necessity for multiplying proofs in a case so palpable and plain. The Old Testament is far from coinciding with Mr. Leeser's strange idea on this subject. His idea is far below what the Bible teaches concerning the nature of the Most High.

We return to a consideration of the first quotation made. Mr. Leeser believes that the "coming of the Jewish Messiah will be the signal for universal peace, universal freedom, universal knowledge, universal worship of the One Eternal," &c., &c. But really, now, does not this seem something more fanatical than one would have expected from a collected and cool-minded Jew? Does it not seem to imply that God will violently interfere by the exercise of sheer omnipotence to suddenly produce those great effects? Is that God's method of procedure with His moral offspring? It might be very great and glorious things to do, but it implies a method too merely mechanical for application to such beings as we are. Even if all those purposes were once secured, what evidence is there that the new Paradise, or second Eden, would not become, sooner or later, as unfortunate as the first Eden, by the introduction of disobedience and sin? Are we also to suppose that the Divine power, or the power of the Messiah, would interfere to prevent sinning? If so, mankind would be no longer moral beings, but the slaves of an irresistible omnipotence. That would be a march backward.

We are furthermore told by Mr. Leeser that the great and blessed things herein described are to take place "on earth." And the same is taught by the Jewish Karaites, or scripturists, a class claiming to keep more closely to the Bible than the generality of the Jews, who mix with the precepts of the Mosaic or written law the traditions of the Mishna and Gemara in the Talmud. It is true that a "regeneration" of the earth is spoken of, after which only will those good things take place, but we are left to conclude that none but they who are found upon the earth at the time of the "regeneration" will enjoy them, and that the millions who will have previously died can have no part or lot therein. The date of this "regeneration" is quite indefinite, and may be "thousands of years" yet to come.

This arrangement is certainly a hard one upon the scores if not hundreds of millions of Jews, including those now living with all that shall have died previous to the great change, and who will be just as deserving, though much less fortunate, than those others. For those others will be made peaceable, free, wise and pious by the irresistible fiat of the Almighty. They *must* be good and right whether they will or no. Nothing is said of what shall become of those on the earth at the time of the regeneration,—whether they will ever die, or will continue immortal. In the case of their death, nothing is said about their fate after death. Equally silent is the recital about the further propagation of the race, intermarriages, &c. Much of it seems to be quite conjectural.

Again it is said by Mr. Leeser that the old law as promulgated at Sinai, and that only, will be the law and standard of the future; whence the world will necessarily take a start backward for a restoration of the prospects and ideas that over three thousand years ago ruled the minds and animated the hearts of the immediate descendants of Abraham, Isaac and Jacob. It is not definitely stated whether the "law" that is thus to rule will include the sacrificial and ceremonial as well as the moral law, but from the observation that it is to be "the law which was at first given," all the forms are included. And this is confirmed by statements in other parts of Mr. Leeser's exposition.

Now about all this it is obvious to remark—and we do it reverently—that if God be the patron of those things, He seems to have left Himself not much scope for direction and command to the coming prophet. The past supplies substantially all that the future can need. If the old law and the old covenant, of which the law was a part, are to be the everlasting standard and rule, it will be of interest to know what the Prophet Jeremiah could have meant in his 31st chapter and 31st verse, when he reports Jehovah as promising a *new* covenant, not like the old one established at the exodus from Egypt, at Sinai, &c. The establishment of a *new* covenant involves essentially an abrogation of the *old.* Are not Jeremiah and Mr. Leeser, therefore, at decided odds on this subject? So, indeed, it would seem.

There is another point in which some considerable discrepancy is involved between what the Israelites of old thought and felt, and what Mr. Leeser opines relative to a "display of the Divine glory before the eyes of all flesh," such as that "manifested at Sinai." They saw it, but did not wish a repetition of the sight. Mr. L., on the other hand, exults in the prospect of this "visible display" being enacted over again. Inasmuch, however, as neither Jehovah nor the Israelitish people favored another instance of that display, it is not likely to be ever repeated. See Exod., 20:19, and Deut., 18:16 and 17.

Whilst our author for himself, and as coinciding with the great Moses Ben Maimon, or Maimonides, called the "lamp of Israel," acknowledges a future King Messiah and a resurrection of the dead, he keeps the ideas of both so distinct and apparently independent as vastly to weaken their effect. Thus the Messiah's field of operation is to be "the world and the people of Israel"—nothing connecting him with the resurrected mass of mankind. The light shed by the prophet Isaiah, especially in that passage which we have quoted from his ninth chapter, is not availed of but evaded, and therefore made unprofitable. Our Jewish friends sometimes belittle and nullify the very scriptures in which they profess to confide.

It must be regarded as a surprising fact that the Jewish people, notwithstanding all their bitter experience, do not candidly enough consider the teachings of their own prophets as they are spread forth in the Old Testament. Take, for instance, the concluding half-dozen verses of the ninth chapter of the book of Daniel. The mention, as by the mouth of the angel Gabriel, of so many weeks, each week obviously representing seven years, lends a precision to the prediction of the events to which they refer wholly unlike the almost wild indefiniteness of such writings as those of the honest Leeser. The allusion to "finishing the transgression, (of the race), to making an end of sins and a reconciliation for iniquity, to bringing in everlasting righteousness, to sealing up the vision and prophecy and anointing the Most Holy," is matter of the profoundest interest to us all, no matter who or what we are. The rest is as much history as prophecy, as those who have some knowledge of the awful sufferings of Jerusalem and her inhabitants will not dispute. In the same serious spirit we earnestly commend a careful attention to the last chapter of the book so closely in keeping with the Christian scriptures. It is of an apocalyptic character, and cannot but produce a salutary impression upon every unprejudiced mind.

We have now gathered very pertinent testimony from Moses, David, Isaiah, Jeremiah, Ezekiel, Daniel, Micah, Haggai, and Zechariah, and might have added Malachi—sufficient to make good the genuineness of the New Testament as an inseparable constituent of the Word of God. Each Testament is interlocked with the other, yielding mutual support. Both can point to the general history of mankind for proof of their title to our reliance, for the great facts of both are incontestable.

The Christian world, whatever their differences on other subjects, regard Jesus of Nazareth as their spiritual prophet, priest, and king, both for the present life and the boundless existence that is to follow it. That Jesus was and is such a priest, David taught when he declared God's appointment of him in the words, "Jehovah sware and will not repent, Thou art a priest forever after the order of Melchisedec." That he is and will be a king to the whole human family we have already seen from his institution by God to a rule extending to the uttermost parts of the earth. That he is the veritable prophet of whom Moses spoke may be shown from his miraculously precise predictions of the destruction of Jerusalem and the temple within it; of the prodigies that preceded and attended that destruction; of the unparalleled sufferings and miseries of the Jewish people during the siege of their capital; of the dispersion of the comparatively few remnants; their present scattered condition throughout the earth, and their future restoration, which they and we take for fact.

Before we come to pen our last paragraphs, we will offer a summing-up of the case of the Jewish people, as presented by a man of genuine learning who lived in the eighteenth century. We commend it to the sedate and candid consideration of all concerned. He says as follows, in commenting on a portion of scripture in Matthew 21: 42:

"'Did ye never read in the scriptures (Psalm 118: 22) The stone which the builders rejected, the same is become the head of the corner: this is the Lord's doing, and it is marvellous in our eyes? Therefore (saith Christ) I say unto you, The kingdom of God shall be taken from you and given to a nation bringing forth the fruits thereof: and whosoever shall fall on this stone shall be broken; but on whomsoever it shall fall, it will grind him to powder.'

"The kingdom of God, as may be collected from what is thus said, denotes the spiritual or moral dominion of God over moral subjects, that is, free agents, and by the people of God are signified such free agents as freely and voluntarily acknowledge the sovereignty of God by worshipping Him, and receiving and obeying all those laws, whether natural or revealed, which appear to have been enacted by Him. The Jews, therefore, by rejecting Jesus Christ, who proved himself to have been commissioned and sent by God, not only from the testimony of Moses and all their prophets, the holiness of his life and doctrine, and the numberless miracles he wrought among them, but still more plainly, if possible, by his rising from the dead, and empowering his disciples to work the same mighty signs and wonders in his name,—the Jews, I say, by rejecting this messenger, this Son of God, and refusing to receive the laws which he proposed to them in his Father's name, evidently renounced their allegiance to God, and ceased to be his people or subjects. And the Gentiles, on the other hand, by renouncing their vices and idolatrous superstitions, returning to the worship of God, and receiving His Messiah, together with the laws proposed to them by him in the name of God, as evidently put themselves under the dominion of God, acknowledged his empire, and became the people or subjects of God. And hence appears what is meant by the kingdom of God being taken from the Jews and given to the Gentiles. God removed the throne whereon David and his posterity had sat as his substitutes and viceroys, from among the Jews who had renounced his authority, and from earth to heaven; and placing it at his right hand, and setting upon it *His* Messiah, his only Son, gave him for his subjects, not one nation only, but all nations and kindreds and people, and all the ends of the earth for his dominion. That the kingdom of God was in this sense and in this manner actually transferred from the Jews to the Gentiles, is too notorious to need any proof. The Jews as a nation rejected the gospel, and persisted in their refusal of the Messiah until the final destruction of their holy city and temple; and what is yet more strange, *still* persevere in their obstinacy. Whereas the Gentiles embraced it so universally, that within a few centuries after Christ, almost the whole Roman empire—that is, almost all the then known world—forsook idolatry and became Christian. And God, on His part, testified that He entered into covenant with them and accepted their allegiance by pouring upon them the gifts of His Holy Spirit; as He signified on the other hand, His renunciation of the Mosaical covenant by not only suffering the seat of His empire, the city and temple of Jerusalem, to be utterly destroyed, but permitting the Jews also to be banished from the holy land, and scattered through all the nations of the earth. And thus was this prophecy most exactly accomplished in all its parts."

Now, those of us who believe in God—and I trust that is the case with us all—will acknowledge that God sympathizes with His creatures, and especially in their aspirations after another life. He commissioned Moses, and put His law into his mouth and into his hands, but that law said nothing of another life. Was not that great matter left to the Prophet like unto Moses of whom the Jewish lawgiver spoke in the 18th Deuteronomy? At least, it cannot be said to be unlikely. And, if so, the Prophet who should speak of another life, and, it may be, an *endless* life, would be much the greater prophet of the two—greater, as the interminable future is greater than the fleeting present.

God, having withholden in His old law any revelation, save a few suggestions, respecting a life to come, plainly designed a new law in which such a revelation should be made, and made in that clear, complete, and practical way which characterizes all the works of God. Common sense dictates that the very best way to demonstrate that man can live again after death, would be to bring to life a man who is known to have died. And this practical, common-sense method God adopted in the case of Jesus of Nazareth, who was known to have been put to death in a most public manner on Calvary, near the populous city of Jerusalem. Jesus of Nazareth rose again from his tomb within three days after being buried. In his resurrected state he was seen, heard, talked with, personally examined and handled, partook of food and drink, and gave all possible evidence of his resurrection. That his body had gone from the sepulchre, which had been closed and guarded with jealous and perhaps unexampled precaution, was beyond question; else his dead body would have been exposed by the Jewish rulers to the public gaze in disproof of the allegations of his disciples and friends. At all events the huge boulder lodged at the entrance of the sepulchre had been displaced, the tomb forsaken, and the once-crucified body never again seen by his executioners.

Following this, Almighty God confirmed the promise He had made to Jesus by conferring miraculous powers on his apostles; by pouring out upon them in a visible manner the gift of the Holy Spirit, and by such aids in their efforts at teaching the new religion as should be irresistibly convincing.

Thus we sketch the outline of the establishment of the Christian faith, which showed its divine origin and authority just as were shown the divine origin and authority of the Mosaic system. Each was attested by signs and wonders from on high.

With respect to the interior doctrines of the religion, the first thing to be taught is that the future life of men, if to be happy, must be the result of a special preparation for it. The preparation, or the education, must take place here; in this world. It must consist in making the concerns of the future life the ruling motives of the heart, so that when any conflict shall appear to take place between the calls and the interests of the present and of the future, the future must prevail. The turning point between living for this world and living for the next is signalized by an external ceremony called "baptism," by which are signified the washing away of the existing pollutions and sins of the soul and the commencement of a new and pure life, after the model presented in the life of Christ. This ceremony of passing through the waters of separation is therefore sometimes called a *baptism into Christ*, having an effect parallel to that which passed upon every child of Israel when they crossed the Red Sea, and, having left behind them the carnality and pollutions of Egypt, followed the lead of Moses under the superintending care of God. They were, therefore, said to be "baptized unto Moses."

To the Christian, Christ stands in the same relation that Moses did to the Israelites. Christ is the great Christian lawgiver, though he largely adopts the Mosaic code, especially the moral part of it, and makes it his own. Christ, like Moses, conducts his followers towards the coveted Canaan; but Christ's Canaan is beyond the grave, in the peace and perpetuity of heaven. The Christian, like the Jew of old, is provided with all the necessary appliances of a priesthood and of sacrifice, but they are not, like the Jew's, transitory. They are perpetual, with intercessory agencies that never cease. Moses failed as a leader, for he was not permitted to enter the promised land. Another, of the same prenomen as Christ's, was required to complete the task. Not so with Jesus, who through the most painful and appalling circumstances, forced his way into the heavenly Canaan for himself and for his people, where he now sitteth, not as God, but at God's right hand.

Having said thus much, we will not longer trespass upon your patience and your time, but commend you most especially to that unequalled letter to the Hebrews by the Hebrew disciple of the Hebrew Gamaliel, where all the principles and analogies of the Mosaic and Christian systems are unfolded and explained to the fullest of every sincere inquirer's most fervid desire. We close with the single remark that the study and experience of a life have tended to prove irrefragably one thing, viz., that the true religion for man, and for all men without exception, consists of a Mosaic pedestal reaching down to the centre, crowned with a Christian capital penetrating the skies.

[The foregoing, "To the Jews," was written with a view to repeating it before a Hebrew congregation, but circumstances did not favor the design. The minister was unwilling that his people should hear it, though he expressed a willingness for a private discussion. The manuscript of the foregoing was then placed in his hands, and on its return was accompanied by a courteous note claiming for the Jews the great advantage of having "the original Hebrew text of the Bible" for the source of their information "instead of in many respects a faulty translation"—the original text causing those sentences of the Bible covering the field of controversy to "appear in an entirely different light, while our Christian friends persistently misunderstand and misinterpret the same." The reverend gentleman thoughtfully suggested that "before seeking to lecture to Jews, and to imply wilful obstinacy on their part in shutting their eyes to the light of the gospel, careful inquiry should be made whether the accusation is well founded." He also said, "Our rejection of the New Testament must not be traced to obstinacy, but rather to the same motive which undoubtedly actuated the writer of the lecture in accepting it, viz., a love of truth." Speaking of the late Rabbi Leeser, he said that his "religious views represented in his days—and certainly in our own—those of but a small minority of his Jewish fellow-citizens. Since his death quite a number of books have been published in the (English) vernacular, which, had they been known and read beforehand, would probably have caused the writer to desist from preparing his lecture. Had, for instance, there been read "The Martyrdom of Jesus of Nazareth," by Dr. I. M. Wise, the writer would have been obliged to admit that the Jews indeed are studying the New Testament, but fail to see in it any truth that did not appear to them in the light of their own scriptures, while they cannot shut their eyes to its numerous contradictions and imperfections." He remarked: "In conclusion, let me assure you that the Jew does hardly require a helping hand in his search after truth; and that he always did and always will find that solace, consolation, and good cheer in his religious teachings which will tend to establish and secure his happiness here and hereafter."

A few days after the receipt of this note from the minister, the following was addressed to him in response:

"Rev. A. B.

"DEAR SIR: Profiting by your suggestion I procured a copy of Dr. Isaac M. Wise's 'Martyrdom of Jesus of Nazareth,' and have given it a pretty thorough perusal. The very most striking of the numerous remarkable things it contains is the doctor's modesty in claiming that a book he has 'systematically compiled' from the *Old* Testament is 'a better book' than the New Testament, and that he has 'a perfect right to expect all readers' to acknowledge this. The doctor seems to forget what others might possibly recollect, that God promised that 'the days should come when he would make a *new* covenant with the house of Israel and with the house of Judah, *not* according to the covenant that He made with their fathers when He took them by the hand to bring them out of the land of Egypt.' This looks very much as if God designed to supersede the old law by the new, for there was to be a day when the 'sceptre should depart from Judah,' and when '*another* prophet should be raised up like unto Moses,' who should lead the people out of the land of oppression and darkness into a land of freedom and light. Therefore it is that the doctor's proclivities to retreat upon the plans and policies of 3,400 years ago are neither conformable to the expressed will of God nor coincident with the reasonable feelings and aspirations of mankind in this practical age of the world. Onward, and not backward, *is* the motto. The *Old* Testament deals but sparingly with the things of the life to come which is so close to us all; the *New* Testament is freighted with the things that belong to man's everlasting peace.

Another noticeable point is Dr. Wise's consideration that the gospel of the Evangelist Mark was the *first* gospel that was written, and that so late as between A. D. 120 and 170, or from fifty to one hundred years after the destruction of Jerusalem by Titus, and after the times of the executions of Paul and Peter, who respectively aided in the compilation of the gospels of Luke and Mark. The doctor has left his motive for this singular metachronism a good deal exposed, it being no less than the endeavor to discredit Christ's power of prophecy and to stigmatize the second synoptic gospel by identifying Mark, its Hebrew author, with one Marcus, who was permitted by the Roman Emperor Hadrian (after A. D. 117) to exercise the office of bishop over the Christian church of Ælia Capitolina, the new city founded by Hadrian on the razed site of Jerusalem. Mark the Evangelist was undoubtedly a Jew, the son of Mary who lived in Jerusalem about the year 44, (Acts, 12: 12,) whilst Marcus, bishop of Ælia Capitolina, was of the Gentile race, a Latin, and probably a native of Italy. Of course, then, Mark and Marcus belonged to different centuries. The oldest authorities, Papias, Irenæus, and the learned Origen agree in stating that the gospel by Matthew was the first penned; in large part from facts ascertained by Matthew during his experience as a disciple. It was written in Hebrew, or Syro-Chaldaic, for the use of Jewish Christians, and perhaps about a score of years afterwards was translated into Greek, constituting the Greek gospel now in our hands. Then the gospel of Mark was written down, probably for direct use in Peter's ministrations, Peter being personal authority for its statements. It was independently written, though by the similarity, or even identity, of much of what it says with the already promulgated gospel of Matthew it gave confirmation thereto and established the genuineness of both. Thirdly, the composition of Luke's gospel was undertaken with the counsel and co-operation of Paul; and lastly, John's gospel was composed a few years before the termination of the first century, with the synoptics before him, which he supplemented and made beyond appraisement from his own personal knowledge, his close intimacy with Christ, and profound spiritual experience. John outlived the other apostles and died about A. D. 101, aged one century. Dr. Wise says 'none of the gospels were written in the first century.' Contrariwise, the evidence is they were *all* written within it.

The doctor betrays a manifest craving to put the fact of Christ's crucifixion in doubt. He suggests that Christ might have been *hanged* only; or possibly, not executed at all. He insists throughout his book that it was Roman and not Jewish policy that put Jesus to death, and that the Roman military power terrorized or corrupted a dozen or two of the Jewish priesthood, including Caiaphas the high priest and some scribes, to aid them in the commission of the crime, and at a time when the mass of the Jewish people were away on Mount Moriah engaged in religious exercises. He intimates that it was a comparatively small Jewish mob which cried 'Crucify him; crucify him; release unto us Barabbas;' and to Pilate, 'if thou let this man go thou are not Cæsar's friend.' He makes no effort to account for the intention to precipitate Jesus down the steep on the occasion of that gracious first sermon at Nazareth, nor to apologize for the flagitious scheme of the priesthood to put to death both Jesus and Lazarus, whom Jesus had raised from the grave, nor the many other such like purposes of violence and cruelty. In covering those wrongs he almost inculpates himself.

The doctor makes Christ the voluntary cause of his own immolation out of a generous desire to save thereby the lives of his immediate disciples and friends and a portion of the Jewish people who were urging him to set up for king, which Christ well knew if attempted would bring down certain destruction on them all. Seeing this, Christ concluded to die out of the way and thus put a stop to the whole design. The doctor thinks Christ acted meritoriously in this matter to the extent of 'eliciting admiration,' but no more. The benefits from his death extended to his disciples and friends above mentioned, but went no farther. They had no effect as regards the future life. In all this it did not seem to occur to the doctor to explain why Jesus did not seek to attain the purpose he ascribes to him by a simple suicide, and so avoid the unnecessary horrors of crucifixion.

The doctor discredits Christ's resurrection, and attributes the report about it to Paul's ingenuity and authority. The belief in the ascension must, of course, go the same way. Touching such phraseology as 'Christianity is no religion—a big bubble—a misfortune for weeping humanity—Jesus was not accused of saying or teaching anything original—all biographies of Jesus are works of fiction'—&c., *Parcius ista viris tamen objicienda memento.* Still, Christianity, disfavored by Jewish priestcraft and Roman pride and power, by philosophic conceit and heathen besottedness, managed to steer on against wind and tide till it rooted itself throughout the civilized and in some parts of the uncivilized world. The genuine touch of it changed the fierce and persecuting Saul into the meek and long-suffering Paul. Its effects were similar in numberless cases. As a model for precept and example, and of both combined, can the brightest intellect on the face of the earth conceive of a superior to Christ; nay, of an equal? If men claiming the honor of the Christian name have defaced and dishonored the pure Christianity, what good institution that ever existed has not human proneness to wrong more or less abused or perverted?

The doctor blames the eucharist as a most fruitful 'cause of hatred, persecution, outrage, and bloodshed,' and says 'if the doctrine underlying this observance be religious, then the Hindoos' car of Juggernaut may justly be called a religious institution.' Can there be any fairness and justice, to say nothing of decency and courtesy, in thus running a similitude between the memorial table of the supper instituted to perpetuate a recollection of Christ's self-sacrificing love, and the most inhuman and abominable development of Hindoo superstition? Will the generality of the children of Israel approve so dishonoring a comparison?

The doctor is very emphatic in his reprobation of the doctrine of Vicarious Atonement. It is true that no such word as 'vicarious' is found in the Bible, and it is not unlikely that a good deal of extravagance and error might be held in connexion with it; still there is a substratum of truth and soberness in the doctrine which no candid believer in either book of the Bible will undertake to deny. The Mosaical or Jewish religion was ushered into existence by the universal sacrifice in every Jewish household of a blemishless lamb, by the display of the blood of which upon the lintel and door-posts of the house of the enclosed family they were saved from the visitation of the destroying angel. Few, if any, of the departing Israelites were acquainted with the philosophy of the command; they simply obeyed the order of Moses, and were saved. Their faith in God and in Moses saved them. They were saved by faith, which manifested itself in their work of obedience. They were saved by the vicarious or objective instrumentality of the lamb's blood, appointed for them by God, and evidenced by their actual protection. Why an offering of blood was selected might, perhaps, be accounted for by the fact that life, or its symbol and representative, blood, indicates the presence and supremacy of God; for the production and sustainment of life, in every form of it—spiritual, animal, and vegetable—imply the presence and power of God. He is the Living God and the God of the living. When man first sinned, the penalty he paid was the return of his life to God, who only could produce it. The luxury of sinning must be paid for by the penalty of death. This idea is present in all the sacrifices of the Mosaic institution. Now, the Christian institution retains this idea, only it extends it, and makes the sacrifice not a continuous succession of petty sacrifices in one place only, but a universal sacrifice answering for all lands and all times, and the sacrifice not of brute beasts, but of the blood of a rational being, demanded by God as His inherent right, if He wills to call for it. If He so wills, man must obey, and obedience is shown both by and without sacrifice. All men die, for all men have sinned; but in the resurrection those only will be preserved from the destroying angel who have been careful to be protected by the blood of that Lamb whom God has selected for the purpose—holy, harmless, and undefiled, and separate from sinners. Blood for sin. By paying blood, sin is remitted. (Leviticus, 17:11.) The only blood God will accept is pure, uncontaminated blood. There is no blood but Christ's that is uncontaminated. He is willing to accept that, of which each one of us can avail himself by baptism *into* Christ, by obedience to him as a lawgiver, and accepting his advocacy as our high-priest offering for us his own sacrificial blood. Therefore Christ, the Lamb of God, is the paschal lamb, the sin-offering, and the priest, all in one. Therefore vicarious atonement means an atonement which another offers on our behalf. If God will graciously accept it, so much the better for us.

The doctor demurs to the prophecy of Daniel. Why? Does Daniel drift too decidedly against the doctor's views?

Omitting minor points too numerous to deal with, the

great flaw with Dr. Wise, as with Mr. Leeser, is the vague notion they have of the future after death, for Jews die as well as other people. This has a bad effect, in deadening their interest in divine things and making them satisfied either with trust in a few effete and exploded ceremonies, circumcision to wit, or casting them upon a cold, barren, deistical morality. It is in the nature of man to have hopes. If he will not take the hopes God offers, he will fabricate hopes of his own, however ill-founded. Thus Dr. Wise is happy in expatiating about a visionary 'gorgeous temple of humanity, one universal republic, one universal religion of intelligence, and one great universal brotherhood.' He keeps out of sight the indelible fact that subsequent to this 'gorgeousness' there must follow death, burial, resurrection, judgment, and final sentence, one way or the other. The glory God has provided for the faithful *beyond* the grave Dr. Wise appears to have no taste for.

By way of reciprocating your kindness, I respectfully suggest to you a perusal of the works of an author noted for 'knowledge, probity, charity, and meekness.' I mean Dr. Nathaniel Lardner, whose 'Credibility of the Gospel History' and 'History of the Apostles and Evangelists' are justly approved. I add to these the 'Evidences of the genuineness of the Gospels' by the painstaking Professor Andrews Norton. They may, perhaps, do something to modify, at least, the extreme views of Dr. Isaac M. Wise in which you appear to participate.

Very truly and respectfully."]

THE METHODIST EPISCOPAL CHURCH in North America may be regarded as the same body of Christians that in the British Islands is called Wesleyan Methodist. The latter may, perhaps, be the more correct designation, for the organization is stamped throughout with John Wesley's lineaments, spiritually, morally and mentally, and its structure was his handywork. This distinguished man was the second born of a family of six, three boys and three girls, all well endowed in body and mind. The parents lived at the little town of Epworth, in Lincolnshire, England. The father of the family was the Rev. Samuel Wesley, rector of the parish, and of course a member of the English Established Church. His eldest son, Samuel, was educated at the University of Oxford and intended for the same church; and the other two sons, John and Charles, after their preliminary education, were sent to the same university. John Wesley was born June 28th, 1703; Charles five years after. In the year 1709 the family parsonage was burnt, believed by incendiary hands, when the life of the boy John was preserved almost by miracle, an event supposed to have had a profound effect upon his mind in after life, and much to do with the deep seriousness that was the masterspring of his soul. The Wesley family, mother and all, though church people in the head, were considerably puritan at heart, and by word and deed made consistent protest against the loose and vicious living of the people around them. This was what most probably provoked the incendiarism.

Whilst at Oxford the brothers did not relax from the cautious and strict life in which they had been brought up, but standing aloof from the prevalent practices and habits of the young men around them, placed themselves under an exceedingly rigid regimen of body, mind, and time, which brought down upon them and the few companions they had succeeded in acquiring a general unpopularity. Under such circumstances there must, of course, be a nickname for them. It might have been worse. They were called *Methodists*, it has been said, from the Methodici, one of the classes of physicians in old Rome, so styled because they "affected to depart from all other physicians and to follow a peculiar method of their own." James Hervey, the author of the Meditations among the Tombs, "was a member of Lincoln College, the same to which John and Charles Wesley belonged, and often took part in their religious exercises. But the most valuable acquisition was George Whitefield, son of an innkeeper at Gloucester, a member of Pembroke

College, and a young man of uncommon eloquence and fervor. Their reading fed the flame already aroused in their souls. William Law's "Serious Call," Thomas á Kempis's "Imitation of Christ," Jeremy Taylor's "Holy Living and Dying," and such works, guided their thoughts and actions. John Wesley took priest's orders, and for a few months assisted his father at Epworth. In the year 1735, his father having died, John Wesley accepted an invitation to go out to Georgia, in North America, to dispense a knowledge of religion to the colonists and the Indians. He was then about thirty-two years of age, and was accompanied by Charles and by Whitefield. The much that was expected of him was by no means accomplished, for he involved himself in ill-judged strifes and controversies in the effort to force people into acceptance of his peculiarly strait-laced notions and practices. Whilst on the ocean and in Georgia Wesley had become acquainted with the Moravians, and was deeply impressed with many of their views. Wesley remained in Georgia about three years, and on returning to England undertook to preach in some of the churches of the Establishment; but his manner and matter not suiting the tastes of many of the clergy and the better educated and wealthier classes of the laity, Episcopal pulpits soon became closed to him. He preached in some Dissenting chapels, but was not a favorite even with dissenters. In 1742 he revisited old Epworth, and offered to the curate of the place to take part with him in the church services. But this was firmly declined. Wesley was, however, resolved the people should hear him, and so got it published abroad that at six o'clock on Sunday evening he would preach in the grave-yard. Wesley was present in due time, and also such a crowd as Epworth never saw before. He spoke standing on his father's tombstone, and the effect of his preaching was to bring forth groanings, tears, and lamentations from the great assembly. So he went on and on, and, forced by events he could not control, became the Moses of a new Israel, performing labors as preacher, writer, theologian, ruler, guide in a hundred ways more than can now be hinted at. His exertions were chiefly in England, but Scotland and Ireland were by no means neglected. Thus he went on, almost a wonder of the world, till the end, on the 2d March, 1791, still found him fully employed in his Master's service. At his death there were in his connexion about three hundred itinerant preachers, about one thousand local preachers, and a regular membership in the British islands of eighty thousand.

There are at the present time in North America about seventeen organizations sprung from the Wesleyan stock. They have about 360 conferences, 28,000 travelling and 38,000 local preachers, and not far from 5,000,000 lay members, with perhaps twice as many attending listeners. Of the seventeen organizations some are white, some colored, some Arminian, some Calvinistic.

The principal offshoot is the *Methodist Protestant Church*, which was born November, 1830. It has now over forty conferences, about 1400 travelling and nearly a thousand local preachers to about 120,000 lay members. Their doctrinal system is the same with that of the Episcopal Methodist, and, as they dispense with bishops, approximate Congregationalism. Touching foreign missions, Sunday schools, educational and publishing institutions the Methodists are the reverse of backward or slackhanded.

Whitefield and Wesley did not long continue to work together. The former was Calvinistic, the latter Arminian; though each respected the moral and spiritual character and sincerity of the other. So John Wesley dropped the close intimacy that one subsisted between the Moravians and himself. He had his frailties like other men, and some of them appear quite puerile and weak, yet his name will compete with almost any as teacher, preacher, and missionary, as well as head of a vast eccelesiastical establishment.

Inasmuch as John and Charles Wesley never dissented from the mother church of England, they necessarily inherited her ideas on fundamental theology. As to the soteriology, John Wesley had a system of his own. Let us give it some examination.

The scripture doctrine as to Christ's death, and the manner in which it becomes available for the remission of sins, shows, *first*, that Christ died only for those who choose to belong to him, that is to say, for those who have believed and been baptized into him so that they have become part of him as they formerly were of Adam. Christ thus becomes the representative of his people before God, who acknowledges the validity of this representation, because plain justice dictates that as many as desire to get clear from Adam and Adamic influences, into which they were helplessly born, should have full opportunity to do so. Christ therefore stands forth in the Divine presence for his people. His acts on their behalf are accounted in God's sight as their acts, and of which, their will concurring, they obtain much of the benefit. When, therefore, Christ died to fulfil the will of God, which will was that he should become a victim or sacrifice for the remission of sins in conformity with the pattern of the old law, (for the bloody sacrifices of the old law were a perpetual reminder that the forfeiture of life—typified by the sacrificial shedding of blood—was inseparably fixed to the commission of sin,) he died for himself and for all his actual followers, who are therefore accounted to have died with him. This obedience to the will and law of God was a propitiation for the past sins of every member of Christ's church and a clear deliverance from those sins; current involuntary transgressions and frailties (confessed and forsaken) being cared for by Christ's unceasing mediatorial priesthood before the throne and mercy-seat above.

Accordingly, then, the propitiation and deliverance from the burden and stain of sin enjoyed by Christ's people have always hinged on Christ's crowning compliance with the Divine will, which compliance is therefore the basis of our chiefest gratitude to Christ, (yet never forgetting his previous wonderful teachings and exemplary life,) as it has always been the ground of God's supreme approval of Christ and consequent exaltation of him to God's own right hand. Still, nothing is more assured than that the salvation by Christ, and Christ himself, are wholly ascribable to God's prevenient purposes of grace and mercy to man. Such, we believe, so far as it goes, a just statement of scripture teaching.

It is observable that Methodist preachers and writers are quite exuberant in their reference to Christ's "merits," so that one might think the Bible teemed with repetitions of that word. Yet, like other favorite Nicenist terms and designations, the word "merit" does not once appear within the lids of the Bible. There is much difference between the Bible doctrine and Nicenist ideas on the subject of Christ's work for man's reconciliation with God. Perfect as were Christ's obedience and service, and infinitely as they are and ever will be rewarded, they were still but a compliance with the Divine will. Doubtless, that is genuine merit and excellence, yet we must not combine with it any idea of supererogation. Ecclesiastical history contains a memorable chapter on the abuses of the doctrine of "merits," and its being made the foundation for the shameless trade in indulgences. The doctrine is much restricted in Protestant hands, yet when ignorantly accepted may become dangerous. A blind trust in, perhaps, a mere form of words, whereby, as has been said, "thousands on thousands have been renewed in a moment, as in the twinkling of an eye," may be quite a different thing from a real and well-grounded conversion. Where a very great boon is offered upon unexpectedly easy terms, it might not be very surprising that it is multitudinously accepted. Hence the readiness with which in Methodist expositions parallels are run between the results of Methodist exhortations, and the effects from Peter's preaching on the day of Pentecost, is not quite justified. A great and amazing miracle, or, rather, series of miracles, had taken place; Christ had been crucified but a short time before, and Jerusalem was profoundly stirred. Peter charged home upon his hearers their share of the guilt and responsibility of Christ's unrighteous immolation, and made them feel, individually in numerous cases and nationally in all, a degree of poignancy that pricked them to the heart, convinced them of their criminality, and brought out the confession and the cry, "What shall we *do?*" Peter promptly answered, "Repent and be baptized into the name of him whom you crucified, and your sins shall be remitted and the Spirit of God poured out upon you." Would any Methodist minister, if precisely those hearers of Peter were reproduced before him, feel authorized to demand no more than Peter did? Would he not say, "Oh, you are Jews, you believe in One God and that there is no other but *he.*" This won't do. You must believe in a God "under a threefold distinction or personality," one of which personalities contains two natures, a divine and a human; hence one part of the God you must worship is a man, is human. After you have accepted this and discarded your monotheism, you can repent of your sins and be baptized.

To be consistent with his published creed, the creed of his church, the Methodist teacher would naturally thus speak. But it would arouse controversy and not contrition in his Jewish audience, and therefore no such penitential results would arise as took place on the day of Pentecost. Therefore until apostolic preaching and methodist are about the same, let not methodists claim the success of the Apostle Peter as if it were due to the preaching of Methodism.

In his second epistle to Timothy, Paul, nearing the termination of a most faithful life, reported himself "ready to be offered, and that the time of his departure was at hand. I have (said he) fought a good fight, I have finished my course, I have kept the faith, henceforth there is laid up for me a crown of righteousness, which the Lord, the righteous Judge, will give me at that day." Here are several considerations other than simple reliance on Christ's "merits," one of which is that Paul had kept the faith, the true Christian faith, as to which his voluminous writings give many testimonies, but, since they all agree, the single one in 1st Corinthians, 8:6, will suffice. And that, as we have seen in Peter's case, is altogether different from the "three-fold distinction or personality" in God, which "Methodists believe." So that the question arises, Whether, before Methodists resign themselves almost or quite entirely to the mere acceptance of a single point of doctrine, it would not be wise and becoming in them, as men and professing Christians, to examine generally the foundations of their faith, and see, if in accepting unquestioned, in a lump, the mass of Nicene dogmas and decrees, they were not less cautious and circumspect than they ought to have been? The one simple circumstance that it was the habit of Christ and his Apostles to teach in the Jewish temple at Jerusalem, and in the Jewish synagogues elsewhere, is not without significance. It means that upon fundamental doctrines Christ and his apostles and the Jewish public agreed. The differences that arose related to Christ's messiahship and resurrection. Not a vestige of any such doctrines as are prevalent in these days, as the three persons in the godhead, pre-existence, incarnation, and their adjuncts, were ever broached in the temple or the synagogues of the Jews! Yet these are the staple of the doctrines and teachings of the present time, which date not from the days of prophets and apostles or from the land of Judea, but from the fourth century after Christ and from sources distant from Palestine.

It has been proposed, apparently in an authoritative quarter, to make the centennial anniversary of John Wesley's death in 1791 the occasion for a grand ecumenical or worldwide conference somewhere in the United States. How admirable would such an occasion be for the public renunciation by the Methodist body of the errors and follies with which Constantine's assemblage at Nice enshrouded the pure and simple elements of the Christian faith. The twentieth century ought not to find the professing Christian church still groping among the blunders and darkness of the fourth.

But perhaps it might be thought that we have not sufficiently and satisfactorily accounted for or responded to the great cardinal doctrine which so occupied Wesley's thought and by the power of which, it is inferred, he was enabled to sway the myriads upon myriads of men that listened to his sermons. We find copied from one of Wesley's self-disparaging confessions the statement that he regarded all his religious exercises, his self-renouncements and denials, his fastings and preaching and prayers, and the charitable deeds that he did previous to his 35th or 36th year, as "altogether corrupt and abominable; that his works, his sufferings, his righteousness, so far from reconciling him to an offended God and making any atonement for the least of his sins, needed atonement themselves, or they could not abide God's righteous judgment; so that he had no hope but that of being justified freely through the redemption that is in Jesus." He implored for faith "that through the merits of Christ his sins would be forgiven." He claimed that "trust in Christ and in Christ *alone*, for salvation," granted to him as an actual experience, was that which *alone* took "away his sins" and "saved him from the law of sin and death."

We would be the very last in the world to seek to deprive John Wesley, or any of his followers, or anybody else, of anything which might seem to them an assurance of the Divine acceptance and favor. God forbid it should be otherwise. God's gifts come to his creatures in infinite variety. That is not the point; but the point is that since men may and do make mistakes; since they are not unfrequently enthusiastic—we do not say fanatical—it will not be always safe to adopt for a basis of expectation of the Divine favor anything which is devoid of the express indorsement of the Divine Word. No Bible text can be shown where the "merits of Christ" are proposed as that through which "alone" "sins can be forgiven." Millions may, indeed, say so; but millions are not the Bible; nor can millions save us.

Just before Christ's departure from the mountain in Galilee to the heavenly world, he informed his disciples that all power (essential to his Christhood) had been granted to him, whereby free scope of action, no longer confined to Judea, was everywhere given to him, and, through him, to them. He then commissioned his disciples, now fully his apostles, to go forth in every direction and "teach *all* nations" by an immersal of them into the name, that is to say, into the doctrine or knowledge, of the Father, and of the Son and of the Holy Ghost. This is in Matthew. In the synoptic Mark the parallel passage reads: "Go ye into all the world and preach the gospel to every creature. He that believeth and is baptized shall be saved, and he that believeth not shall be damned." Now in both these passages of scripture, which mean the same thing with a variation in expression, the preliminary consideration is that something is to be taught or communicated. That something is the knowledge of God, of His Son and His Spirit, or, in one word, the gospel. After this is accepted and understood, in other words, after the gospel is taught and believed, there will come the duty of public acknowledgement of it by the rite of personal baptism of the body, directly enforced by Mark and impliedly by Matthew, either by indoctrination into the knowledge of "the Son" or the observance of the "all things whatsoever." With belief and baptism salvation is connected; without them, damnation is denounced.

In the seventeenth chapter of John's gospel Christ defines "life eternal" to consist in the knowledge of the "Only true God, the Father, and of Jesus Christ whom the Father had sent." Taken in connexion with the above-mentioned texts in Matthew and Mark the inference must be just that "salvation" and the "knowledge of the true God and His Son" are convertible and equivalent, or that the one is identical with the other.

Now, then, if salvation, or, which is the same thing, life eternal, are the reward of a knowledge of the true God and of His Son, with the sequence of outward baptism in the world's face, why did Mr. Wesley put these things behind his back and cast his hopes upon Christ's "merits" *alone*, irrespective of all belief and all action besides?—And especially as no such thing is anywhere proposed in the Bible? Was he not in respect to his decision determined rather by his reading of William Law and Jonathan Edwards than by the calm trust of the royal Psalmist, or of the Apostle Peter and his fellows in the apostolate? That passage, 2d Cor., 5: 18, which tells us that "all things are of God, who hath reconciled us to himself by Jesus Christ, to wit, that God was, in Christ, reconciling the world unto himself, not imputing their trespasses unto them"—we suggest that this passage of the scripture would have shown Wesley that God should have had a share in his "trust" and not Christ *alone*, just as a saving knowledge of the gospel is not a knowledge of Christ only, but of the Father and operative Spirit also. It seems hardly to be questioned that the gratitude and praises addressed to Christ *alone* which comprise so large a proportion of the contents of most hymn books and poetical compositions must be referred to the ideas in which Wesley shared. It will be no diminution of the thanks, honor, and praise we owe to Christ for his free-will sufferings and death on our behalf, to keep ever in rememberance that thereunto was he appointed by His Father, for "all things are of God" who, by means of Christ, reconciled us unto himself through a merciful omission to impute to us the guilt of the trespasses we have committed—that is to say, by the exercise of His divine Sovereign forgiveness. "By grace are ye saved, through faith; and that not of yourselves; it is the gift of God."

In this doctrine of forgiveness, exercised by God the Father, it seems to us, (and we hope to be forgiven for saying so,) neither Wesley nor many others with sounding names have a very vigorous, or even a real reliance. There seems to lurk in many of their declarations more or less of the idea that God the Father is a stern and severe creditor or taskmaster, who will exact the uttermost farthing, and that therefore it is through Christ's leniency, compassion, and generosity *alone* that mankind have any just ground for hope of final salvation. They do not seem to see that notwithstanding Christ's sacrifice of himself there was and is still left very broad need and room for the exertion of the Divine forgiveness. "If we confess our sins, God is faithful and just to forgive us our sins and to cleanse us from all unrighteousness." It is most true that "if any man sin, we have an advocate with the Father, Jesus Christ the righteous, who is the propitiation for our sins; and not for ours only, but also for the sins of the whole world." But these consoling and invaluable utterances of the Spirit of God show that though we and all the world have an advocate with the Father, yet he, the advocate, is not the final resort, but a mediating agent for us with Him who sitteth on the throne of judgment. The transgressions that require pardon are transgressions not against Christ, but against God the Father, with whom Christ treats for our forgiveness, pleading before the throne of God whatever may be alleged in extenuation of our demerits and sins. It is God who must finally forgive or refuse forgiveness, and the ground, or at least a very principal ground, for forgiveness is our confession of our sins. No pleading of Christ's merits is presented as a ground of forgiveness, whilst, undoubtedly, it was the meritorious fidelity and excellence of Christ that gave him the position of advocate. Christ's worth and vast weight in God's esteem will, we may be sure, give the greatest value to his pleadings in our behalf, yet, after all, the final decision is with the mind of God, and with that *alone.* Is not this demonstrated in our daily prayer to Our Father, "forgive us our trespasses"? Was not Christ's prayer to the Father when he implored forgiveness on his murderers, "Father, forgive them, they know not what they do"?

We very readily admit that in his capacity of our representative, or our "federal head," as Christ has been termed, or the head of his body, the church, (of which those who have been baptized into Christ are the members,)—we very readily admit that we may point the Divine consideration to Christ's perfect obedience, and urge its worth, yet that can only be effectually done by those who have an honest consciousness of having striven to be, to the best of their ability, faithful workers of the Christian law. And could not John Wesley have with entire truth and honesty claimed, even in the sacred presence of God, of Christ, and of his own solemn conscience, that at least those religious exercises, self-renunciations, preachings, prayers and charitable deeds which he did previous to his 35th or 36th year, were at least sincere and well-intentioned and designed at the time for service to God? We fully believe he could, and can see nothing to raise a doubt that those works would have been so accepted. His first thoughts on this point appear to have been his best, for the second thought seems to lack any scriptural basis. And we think it by no means unlikely that the second thoughts were the fruit of perusal of writings at that period more fashionably ecclesiastical, perhaps, than they were apostolic.

As an instance of the wrongfully prevailing tendency among many churches and religious people to place the dignity and supremacy of God the Father in a position of actual disparagement, we will run the risk of a reference to the history of the earthquakes that in the year 1886 produced such havoc in and near the city of Charleston, South Carolina. At such times, and in all times when mankind are driven beyond the ordinary conventionalities, the beatings of the popular heart can more surely be learned from the common people than from the educated and refined classes. The colored population of Charleston exhibited during the terrors of the earthquake the ultimate meaning of the religious teachings they had all along been receiving. In the depth of their fright, with their souls probed to their centre, they showed who was their final reliance; who was truly their *God*. The public press reported that "the name of Jesus was most frequently used, and, as if supplicating God face to face, they shrieked out in the very helplessness and pathos of despair, such sentences as "Do, my Master, Jesus, have mercy on me." "Oh, sweet Jesus, save me, save me." "Let me live through this night, my God, my Saviour." "Hold me up once more, thou blessed Christ, my Master." The large majority of the hymns sung in their churches—and the hymns make the deepest impressions on their minds—are in praise of Christ,—God, as a being distinct from Christ, scarcely ever practically entering their thoughts. The human heart seems capable of having in reality but *One God;* no matter what the brain may argue or the tongue be taught to articulate, the heart kneels to One God alone. It might be Jesus, it might be the virgin Mary, it might be some other, it might be the true God, but it is always *only One*, for the mind instinctively rejects distraction. In respect to *baptism*, it might be incidentally remarked, the bulk of the colored people seem to be instinctively right. Regarding baptism as the sign of a sincerely religious purpose, and that in baptism we propose to "*put on* Christ," they use immersion of the *whole* person.

Wesley's affection for the English Episcopal Church led him blindly to adopt the system of Pædobaptism. This was to the serious injury of his own system, thereby left incomplete. The tenth chapter of the Acts of the Apostles illustrates this. Cornelius, the Gentile centurion, approved of God and man, was by the Divine will to be inducted into the Christian church, to become a member of Christ and an heir of salvation. Appropriate means were adopted, and Cornelius and his party were instructed in the leading principles of the Christian faith by the chief of the apostolic band. The procedure was divinely crowned by a general outpouring of the Holy Ghost. Just here, according to Methodist principles and practice, the business was, to all intents, at an end. Able Methodist preaching informs us that when "sinners have been invited to methodist altars, and they have been directed to their atoning Saviour and bidden to look and live, thousands and thousands of them have been renewed in a moment—as in the twinkling of an eye." And here the matter of Christian induction by the Methodists appears to stop. The sinners have become "believers," but they have fallen short of fully obeying Christ's dictum, in that they have not been "baptized." Now, we may certainly suppose that the outpouring of the gift of the Holy Ghost (accompanied, too, by miraculous powers) was at least equal in salvable force and efficiency to any "renewal" ever accomplished by Methodist agencies. Yet that outpouring was not sufficient. Peter appealed for something else. He demanded a closing process, and thereupon commanded the converts "to be *baptized* in the name of the Lord." This terminated the matter. Nothing further is anywhere said of Cornelius or his friends. No more needed to be said. They had been born again out of Adam into Christ; had "put on" Christ, which is a far more real and thorough thing than "looking" at him, and nothing was now left them but to live lives to the end consistently with those new relations they had assumed.

The Methodist deficiency thus becomes easily perceptible. The inward "renewal," which is the equivalent of "believing," must be followed by practical baptism with water in, or into, the name of Christ. It will not do to say that the Methodist converts were baptized in their infancy, or babyhood, perhaps, and that that was and is enough. The only baptism that can be efficacious must follow, and not precede, the "renewal" within, or the "believing;" and the baptism must be the result of the convert's own intelligent and earnest desire, and not merely that of his parents, kindred, or friends.

THE UNIVERSALIST CHURCH in the United States appears by a report in 1884 to have had within its control 1 national convention, 22 State conventions, 73 ecclesiastical associations, 948 parishes, 669 ministers, 4 colleges, 2 theological seminaries, 6 academies, and 34,349 church members. Since 1884 there has probably been a proportionate augmentation of these figures.

The idea around which this denomination is gathered has come down from the early days of Christian history. Origen, who was born in the Egyptian city of Alexandria in the year 185 after Christ, and a man of immense learning for those days, both sacred and profane, advocated the idea that the torments of the damned would at some time cease. He held, however, some remarkable notions which much interfered with the popularity of his doctrines. Amongst these may be mentioned that the souls of mankind exist before men appear in this world, to which they are sent in punishment of sins committed in a pre-existent state. Also that the sun, moon, and stars have souls; that after the general resurrection all bodies will be round; and that as Christ was crucified on earth to save mankind, he will be crucified in the next world to save devils. Gregory, of Nyssa, was an admirer of Origen in some respects, and appears to have adopted his views about restoration. Theodore, of Mopsuestia in Cilicia, is supposed to have thought the same way. Of reputed authors and thinkers among the moderns who have favored the restoration doctrines, Archbishop Tillotson was one; Dr. Gilbert Burnet; Bishop Thomas Newton; the celebrated William Whiston; Soame Jenyns, author of the Internal Evidence of the Christian Religion; David Hartley, who so strenuously opposed the war against the American colonies, and was appointed on the British side to negotiate with Dr. Franklin the terms of peace; William Law, author of the Serious Call; and nearer our own day Thomas de Quincy and Professor Maurice. John Foster, the Baptist, wrote against the doctrine of endless punishment. The same doctrine was publicly taught in this country by Dr. Jonathan Mayhew, in Boston, 1762, and the first church built in the restoration interest was in Gloucester, Mass., in 1780, of which the Rev. John Murray was pastor. What is called the Winchester (New Hampshire) confession was adopted in 1803. It declares, 1st. We believe that the Holy Scriptures of the Old and New Testament contain a revelation of the character of God and of the duty, interest, and final destination of mankind. 2d. We believe that there is One God, whose nature is Love, revealed in One Lord Jesus Christ by One Holy Spirit of Grace, who will finally restore the whole family of man to holiness and happiness. 3d. We believe that holiness and true happiness are inseparably connected, and that believers ought to be careful to maintain order and practice good works; for these things are good and profitable to men. Accepting this confession, the Universalist Church claims to be thoroughly Christian in belief, holding inflexibly to the authority of the Bible, the divine mission and office of Christ, the absolute necessity of a holy life, the certainty of a just retribution for sin and the assurance of the final triumph of good over evil and holiness over sin, in all worlds and all souls.

The Universalists are not exactly a unit in point of doctrine. Some believe in a final restoration to holiness, to be effected subsequently to the general resurrection of the dead, either all at once or successively as fitness in each case might dictate. So they believe in a state of probation after death. Others hold that so great a change will be effected in human character by the simple process of death or resurrection, or both, that no matter how unregenerate and ungodly a man might be at death, he will rise from the grave in a state of fitness to enter the perfectness and bliss of heaven. Perhaps the first-mentioned class of thinkers predominate in Europe; the latter in the United States. Referring to the latter class, we find them taking pretty high ground. It is argued that God's omniscient foresight beheld, before the creation, the historic profile of every individual of the coming race. He saw the end of all prior to their beginning. As a Being of infinite benevolence they claim that it became the Creator either not to create at all, or so to ordain every human life that after all its trials, temptations, misfortunes and sufferings its end should be everlasting peace and joy. Those trials, temptations and sufferings are disciplinary only, intended to teach and to warn. The Divine foresight, it is assumed, "is a solemn pledge on God's part" that every life He originates "shall prove a final blessing to its possessor." The justice of God, it is argued, could not mete out to temporary and finite sin a punishment out of all proportion greater than itself; besides which, God cannot suffer anything by the sin. He is above and beyond all human reach. Why, then, should God inflict the awful vengeance of eternal suffering on his "helpless children"? Say they, "God's justice demands an end to punishment and the final redemption of all." Even Satan, it is urged, could do no worse than is affirmed of God's purpose against a part of mankind; God cannot and will not do anything but the very opposite of what might be presumed of the devil.

God's love and goodness stand evidenced in the material creation, and Christ's mission was to save his people from their "sins and iniquities" "in this present evil world." This proves God's care for not only the bodies but the souls of men, for we cannot believe that the never-dying soul would be less cared for than the transient and perishing body. Now if this "present evil world" is the scene of Christ's saving work, then it is not from the evils of any *future* world that he seeks to save. From this the "final holiness and blessedness of all men" is inferred.

God commands men to "overcome evil with good." Will God Himself do less? Will the God who commands men to forgive their enemies eternally torment His own? It cannot be. God punishes only to correct. He does not willingly afflict the children of men. It was God's purpose to reconcile all men to Himself by the blood of Christ's cross. Christ is the propitiation for our sins and not for ours only, but for the sins of the whole world. The Father sent the Son to be the Saviour of the world. God promised to Abraham that in him all the families of the earth should be blessed—that is to say, through Christ, who was to spring from the loins of Abraham. The resurrection that was brought to pass in Christ's person will happen to all, and will be not a mere resurrection of the body, "but be a moral and spiritual uplifting, exaltation, or raising of the *whole being* into the Divine or heavenly likeness." Since all (not only saints, but *all*) will be changed in the twinkling of an eye from corruptible to incorruptible, the good and evil alike will rise from the grave freed from all sin and tendency to sin and "universal blessedness and holiness" pervade every soul. As the spring returning every year brings back to the face of nature life and freshness and beauty, so will the resurrection morning open upon an entirely redeemed and perfected world.

Such in the main and in brief is the Universalist doctrine. Is there objection to it? There seems to be. In the first place, the Universalists apply to all mankind, without discrimination, those gracious provisions and merciful promises which are designed for the faithful servants of God and followers of Christ *alone.* In their view the Bible regards all men as "the sheep," none of them "the goats." Thus we find them quoting with much satisfaction the passage in Romans, 8: 38 and 39, where they should note that the "love of God" spoken of is that which "is in Christ Jesus our Lord," meaning that *out* of Christ Jesus our Lord none can confidently hope for the love of God. There are circumstances, however, when "our God is a consuming fire," of which both Old and New Testaments testify. There is also a "wrath to come," from which we are admonished to flee. Likewise wheat for the garner and chaff for unquenchable fire. The Universalists permit themselves to look on one side only of the Divine character and administration.

Universalists speak a good deal about the "moral and spiritual world." Judging by their general views their "moral" world must be a very ineffective state. Death and resurrection, one or both, are incomparably more effectual to prepare mankind for eternal holiness and happiness than any moral or spiritual education that appears anywhere. That death and resurrection, one or both, should produce such effects must be regarded as the greatest and most unaccountable of prodigies. No metamorphosis in ancient mythology surpasses it in extravagance.

Universalism is inconsistent with itself. It asserts that every transgressor must suffer the punishment of his own sin. But what opportunity can there be for this in the case of transgressors who are struck dead in the very act if, when they rise at the great day, they shall be "raised in their whole being in the Divine or heavenly likeness?" They must certainly escape altogether. Can so lucky a fate be predicted for the inhabitants of Sodom and Gomorrah ; or Korah, Dathan and Abiram ; or Ahab and Jezebel ; or Judas Iscariot ; the proud and self-worshipping King Herod ; how the abominable Nero ; the hideous Domitian ; Commodus; Caracalla ; Heliogabalus; the third King Richard,—nay, has not every one recollection of instances in which transgressors have been cut off in the very bloom of their wickedness? Are we to understand that because these and such as these will in the order of Providence rise again at the last day, they will therefore be raised in the Divine likeness? If so, why submit anybody to the painful and unprofitable processes of trial, tribulation, and moral ordeal, when death and resurrection will of themselves in some way perfectly restore, or rather *create*, holiness? If the Universalist doctrine is true, Solomon and Christ were very wide of the mark when they taught that in the silence of the grave and the night of death no device or work could be performed.

It will be to no purpose in any effort to answer these objections to quote scripture predictions of what will take place in the case of the servants of God and the followers of Christ. It should not be forgotten that much the larger part of the New Testament is addressed, not to the worldling and the godless, but to those who have enlisted in truth and verity under the Christian banner, and rest quietly beneath their master's yoke. Even the Lord's prayer was spoken to, and is yet the special property of, Christ's disciples. Therefore most of the scripture quotations applied by Universalists to *all* mankind were meant to be restricted to Christians, or believers, alone.

They seem to infer that the resurrection will be simultaneous for all. But this is also a mistake. Christ, our elder brother, has already risen, being the first fruits of them that slept. Those who are Christ's will rise at his second coming, for in the resurrection to come the dead in Christ will rise first, and take their place in the blessed first resurrection. Afterwards will rise the dead who are *not* in Christ ; to more or less of whom may appertain that infinitely awful destiny, the *second* death. Perhaps it was at this that Felix trembled when Paul reasoned with him of righteousness, temperance, and judgment to come.

Did Universalists never reflect on the consequences to

mankind of a simple non-preparation for the scenes of another world? Suppose God entirely withholds the torments of which they speak, will the negligent still be safe? Nowhere do we read of an intermediate state between heaven and hell. If, then, the careless passenger through this life misses heaven, where will he alight? Will not the simple loss of heaven be remorse and wretchedness enough to fill his soul with woe? Would not that disappointment be quite hell enough? How would a farmer feel at the close of the year if, wedded to sports and pleasures through the working seasons, he neglected the plowing and planting, the digging and seeding, and the other various occupations incident to the cultivation of a well-ordered farm? Having produced nothing, how could he and his family subsist through the winter? Would not their bitter cry be, "The harvest is past; the summer is ended, and we are not saved?" And how otherwise can it be with them who pass their life-year after the same careless, idle manner? With them "who despise the riches of God's goodness, and forbearance and longsuffering, not knowing that the goodness of God should lead them to repentance? Who, in their hardness and impenitence of heart, treasure up wrath against the day of wrath and revelation of the righteous judgment of God, who will render to every man according to his deeds: to them, who by patient continuance in welldoing seek for glory and honor and immortality, eternal life; but to them who are contentious and do not obey the truth, but obey unrighteousness, indignation, and wrath, tribulation and anguish upon every soul of man that doeth evil; of the Jew first and also of the Gentile, for there is no respect of persons with God." That is Paul's picture; does it savour of Universalism? Can any one justly regard that system of religious thought to be favorable to a growth in righteousness which secretly hints to the sinner's heart that, after all, it might be pretty good policy to cultivate cunning and artful dishonesties, and occasionally indulge in pleasant immoralities, even down to the instant of death, because death and resurrection will in some way effect all the moral and spiritual change that is necessary to start one upon a new career of holiness and blessedness in the next world? Knowing, as we do, the deceitfulness of sin, and the foolishness and corruption of the unregenerate heart, will it be wise to furnish it with a system of belief that is itself as great a temptation to unfaithfulness as could well be imagined?

Another inconsisteney in Universalism is that it saves men against their will, or at least, without consulting their wishes in the matter. Even if the dying sinner has gone down into the grave cursing God Himself in his heart and upon his lips, Universalism alleges that with the resurrection there will come "a moral and spiritual change which will remove all the elements of the earthly and renew his soul in the likeness of God."

Universalist teachers are not forward to suggest to their hearers and readers that all, without exception, must stand before the judgment-seat of Christ. Nor, with the doctrines they hold, is this to be wondered at. For what can a judgment-seat find to do if every human being, as he or she rises from the tomb, comes forth "uplifted, exalted, or raised, throughout the whole being into the Divine or heavenly likeness"? Each soul, having become "spiritually a child of God," will require no tribunal to determine its quality and character, for that will be stamped upon each in the sight of the whole universe. As well think of gathering Gabriel and Michael, the seraphim and cherubim, for trial and judgment around Christ's tribunal, as the family of mankind who have, simply by resurrection, become "children of God and equal unto the angels." Under circumstances such as these, Christ's judgment-seat must, if Universalist ideas be correct, become a useless display whose object has been anticipated. It is true that Jesus told the Saducean Jews (Luke 20th) that certain of those who will rise from the dead will not "die any more, for they are equal unto the angels and are the children of God, being the children of the resurrection." They are not, however, the "children of *this* world," but such as shall be "*accounted worthy* to obtain that world and the resurrection (presumably the *first* resurrection) from the dead"—a restricting clause which is resented by a leading Universalist author, who thinks that because Matthew in the parallel passage omits the clause, he attached no weight to it. It is highly likely, nevertheless, that Luke gives it as Christ spoke it, for the whole text consists of an antithesis, or contrast, showing the difference that would be observed between the children of "this" world and of "that." Then, in speaking of those who shall be "*accounted* worthy," a perfectly distinct intimation is given of a day of account.

The advantage to Universalism sought for in the simile proposed between the renewal of the earth's face in the spring-time and the great moral renewal of the world of mankind at the resurrection does not really exist. If mankind at large were as obedient to the Divine laws as material nature is, such a simile might have place; but, as man is to a great extent rebellious, the parallel does not hold good, nor is any illustration furnished by it.

We close these cursory remarks by simply noticing the tone of Universalists in seeming to dictate what God ought to be and to do. There is contained in this a virtual censure of the deluge; of the overthrow of the cities of the plain; the punishment of the disobedient Israelites, and, in fact, almost the whole history of God's dealings with sinful mankind recorded from Genesis to Revelations. God is truly love and mercy to those who meekly trust in Him; but to the contentious and disobedient God is not unrighteous in taking vengeance. Lastly, If the righteous scarcely be saved, where shall the ungodly and sinner appear?

The last church organization we propose to consider is THE UNITARIAN, which is so called because its distinguishing tenet is that the Godhead of the Universe is not divided up among two or three or more personalities, but is filled by One Infinite and Eternal Being, whose intellect is all comprehensive;—whose goodness is absolutely perfect, and power illimitable. An ancient Grecian philosopher, who lived more than 500 years before Christ, arrived, by the bare exercise of his reasoning faculties, at the conclusion that there can be only One God, because if there were more than one, neither of them could be perfect; neither would be God. The illustrious Plato, who flourished between 400 and 500 years before Christ, was a believer in the Divine unity, but, from a lack of that fidelity to honest convictions which is no less a duty than a glory to every man, he did not give the prominency and force to the results of his thinking which he ought to have done, but kept his purer and nobler ideas in comparative concealment, out of unworthy deference to the ignorant and corrupt notions of his day.

Greater than any Grecian sage the divinely-instructed Moses, leader of the Hebrew people not only out of corporeal bondage, but from heathen darkness into mental truth and moral light, taught his people, under the ordination of God Himself, the massive and elevating doctrine of the simple unity, the absolute oneness of God. He reported to the Hebrews the name which the Great Supreme had chosen for his own designation—"I AM THAT I AM." Thus shalt thou say (said God to Moses) unto the children of Israel, "I AM hath sent me unto you;" that is to say, the simple, sole, individual, self-existent, eternal JEHOVAH. And again, in fuller description, he declares unto the people of Israel that "Unto them it was showed, that they might know that Jehovah is God; there is none else beside Him." And, as if to remove every conceivable idea that might infest their minds contrary to this oneness of the Deity, and that He, and He alone, inhabits the universe and is the sole and only God in heaven, he quotes God's own words and warning, "See now that I, even I, am He, and there is *no God with me.*" (Deut., 32 : 39.) Can Trinitarians, learned or unlearned, construct language more pointedly and completely expressive of the personal oneness of God than this? And if there were, at the time this utterance was made, and had been from all eternity, three equal constituents in the Divine personality, could it be truthfully said that the utterance was a correct description of the nature and being of God? Did God, in that utterance, declare the truth, the whole truth, and nothing but the truth? Does not an assertion of the doctrine of the Trinity imply essential unfaithfulness in God's account of Himself, or (if our Trinitarian friends are right) of *them*selves?

Of the testimonies of the great prophet Isaiah, who reports God as saying (Isaiah, 44 and 45), "I AM JEHOVAH and there is none else; there is no God besides me," we have already sufficiently spoken. The testimonies of Christ and his Apostles are all to the same effect, teaching the unity of God as "the first and great commandment of all" in precisely the same unperverted sense in which that unity has always been understood and accepted by the Jewish people now and in all past time. (See Mark, 12 : 29 to 34.)

Holding thus to the unsophisticated doctrine of the Divine unity, the Unitarians permanently wonder at the prevalence among Christians, in this comparatively enlightened age, of doctrines utterly untaught and contradicted by the Bible. It could not be out of any design of casting contempt or ridicule upon the opposite Trinitarian doctrine that Archbishop Whately thus discourses in his book on logic: "Nothing," he says, "can be more indistinctly explained than is the doctrine of the Trinity in scripture; nor are we, perhaps, capable, with our present faculties, of comprehending it more fully. Theology (that is, Trinitarian theology) teaches, says a passage in a Protestant work, that there is in God, one essence, two processions, three persons, four relations, five notions, and circumincession, which the Greeks call perichoresis." Nevertheless, the good archbishop clings to the scripturally unexplained and humanly unintelligible Trinity, showing, besides, a facility at misinterpreting very plain and obvious passages of scripture that should bring a blush upon the cheek of a youth in his Greek primer, if found equally at fault. Whilst the excellent archbishop doubts the competency of the human faculties to comprehend the Trinity more fully than the indistinct explanation of the Trinity in the scriptures now permits, (unless the trouble lies in the "indistinct explanation,") it might be brought to mind that the Apostle Paul said to the elders of the Ephesian Church that he had "kept back nothing that was profitable" unto them, and had not "shunned to declare unto them all the counsel of God." Supposing Paul to have uttered the truth, the inevitable inference must be that the doctrine of the Trinity was not, in Paul's judgment, either "profitable," or any part of "the counsel of God." Can we be surprised that such a doctrine is most "indistinctly explained" in the scriptures, or that it is not explained at all? The conclusion justly follows from both St. Paul and Dr. Whately that there is in the Bible no such doctrine as a Trinity of the Godhead, and therefore nothing about it to be explained, either distinctly or indistinctly.

With respect to the nature and person of Christ there have some differences among Unitarians. They all, however, agree that Christ is not God nor demi-god, angel nor spirit, but a human being, no more and no less. He is not, what some are pleased to call, a "mere man," but the Son of God by special generation, to whom the Holy Ghost was imparted "not by measure." He was the divinely-commissioned teacher, master, and Lord of God's people;—the very prophet foretold by Moses that should arise like him out of the midst of the Jewish nation, to whom all, Jews and Gentiles, should give heed at the risk of the penalty of utter destruction. The belief of all Unitarians seems to be comprehended in what is known as *the Apostles' creed*, which John Milton justly describes as "the most ancient and universally-received compendium of belief in the possession of the church." Of course, then, Unitarians reject that travesty and perversion of the Apostles' statement which is called the Nicene Creed, so called, but not with entire correctness, for though it was commenced at the council of Nice in the year 325, was not completed till the year 381 at the second general council of Constantinople.

Even then it was not in the same shape in which we now have it, for an important and, as the event showed, an almost fatal addition was made to it afterwards. The decision of the council of Nice has been described by an eminent Episcopal bishop as "the greatest misfortune that ever befel the Christian world."

On the subject of Baptism Unitarians are not unanimous, some holding to immersion, whilst, perhaps, the majority are satisfied with aspersion or affusion. The rite of the Lord's Supper is now and always has been observed by them.

The eschatology of the denomination is various. Many, particularly in Europe, are Restorationists, but in this country those views are not put prominently forward, and are not, I believe, at all in favor with the best thinkers of the church. The Unitarian Bernard Whitman's "Friendly Letters to a Universalist" is a powerful testimony against the truth of Universalism.

Rather than present statements of our own, we offer the following comprehensive sketch of the earlier history of Unitarian opinion from an "orthodox" publication, the International Cyclopædia: "There have been," says that work, "Unitarians from the earliest period of ecclesiastical history. Until the middle of the second century there seems to have been no controversy on the subject; but from that time to the end of the third century there was a succession of eminent teachers who maintained against the ecclesiastical doctrine of the Logos, the undivided unity, or, as they expressed it, the *monarchy* of God. From their use of this word they are known in ecclesiastical history as the *Monarchians*. There are generally understood to have been two classes of them; those who taught that Christ was God in such a sense that it was the Father who became man and was born and suffered, and who were on that account called *Patripassians;* and secondly, those who held that Christ was in nature a mere man, but exalted above all others prophets by the superior measure of Divine wisdom with which he was endowed, and who, therefore, corresponded more nearly with the modern Unitarians. It is right to notice, however, that the doctrines of the Monarchians are known to us only through the statements of opponents, and it is probable they would have disowned the more extreme views ascribed to them. To the former of the two classes we have mentioned, belonged Praxeas, against whom there is a treatise by Tertullian and Noetus; and, at a later period, about the middle of the third century, the famous Sabellius taught very similar doctrines. The Monarchians appeal in support of their doctrines to the Old and New Testaments, and to the early opinions of the church. They are said by Tertullian to have consisted of the simple and unlearned, 'always,' he adds, 'a majority of the faithful,'—a statement which shows that they must have been tolerably numerous in his time."

So says the Cyclopædia; but if, as Tertullian avers, "a majority of the faithful" were Monarchians, that is to say, Unitarians, the words "tolerably numerous" belittle the truth in the case. What Tertullian says amounts to this: that a majority of the Christian masses in his day, which was between A. D. 160 and 245, were Unitarians. If inquiry were made for the distinguished sources under whose authority those Monarchians believed, their own answer of the Old and New Testaments and the early church would be the true one. The "monarchy" meant the supremacy of the One God, the Father.

In more modern times many men, whose names will never be forgotten, have declared themselves worshippers of the Father as the only true God. Anything like a tolerably full list would be too voluminous here and now. A few only can be given to suggest their respectability. Christopher Cellarius, a learned German, professor of history at the University of Halle, suffered imprisonment for his opinions and finally escaped to freer Switzerland. He was a friend of Luther and Melancthon. Gentilis, an Italian, escaped to England. He was of a distinguished and learned family. The two Socini, Lælius the uncle and Faustus the nephew, were men of superior intellect, learning and pure character; of whom the latter is the more famous, for of him it was written on his tomb in Latin, meaning thus:

"Luther destroyed the roofs of Babylon;
Calvin the walls; but Socinus the foundations."

The martyr Michael Servetus, of whom we have heretofore spoken as burnt under the auspices of John Calvin. John Crellius and the able band called the Polones Fratres, or Polish brethren. In England, John Biddle, a brave and able man in the time of Charles First and of Cromwell, bore the brunt of Nicene enmity till his death in 1622. Biddle built a church in London in which were taught Unitarian principles. The excellent Thomas Firmin, the friend and helper of the persecuted Biddle, whose Christian charity and general benevolence captivated all hearts, so that, as the biographers state, "Archbishop Tillotson and other eminent prelates were proud of his friendship." His charity was bounded by no sect or party, but extended to all. His useful life terminated in 1697.

The great patriot and poet John Milton; the philosopher and astronomer Isaac Newton, whose comprehensive intellect grasped all truth, so that it was written—

"Nature and Nature's laws lay hid in night;
God said ' Let Newton be,' and all was light."

To these we can add the eminent moral philosopher, John Locke, whose essay on the Human Understanding and the Reasonableness of Christianity did so much in their day in support of the Christian verities. The worthy Theophilus Lindsey, who, out of pure conscientiousness and love of truth abandoned a comfortable connexion with the English church to stand up for an unpopular profession of faith. The learned and industrious Nathaniel Lardner, who, as a champion of Christianity, has hardly been exceeded, if equalled, and on whose labors the candid and ingenious Paley, of the English establishment, so steadily relied. Dr. Samuel Clarke, a man of thorough erudition and a believer in and writer on the Divine Unity, though still a member of the Church of England. Dr. Richard Price was an able and excellent man and an earnest advocate of the doctrine of the Divine Unity. His two brave pamphlets, in opposition to the course of the British ministry, which led to the war with the American Colonies, (now the United States,) were so highly approved by the corporation of London that they voted him their thanks and a gold box. The University of Glasgow likewise conferred upon him the academical degree of Doctor of Divinity. The great English war minister, William Pitt, son of the Earl of Chatham, was so impressed with Price's abilities on the subject of finance that he applied to him to assist in the design of liquidating the British national debt. Out of their conferences grew the adoption of the sinking fund system. Such was Dr. Price, but he maintained throughout life the pastorate of the Unitarian congregation at Hackney, a suburb of London. Dr. Joseph Priestley, the personal friend of Price, Benjamin Franklin, and James Watt, was an eminent defender of the doctrine of Divine Unity, and, like Price, a preacher thereof. He was a very prolific author on a great variety of subjects in literature and science. As the discover of *oxygen* his name is immortal. He also pursued the study of electricity with great ardor. Priestley was one of the manliest and most straightforward of our race. Kings and princes, priests and populace, were to him as the small dust of the balance in comparison with sincerity and truth. Deceived, as many distinguished men were by the opening aspects of the French Revolution, Priestley gave it the endorsement of his heart and voice, so that he was complimented by the French with the honor of being made a citizen of their republic. This naturally brought him a widespread and active enmity in his own land, the end of which was that the excited populace of Birmingham burnt his dwelling-house, library, manuscripts, and philosophical apparatus, and put him and his family in great personal danger. This was in 1791. The French Revolution not progressing after his hopes and expectations, he resolved on emigrating to the United States, and, in 1794, selected Northumberland, in Pennsylvania, as the place of his future residence. He was an earnest political friend and supporter of Thomas Jefferson, and died at Northumberland in 1804. We here leave our sketch of eminent English Unitarians, mentioning further only the following additional names of Belsham, Aspland, Carpenter, Higginson, Tayler, Beard, Southwood Smith, Wellbeloved, Yates, and James Martineau; nay, since he died in England, we will give place to the able East Indian rajah, Rammohun Roy, Christian convert and Hindoo reformer, whose defence of the Divine Unity, in his controversy with the Baptist missionary, Dr. Marshman, of Serampore near Calcutta, is a monument of his effective intellectual force and wide learning. He died September, 1833.

Before simply naming some leading American Unitarians of the present century, we give insertion to the opinion of the English archbishop, Tillotson, in regard to the controversial skill and ability of the Unitarians of his day, amongst whom must be included some, with more or less justice, denominated Socinians. He says: "To do right to the writers on that side, I must own that generally they are a pattern of the fair way of disputing and debating matters of religion, without heat and unseemly reflection upon their adversaries. They generally argue matters with that temper and gravity, and that freedom from passion and transport, which becomes a serious and weighty argument; and, for the most part, they reason closely and clearly, with extraordinary guard and caution; with great dexterity and decency, and yet with smartness and subtlety enough; with a very gentle heart and few hard words—virtues to be praised wherever they are to be found, yea, even in an enemy, and very worthy of our imitation."

The more prominent Unitarian preachers and teachers of this country, deceased and surviving, have been Dr. Gay of Hingham, Mass., about 1732, Buckminster, Henry Ware, father and son, Greenwood, Peabody, Livermore, Sparks, Whitman, Palfrey, Norton, Noyes, Dewey, King, Ellis, Gannett, and the equal of any and admired by all, Dr. William Ellery Channing, born in Newport, Rhode Island, in 1780 and died 1845. His admirable works in divinity and general literature have been translated into every important European language, and have leavened the century in which we live with a spirit of pure devotion, noble aspirations and justness of judgment which must have enlightened the intellects and purified the hearts of thousands in every walk of life.

Able and distinguished for many accomplishments as the Unitarian clergy are in the main, there are some in the connexion who, from overmuch learning, passion for singularity or something, perhaps, several things else, put themselves and consequently their denomination into positions of conflict with well-settled public sentiment and the plainly-stated doctrines of the Bible. This may go a good way to account for the comparative unpopularity of the whole body. Its principles are made to appear to the general eye fluctuating, unfixed. People do not feel it judicious or safe to become attached to so much fitfulness and uncertainty. Whilst nothing like Universalism can ever be heard from many Unitarian pulpits, there are others wherein it is either openly inculcated or furtively introduced. There are also pulpits where even worse and more reckless teachings than Universalism are hazarded. The audacity of a second, perhaps a third, or other successive probations for the unregenerate after death, is occasionally protruded and garnished with more or less direct imputations on the Divine government and character, and glittering scintillations of wit and fancy. Sometimes the assumption is boldly made, as if it were incontestable, that the happiness and perfection of heaven will be a gradual affair, with comparatively small beginnings and accretions, according to the virtue and industry of each individual struggle. All eternity will be insufficient to make the celestial occupant perfect; he will be like the asymptote to a certain curve, always approaching but never really meeting perfection. Such are some of the liberties taken with the letter and spirit of what is taught in the scriptures.

We have already considered Universalism as a system without support from either the Old or New Testament.

What strength it has in the world comes from unwarrantable liberties with the rights of God as the Creator and Sovereign of the Universe, for it calls the Creator to its bar, and summarily demands to know with what justice He can undertake to condemn mankind to everlasting wretchedness for the sins, (or peccadilloes, as sometimes called), of say sixty, or seventy, or even eighty short years on earth?—quite forgetting the essential and inseparable connexion established between obedience and happiness on the one hand, and between disobedience, or sin, and alienation from God, on the other; and keeping out of sight the measures that have been adopted for the recovery of sinners from the error of their ways, and for putting them into the road of salvation and safety, they argue on the basis of a natural right to disobey and of a title to be made forever happy without any sustained exertion towards that end. Hard thoughts of God are entertained as if He were an unfeeling despot managing the affairs of His universe on other principles than those of justice and equity.

Of the same general character are the deductions of the astounding Second Probation advocates. In a sermon preached by a Unitarian minister of acknowledged intellect and ability, in behalf of a second probation, God's character for mercy was sharply arraigned, that is, if there is to be no second probation. Instead of making appeal to the Bible on a subject of paramount interest, no such reference was made, but the speaker sought solace from the opinions of avowed Universalists and the disciples of the vision-seer of Sweden. Thus the Second Probation is pretty distinctly promulgated as *another gospel* for the comfort of those who do not care to take the trouble to avail themselves of the first. The Apostle Paul's ideas about "another gospel" are pretty plainly developed in his first chapter to the Galatians, together with the disposition he would make of the preachers thereof. Where the Second Probationists propose to locate the scene of the second test has not been named; so whether on this earth, or the moon, or one of the other planets, or some great comet, is more than has yet been made known. As the second probation will necessarily be a supersedure of the unfavorable sentences at the judgment-seat of Christ, there should be some mention made of the court that will issue arrests of judgment in the numerous cases that will arise. It is hardly likely that this earth will be the scene, because it will be appropriated for the residence of the redeemed with Christ for their ruler and king. Then nothing has been prognosticated as to the manner in which the second trial is to be commenced. Whether through the intervention of a second father and mother, or by some other means of reproduction, we are not informed. Other considerations present themselves; among which will be the necessity for provision for the vast assemblage of re-embodied beings all at once in the new home. At all events, one cannot but mark some kinship between the ideas of the Second Probationists and the notions of old Origen, the father of Restorationism. And if the second probation should fail, it is not unlikely that a third and even a fourth might be proposed. Can any church organization afford to give countenance to such extravagances?

The other assumption of a gradual acquirement of holiness and consequent happiness in heaven, carries some discouragement in itself, besides being wholly foreign to the Bible. It seems also to involve some imputation on both the power and gracious goodness of God. If God's power was competent to change instantaneously the spirit of the son of Kish, so as to "give him another heart and turn him into another man," why should we think that the Divine arm would be restrained from at once conferring on Christ's redeemed ones a full measure of perfection? "Blessed," said Christ, "are they that hunger and thirst after righteousness, for they shall be filled." "Filled" is Christ's word; not partially, but "filled." Such is God's response to the desire for righteousness. The aged Paul rejoiced in the hope of the "crown of righteousness which the Lord, the righteous judge, would give him at that day"—yes, "at that day,"—not delaying the ineffable gift till some indefinitely or even infinitely-distant day in the later ages of eternity. What, too, does Paul mean by "the perfecting of the saints" and coming "in the unity of the faith and of the knowledge of the Son of God unto a *perfect* man, unto the measure of the stature of the *fulness* of Christ"? So Christ himself, the captain of our salvation, was made perfect through sufferings, by which he was forthwith exalted to the incomparable honor and dignity of a seat at God's right hand. There was no delay, but a prompt, immediate, and full reward. So with Christ's faithful followers; they will find in God's presence not partial or far-off blessedness, but "fulness of joy; and at His right hand pleasures for evermore."

After thus looking into the opinions of the leading churches relative to their theology and soteriology, we will briefly review the testimonies of God's written word in the Old and New Testaments, bespeaking the reader's patience with "the line upon line, the precept upon precept" he may meet in the remainder of the course before us.

If the Supreme Being, as Nicenists represent, consisted from everlasting of three separate intelligences, having the common basis of one and the same essence or nature, then if He saw fit to reveal Himself to any extent to His creatures upon the earth, He would do so either truthfully or untruthfully. That He should reveal Himself untruthfully is not to be admitted, for being infinite in power and majesty and in every way Lord of the Universe and all it contains, no motive is conceivable why He should be ashamed or afraid to be known in any but His real character. If, on the one hand, He were a Unit, undivided and perfect in His single self, why should He represent Himself as a Triple Being? On the other hand, if He really existed in a tripartite form, why aver Himself strictly a Unit in language inappropriate to describe any other than a unit? No sufficient reason appears why an erroneous, not to say deceptive, representation should be made; besides which, the character of the Supreme for simple veracity is not to go unconsidered.

We learn from the Bible that when God commissioned Moses to communicate His will to the Israelitish people in Egypt, Moses desired to know by what name he should designate the sender of the commission he bore. God chose a title for Himself of, verbally, the simplest, yet, in fact, the most comprehensive and sublime. "I AM THAT I AM" was the awful name, implying self-existent Unity. Now, because men, believing God, taking Him entirely at His word, and deeply impressed thereby, have testified to the world this *Self-existent Unity*, they have been vilified, abused, persecuted, maltreated, imprisoned, tortured, and burnt alive at the stake by those who have thereby virtually proclaimed that God meant *not* to say "I am that I am," but "We are what we are," words just as easy of utterance and incomparably more befitting, if the Trinity were true, than the designation really chosen by the Supreme. At the time Moses was commanded to communicate with the people of Israel, the plural sentence, "We are what we are," would have been as thoroughly acceptable to that people as the unitarian designation, for (Exod. 6: 3) their education in divine things was but commencing.

What then must be our conclusion? What can it be other than that God described Himself as the self-existent

Eternal One, with no tinge of plurality in His constitution or manner of being? Nor was this all. It was no mere passing or temporary title for that occasion only, but was ordained to be God's "name forever and His memorial unto all generations;"—why not in *our* generation?

When the law was formally delivered in Deuteronomy, 6:4, the same strict unity was again enjoined—"Hear, O Israel, the Lord our God is One Lord." And when the prophet Zechariah, looking down the long vista of the ages to come, saw the day when "the Lord shall be King over all the earth," he added, "in that day shall there be One Lord and His name One." What Christ and his Apostles so abundantly said to the same effect we have already seen. Where then is triplicity as belonging to, or descriptive of, the Divine personality? Where that invention of Theophilus of Antioch, who in the word "Trinity" sought to gratify the vitiated conceits of those who gravitated to a belief in more divinities than one, yet hoped to placate the Monarchian majority—an invention, as remarks Dr. MacLaine in his Chronological Tables to Mosheim's Ecclesiastical History, for which "the Christian church is very little indebted to Theophilus, for it has produced heresies of the worst kind."

What we have further to say on this greatest of all subjects, and which is only allowable because the divine records invite to a true knowledge of the Most High, will be mainly a retrospect of a learned essay written in support of the doctrine of the Trinity. It can be found in Addis and Arnold's "Catholic Dictionary," published in New York, and which commends itself by its spirit of general candor and fairness.

The article explains the Nicene method of constructing the doctrine of the Trinity. This is effected by means of two propositions, the first of which reads: "The absolute unity of God was and is the great article of Israel's faith, and it is asserted with equal emphasis throughout the New Testament." The second proposition says, " If, then, the New Testament teaches the real, distinct and divine personality of the Father, Son and Holy Ghost, this comes to teaching the Catholic doctrine of the Trinity." The meaning of all which is that the first proposition declares the Bible testimony to what is called "the absolute unity of God"; the second proposition takes for granted (for it does not demonstrate) God's threefoldness, or existence in three separate and distinct persons; therefore, both propositions, taken together, teach God's simultaneous unity and triplicity, or that He is both three in one and one in three. Q. E. D.

But a little examination will suffice to show some faulty logic in this very compendious method of construction. The first proposition speaks (but not with special accuracy of language) of the "absolute unity of God," by which it does not mean, as it ought, God's singleness of person, but sameness of nature in *several persons*, which certainly was not "Israel's faith," nor the doctrine of Christ or of his apostles, or of the New Testament in any part of it. What the first proposition means by the "unity of God" differs nothing in principle from the Hindoo idea of the same "unity," as has been shown in the foregoing pages. Mark's gospel, chap. 12: 28 to 34, proves incontestably the identity of "Israel's faith" with Christ's doctrine, which ever was and is and will be that there is "One God and none other but he," viz., a being absolutely singular or sole both in person and nature; "*He*, and none other but *he*."

The second proposition is not assertive like the first; but merely hypothetical. "If," it says, "the New Testament does so and so, why, then, this comes to so and so." Thus no fact is alleged. Perhaps, it is intended that the following part of the article shall prove that "the New Testament teaches the real, distinct, and divine personality of the Father, Son and Holy Ghost,"—jointly and severally, we presume to be meant. Let us see.

The Catholic Dictionary declares that the doctrine of the Trinity "*appears* in the New and has its *roots* in the Old Testament." Where are the appearances located, and where the roots? The dictionary does not feed the hunger it arouses. It only tells us that "Catholics have naturally been prepared to find *traces*," as in Genesis, 1: 26 and 3: 22, but it seems that the renowned French Jesuit, Denis Petau, or Petavius, will not acknowledge those texts to be "traces" at all, nor will he permit the plural noun *Elohim* (the Hebrew name for God) to have "any allusion to a plurality of Divine persons." "The word for a human master is often plural, and the same plural form of the word "God" with a singular verb is used of the idol Dagon in Judges, 16: 23." And then, says the Dictionary, "To sum up, *Here* and *there* the Old Testament clearly and by itself indicates *portions* of the doctrine; in more, the New Testament helps us to discover certain or *probable traces* of it in the Old, while it is generally held by Catholic divines that *some* favored saints of the old law had a knowledge, *more* or *less* complete, of the mystery." And this is spoken, be it understood, of two books announced to mankind as *revelations*, and particularly of the principal article to be revealed. Most of us have heard of a something very like this argument of the Dictionary, on which, if you put your finger, you will not find it there.

Concerning the doctrine of Christ's pre-existence, or existence before his birth of the Virgin Mary, the Catholic Dictionary says: "Nowhere is Christ's pre-existence, much less his eternal generation, in terms," but "Christ in the synoptic gospels claims attributes which can hardly be less than divine." (Matthew, 11: 27.) Whoever will refer to this text in its place will instantly perceive that if the possession of the knowledge Christ speaks of render him divine, so also will the same knowledge render divine the person to whom Christ shall reveal it. To as little, or even less purpose, are quotations made from Paul's earlier epistles to prove Christ's pre-existence. Christ is quoted as "the image of God." If he is the image of God, as all true Christians cheerfully admit, then he is not the God whose image he is. The picture of a man is not, assuredly, the man himself. Allusion is made in the Dictionary to the controverted text in Romans 9: 5, but it is fair and candid. To claim this text as a proof of Christ's deity lacks little or nothing of the phrenetic. There is scarcely a text in the Bible of plainer import. Paul is writing of his Israelitish kinsmen, whose were the law and its remarkable and glorious accompaniments; whose were the fathers, and of whom, by natural descent, was Christ; God, blessed for ever, transcending all. The passage is a rhetorical climax, much in vogue with St. Paul. For other instances of the climax, where God's supremacy is maintained, see the conclusion of 1st Cor., chap. 3; also 1st Cor., 11: 3. With respect to Romans, 9: 5, the revisers, in producing the new version, acted unmeritoriously. The American committee translates almost precisely like the Catholic Dictionary, "He who is over all, God, be blessed forever." The English committee did worse in going farther away from Paul's meaning than even the Old Version. They could not afford to lose the old prop to a weakening cause, so they concluded to leave it stiffer than they found it. The genuine truth is that the revisers need a good deal of revising.

The Dictionary quotes, "Christ, the beginning of the creation of God." Very well, then; if a part of the *creation*, Christ is *not* the creator. As to the so-called baptismal formula in Matthew, 28: 19, the Dictionary claims it, without proof, as a support to the Trinity; quoting to the same ineffectual purpose the benediction in 2d Cor., 13: 13, but shuns Acts, 5: 31 and 32, and 1st Cor., 12: 4, 5, and 6—texts more definite and instructive. The text John, 10: 30, is quoted as if the explanatory texts in John, 17: 11 and 21, were not in the Bible.

Passing over to the Apostolic fathers, the Dictionary acknowledges that the "doctrine of the Trinity is neither expanded nor reduced to system" by them. "Nor is the Logos used as a personal name.". Going farther off, however, than the era of Christ and his Apostles "to the middle of the second century, we find much fuller statements and an approach (an *approach* only) to a definite theology of the three divine persons." Still, there was yet no such word as "Trinity." It was about one hundred and eighty years after Christ that Theophilus of Antioch hammered out this designation for the rising dogma, before then a something without a name. The Dictionary goes on to admit that the fathers who lived between the Apostolic fathers (viz., Clement of Rome, Barnabas, Hermas, Ignatius, Polycarp, Justin Martyr, Papias, Irenæus, Origen, Tertullian, Lactantius, Clement of Alexandria, Hippolytus, Novatian, Dionysius of Rome, Dionysius of Alexandria, &c.) and the period of the Council of Nice "call the Father *the* God, or God absolutely; the Son is only, or simply, called God." Tertullian speaks of the Father as "ipse deus," that is, God in Himself, the self-existent God. Of the Son he says "*hactenus deus, quatenus ex ipsius Dei substantiâ,*" that is, that the Son is God in so far as he is derived from the substance of the original God;—leaving it to be afterwards determined whether Christ was or was not to any extent so derived.

The Dictionary continues: "But in two ways the teaching of many of the Fathers who lived before the Council of Nice was imperfect and inconsistent with itself. Their belief led them to speak as if the nature of the Son was inferior to that of the Father. Thus Justin describes the Word as a 'God under the maker of the Universe; a God different in number from the God who made all.' Clement of Alexandria attributes to the Son a 'nature most near to the sole Almighty' Father. Tertullian declares that the whole substance of the divinity is in the Father, 'a portion of it only in the Son.' Origen says that the Son is worthy of a 'secondary honor,' after the God of all; that he is 'different in essence from the Father.' Many of these fathers affirm that the generation of the Son happened in time; for instance, Justin, Tatian, Hippolytus, Tertullian, Novatian, and Lactantius. On the other hand, Irenæus maintained Christ's eternal generation. So also thought Dionysius, bishop of Rome, in the middle of the third century. The eternity of the Sonship was not defined in the Nicæan creed, and, for many years after 325 a few even of the orthodox continued to deny it.

Some members of the council of Nice who were orthodox on the divinity of the Son feared to call the Holy Ghost 'God,' partly because they doubted whether scripture justified such a use of language; partly because they feared seeming to confess *three* Gods. St. Gregory of Nazianzen believed that the divinity of the Holy Ghost was to be taught gradually, with great caution, and not to all, and he defended St. Basil the Great for his prudent reserve on that point. Basil believed that the Holy Ghost was God, but did not at the same time say so *openly* in set terms. 'The true divinity of the third person was asserted at the council of Alexandria in the year 362; by two synods at Rome under Pope Damasus, and finally by the council of Constantinople in 381, in a decree accepted by the whole church.'

The fourth Lateran council, held at Rome in the year 1215 after Christ, defines the distinction of the persons from each other, and the absolute identity of each with the one 'individual essence' of God. The council speaks of the incarnation as effected 'by the whole Trinity in common.' Of course the second person only was incarnate, but all works exterior to the Trinity itself are effected by the three persons. They are distinct only in virtue of their relations to each other. The Father alone generates; the Father and the Son alone breathe the Holy Ghost.

All Catholic theologians are agreed that the existence of the Trinity cannot be proved by reason, and although they add that the doctrine is above reason, but not contrary to it, still Billuart, at least, admits that we cannot prove 'positively and evidently' that the doctrine does not involve contradiction. The obvious objection presents itself that we cannot believe what is absolutely unintelligible; and again it might be said that a revelation that tells us nothing of God's character brings us no closer to Him; in no way affects our own life; is not a revelation at all.''

The same dictionary article intimates that if the purpose is that the worship of the Son *must* be maintained, it is necessary to have a Trinity, or else "fall back into polytheism "—a pretty desperate alternative, which may, however, be escaped altogether by not maintaining the forbidden worship.

Thus far we have copied from the singularly honest title on the Trinity in the Catholic Dictionary. At least two important conclusions can be drawn from it. The first is that men, both before and after the council of Nice, who were, we may say, totally ignorant of the commonest principles of natural philosophy and of the composition of the most ordinary substances with which they were surrounded, the rocks, the earths, the elements, and other forms of matter—undertook to define and fix the essence, substance and structure, respectively, of the Invisible, Immaterial and Infinite God, of Christ and of the Holy Ghost. Unable to analyze a drop of the blood in their own veins, or to tell the components of a single pebble lying at their feet, they hesitated not to dissect God and Christ, and to pretend acquaintance with the most abstruse and secret mysteries; with the interior of the Divine organization; and even to describe and limit in each the workings of this or that divine person. That their several guesses should have differed among themselves is no more than might be expected so long as any freedom of thought and expression was permitted, and it was only when the differences between these conjectures betrayed their mutual destruction that imperial political authority stepped in and by such restraints as privation of office, confiscation of goods, imprisonment, exile, and other severe penalties, compelled universal unanimity. Constantine's decree put a quietus upon conflicting speculations, and disgracefully dominates nineteen-twentieths of the Christian world down to the present hour.

The second important conclusion is drawn from the survey of the movement of patristic thought respecting celestial beings. Monotheism, monarchianism, unitarianism, was in full vogue during the lifetime of Christ and of his apostles, and so continued to prevail until gradually encroached upon by the mixing up of Gentile speculations with Bible truth, which ended in such an almost total eclipse of the pure light and incoming of the dark ages, as to justify the sentiment of the English bishop that "the decision of the council of Nice was the greatest misfortune that ever befel the Christian world."

The object of these papers has been utility—practical utility—*i. e.*, in furnishing members of a church with means for scrutinizing the principles of their sect by a comparison with the religion of Moses and the Lamb; of Moses as preliminary, and of the Lamb as completive. Leaving, undiscussed, minute particulars, we have considered only the great points in theology and soteriology. They are expressed, not in language of human construction and arrangement, but in terms dictated by the Holy Ghost, thus: "There is one God and one Mediator between God and men, the man Christ Jesus, who gave himself a ransom for all." One only God, and one only Mediator and Saviour, and that mediator and saviour, a man; capable of redeeming from the bondage of sin and sinfulness in this world, and of furnishing an acquittance from the penalty of former disobedience in the next. A complete Saviour to the uttermost to all that come unto God by him.

If God is one, and the one Mediator stands between God and men, then the mediator is not that one and only God. He is some other being. He is not a Godman, for no such being ever had or will have existence; and all that ever has been or ever will be said about such is simply mythical. The mediator is man; so designed and so constituted by God his Father; born of a woman; born under the law; subject to temptation; therefore potentially not beyond liability to sin, for if not so liable, at least potentially, he would be no suitable exemplar for fallible man; capable of obedience and improvement even to perfection under the discipline of temptation, trial and suffering; actually sinless, because continually remembering the written divine law and prayerfully seeking ever fresh supplies of the Holy Spirit, which God gave him not by measure; whose human body he himself offered on the cross as a sacrifice for sins which God accepted; and lastly, with an expectation, sure to be fulfilled, of being the world's judge, and after that the perpetual High Priest and King over the Israel of God on the restituted earth purged of all iniquity, sorrow and pain.—Daniel, 7: 13 and 14.

But now, as to the way of salvation? The Bible is not lacking of means to answer the inquiry. It prescribes One God and Father of all, who is above all, and through all, and in all whose faces are heavenward; One Lord Jesus Christ, who gave himself a ransom for all; One pure faith, the common profession of all; One baptism following after faith, the participation and joy of all; One Spirit, with the bond of peace, uniting all in an unyielding righteousness of life. Herein will salvation be found.

Throughout all is the prevailing idea of unity. Triplicity, Tritheism, or Trinity, gets neither hint nor "trace." Equally absent are dogmas about eternal generation, pre-existence, incarnation, two natures in the person of a single being, and the mass of dependent errors from time to time elaborated and fastened upon the enslaved minds and confused consciences of men. Whether the world's thought is or is not being lifted up to a better conception of the truth, with a yearning for reunion upon a common basis, is more than we can dare an attempt to determine; yet such is our very earnest hope. Of heresies and schisms the so-called Christian world should be sick to nauseation. The case at present is that of a house wofully divided against itself. Every man's bounden duty is, then, for himself to know the truth, that he may be free, and to extend that truth whenever and wherever he can. Every man is not only his own but his brother's keeper. Remember that those who will sleep in the dust of the earth shall awake, some to everlasting life and some to shame and everlasting contempt. They that be wise shall shine as the brightness of the firmament, and they that turn many to righteousness as the stars for ever and ever.

Modern astronomy, under the guidance of what we everywhere learn of the creative energy and beneficence of the Most High, conducts to the conclusion that the immeasurable heavens are studded with worlds so many as to baffle numeration; stocked, in the main, with countless intelligent and morally-responsible inhabitants. God, the Universal Creator and Preserver, it is not to be doubted, is recognized as such everywhere; subordinate to whom it is probable there is a visible representative in each of most, or very many orbs, of His perfections, answering to Christ, the Son of Man, the future Lord of this whole regenerated sphere. The glories of this restituted globe, there is every just reason to suppose, will be incomparably greater than the blooming beauties and magnificence of the Paradise of Eden. This state, never diminishing in glory, with no breath of malady, visitation of sorrow, or worm of decay, will be for ever and ever. There perfection will reign, for the Lord God shall be Supreme Monarch over all the earth. *He shall be One and His name ONE!*—Zechariah, 14: 9.

BRIEF EXPLANATIONS OF TEXTS SOMETIMES MISUNDERSTOOD.

Genesis, 1: 26.

"Let us make man in our image, after our likeness," &c. This is a familiar mode of expression, (so Mark, 1 : 24,) having no special significance, and furnishing no ground for supposing a plural deity. In the next verse it is said, "So God created man in *His* own image ; in the image of God created He him." Here the singular number is used in close connexion with the name of God. In Gen., 3 : 22, God said : "Behold, the man is become as one of us, to know good and evil." In these cases God most probably speaks as belonging to and representing the invisible spiritual realm, all whose inhabitants are endowed with the knowledge of good and evil. In this incidental way the Word of God early taught the existence of a world superior to this, yet invisible to man. Whoever may wish to know the number of persons in the Deity can find direct instruction on that point in Deut., 6 : 4 ; Deut., 4 : 35 and 39 ; Deut., 32 : 12 and 39 ; Isaiah, 44 : 8, and 45 : 5 and 6 ; Mark, 12 : 32.

Isaiah, 9: 6.

The proper rendering of this verse will be found at page 149, copied from Bishop Lowth's Translation of Isaiah. Instead of "The Everlasting Father," Lowth more fitly reads, "Father of the Everlasting Age," meaning the age beyond the grave, a highly appropriate designation for Christ. The name "Mighty God," by which he "shall be called," does not indicate Christ's deity, but the paramount distinction of "Mighty Ruler" in the future *kingdom* and *government*, according to the Hebrew idiom. (See Exodus, 22 : 28 ; Psalms, 82 : 1 and 6.) Moses was made a "God to Pharaoh," and to Aaron "instead of God." That this title has no reference to any deity in Christ is plain from his being "a child born" and "a son given"—words not compatible with deity. Besides which, the subject of the prophecy is to sit "upon the throne of *David*," through the "zeal of Jehovah of hosts," the "only true God." (See also 2d Kings, 19: 31, and Isaiah, 37 : 32.)

Micah, 5: 2.

"Whose goings forth have been from of old, from everlasting."

A thoroughly unjustifiable perversion is sometimes committed in respect to this portion of scripture, in intimating that it teaches the pre-existence of Christ and his past-eternal deity. It would be difficult to find a clearer instance of swallowing a theological camel. The text simply and really shows that it had been the divine purpose from everlasting to cause the Messiah to be born in Bethlehem, as David was, and go forth from thence. The subject of the prophecy was thereafter to "stand and rule in the strength of Jehovah and in the majesty of the name of Jehovah *his God*, for he (the subject of prophecy) shall be great unto the ends of the earth." That Jehovah is the Messiah's God, demonstrates that the Messiah himself is *not* God. As to who Messiah's God is, see further, John, 20:17 and Ephes., 1:17. In Matth., 25:34 Christ's kingdom is said to have been "prepared from the foundation of the world." Also Ephes., 1:4 and 1st Peter, 1:20, to the same effect as the text in Micah, and giving no tittle of countenance to Christ's alleged pre-existence or deity. The pre-existence had place only in the fore-entertained purpose of the Most High.

Matthew, 1:23.

"They shall call his name Emmanuel, which being interpreted is, God with us."

With all due respect to the old translators and the late revisers, the name Emmanuel, properly interpreted, is, *not* "God with us," but God *is* with us, as may be seen on reference to Isaiah, 8:10. Everybody having any acquaintance with the scriptures knows the Hebrew habit of designating persons and places from some striking circumstance in the history of each. Thus came Adam, Eve, Abraham, Israel, Ichabod, &c., by their names. When Jacob dreamed at a place called Luz (Gen., 28:15) of the ladder reaching from earth to heaven, and received God's assurrance, "I am with thee and will keep thee in all places whither thou goest," he renamed the place wherein he had slept "Beth-el," or the house of God, for he said, surely "the Lord is in this place." The belief, and still better, the assurance, that God was with them was to the Hebrews, and most justly, the greatest possible comfort and support. As another instance or two, see Gen., 21:20; 26:24; 39:2; 39:21 and 23; 1st Samuel, 3:19; Acts, 7:9. Turning to Isaiah, 7:14, we note that the supernaturally-born child of the virgin of that day was called Immanuel, because the miracle of its birth was a token of the then divine presence and supervision. In like manner, the miraculous birth of the child Jesus naturally induced the application to him of the same name, Emmanuel, for it was a distinguished token of the continuance of the divine presence yet among the Jewish people. In Luke, 7:16, the presence of Christ among them was proof to the Jews that "God had visited His people." Nicodemus was convinced that Christ was a teacher come from God, because no man could perform such miracles as he did except God were with him. So in Acts, 10:38, Peter said God was with Christ. Jesus was, therefore, allusively called Emmanuel in this text (though the one only place in the New Testament) because his advent showed that God had not abandoned His once chosen people. Oh, the lamentable blindness and infatuation of the Jews in that they did not hold to their convictions as expressed in Luke, 7:16!

John, 10:30.

"I and the Father are one."

This text furnishes an instance of the Divine prescience in kindly providing for mankind a Greek original. What between the baldness of the English translation and Nicene partizanship, the general reader's chance to learn the truth is none of the best. The unity spoken of in the text is not a unity of person or being, but of soul, heart, counsel or cause, and it was said in order that those Jews might understand that any assault on Jesus was equally against God, for that the Father and Jesus were united in one and the same design and work of human redemption. The correctness of this will be evident from an examination of the 11th, 22d, and 23d verses of John 17th, where a unity of person or being would make nonsense. The kind of oneness or unity subsisting between God and Christ is the same as that prayed for between the individual disciples, for, says Christ, "I pray that they may be *one*, as *we are*," or "even *as we are one*." The unity is "of one heart and one soul," as in Acts, 4:32. If there could be any doubt about this, the Greek original would dispel it, for God and Christ—and God and Christ and the disciples—are not ($εἱς$), but ($ἐν$); not one person, but one thing. Most certainly educated preachers and writers are entirely aware of all this, yet most of them let the old error continue on and on because it makes for their side. Thus also did the revisers.

John, 8:58.

"Before Abraham was, I am."

This text has been elsewhere explained, but it might be

here remarked that the only mistake that has arisen about it is due to unfaithful translation of old under King James, and now under Queen Victoria. This is less to be excused from the fact that the translators did what was right in verses 24 and 28 of this chapter; in verse 9th of the next chapter; in verses 5th, 6th and 8th of the 18th chapter, where they inserted the pronoun (he) to make sense, and in other places. "He" in this chapter means Christ, and had that word been put after "I am" in the 58th verse it would have meant Christ, showing that in the divine counsels Jesus had been appointed "the Christ" before Abraham existed. In Mark, 13:6 and Luke, 21:8, the noun "Christ" is bodily inserted after "I am" by the old translators. The trouble with the Jews was that they refused to identify Jesus as the divinely-appointed Messiah or Christ. The peaceful Jesus did not suit—they wanted a warlike, conquering hero.

John, 1:6.

"There was a man sent from God whose name was John."

If John the Baptist was a subject of prophecy centuries before his birth, (Isaiah, 40:3, and Malachi, 3:1,) and that birth, fairly supernatural, was pre-announced by the angel Gabriel, we may be sure that John was an integrant in the train of agencies for the redemption of the world. Ordained, prepared and sent from God,—constituted a divine commission for him, similar, though humbly subordinate, to Christ's. We are reminded of James's epistle, which says: "Every good gift and every perfect gift cometh down from above." God is not a visible Being, but His visible gifts come to us through the media of providence and grace.

John, 8:31 and 32.

"Said Jesus to those Jews who believed on him: 'If ye continue in my word, then are ye my disciples indeed, and ye shall know the truth and the truth shall make you free.'"

Christ well knew the craving in every Jewish heart for freedom from the Roman yoke. He told them that by becoming his disciples they would attain a freedom indeed; a freedom they would find to be personal and individual; a freedom from the dominion of sin with its ignominious ignorance, darkness and slavery. The soul would be emancipated and the effect extend to all the concerns of life, so that there might come even in the case of the subjugated Jew a deliverance from the sense of submission to

Rome, with a flow of light and liberty overspreading his whole being. To all those who in this or any age of the world are under the dominion of evil habit and sin, Christ addresses himself as forcibly as at first.

1st Timothy, 3 : 16.

"And without controversy, great is the mystery of godliness; God was manifest in the flesh," &c., &c.

This text was formerly much relied on to prove the deity of Christ. But since the Revised Version has succumbed to the evidence long ago presented (as by Sir Isaac Newton) that the word "God" was incorrectly put by the old translators for "he who," the text has passed out of controversy, and we therefore read "he who was manifest in the flesh." Similarly, in Acts, 20:28, the words "church of God" should read "church of the Lord," according to the weight of the best manuscripts. The "blood" of God, sounds more heathenish than scriptural.

1st Corinthians, 1: 23.

"But we preach Christ crucified; unto the Jews a stumbling block, and unto the Greeks, foolishness."

"Christ crucified" was a stumbling block to the Jews because their hearts were set upon having in their Messiah a great national champion, much, perhaps, after the pattern of the patriotic Judas Maccabæus, who should sweep the earth of Roman supremacy and repeat the glories of David and Solomon. They did not bow to and accept the divine purpose of extending spiritual and moral conquests in individual souls, though the miracles of Christ were ample notice of where the divine purpose was to be read for certain. We fear that the Jews of the present day are victims to the same delusions that betrayed their ancestors, for they mistake the true purpose of man's education and probation on this earth, and regard as a "faith" to be hugged to their hearts, expectations absolutely groundless. The 13th chapter of the Acts of the Apostles is scarcely less to the purpose for the Jews of this nineteenth century than it was for those of the first.

To the Greeks the cross was "foolishness," because, besides their disbelief of the resurrection, they had no appreciation of the inviolability of the divine law and its demand for atonement in case of the breach of it. They had no just conception of the divine majesty and purity. Their mythologies were all dreadfully misleading, and their sacrifices and services, for the most part, abominations.

They could not perceive any reason why the blood of an unoffending benefactor of his race should be shed for the atonement of men's sinful souls. They knew nothing of the obligations and the philosophy that dwell in the single text, Leviticus, 17:11. They had not been initiated into the pure yet lofty mysteries inhering in the Mosaic and Christian systems.

Mark, 2: 7 and Luke, 5: 21; also Matth., 9: 6.
"Who can forgive sins but God only?"

Though put by the unfriendly scribes and Pharisees, this question was not without pertinency. The remark to the sick man was purposely made by Christ to bring out an opportunity to promulge the fact that he was charged with power *on earth* to forgive sins. Nothing could more certainly attest the divinity of his commission and messiahship than his being entrusted with such a power. But Christ faithfully took care to describe the scope of that power; it was "on earth" alone, and so all three of the evangelists pointedly record. On Christ's bodily departure from the world, after *all* power concerning his church had been given him, the same pardoning power was confided to his Apostles. (John, 20: 23.) The Apostles could either remit or retain sins.

Yet the Pharisees were right in the abstract, as Christ indirectly acknowledged, and were wrong only in their indisposition to own that the pardoning power had been conferred on Jesus. The power of forgiving sins still rests finally in God alone; yet as Sovereign Lord of all He can delegate the exercise of that power to whom He will.

Though the ability to forgive sins was given to Christ whilst on earth, it does not appear to be properly his now in heaven. He is now, because of his righteousness, mankind's mediator and advocate, (1st John, 2: 1,) man's High Priest, but not his judge. He now stands *before* the judge to act in cases requiring current adjudication. At the great day of account Christ's present lofty office will merge into the yet loftier office of delegated Universal Judge, involving the prerogative of weighing evidence *pro* and *con*, and making irreversible decisions. And to his faithful Apostles, who on earth participated with him in the power of forgiving sins, it is promised that they shall, in the day when the Son of man shall sit in the throne of his glory, also sit upon twelve thrones, judging the twelve tribes of Israel. (Matth., 19: 28; Luke, 22: 30.) Under God, the last judgment will be conducted by *men*.

The sins of mankind are committed against God, the Universal Lord. He is the party who has been offended, whose laws have been broken, and it is for Him only to forgive; therefore St. Paul testified at Miletus "repentance toward God." It was different in respect to "our Lord Jesus Christ," toward whom "faith," as in a divinely authorized teacher and atoning Saviour, was enjoined. Men are forgiven by God in, or through, "putting on" Christ. (Ephes., 4: 32; 1st John, 1: 9.) In the Lord's prayer the Father only is invoked to forgive. When on the cross Christ prayed the Father to forgive his murderers.

In one of Dr. Isaac Watts's hymns, after glorifying Christ's atoning sacrifice, the doctor says: "My Father *must* forgive,"—involving an idea very prevalent in Nicenist preaching and poetry, and also to be found in Universalist teachings—that Christ's work, sufferings, and death override every other consideration, and compel universal redemption. It ought to be remembered, however, that there are some sins for which Christ will refuse to offer atonement; of this kind is blasphemy against the Holy Ghost. (Matth., 12: 32.) So in the Old Testament we read that the sins of the house of the High Priest Eli were so heinous that God disallowed their being "purged with sacrifice or offering forever." It will, therefore, be a very perilous mistake to lean upon anything but faith resting on submission of heart and obedience of life, for pardon and acceptance with God. The case of every individual soul must stand in the full light of the divine cognition, for, *finally*, none can forgive sins but God only; and He is no respecter of persons. (Acts, 17: 31.)

The text 1st John, 5: 7, that for successive ages and centuries disfigured the common version, has, after many a remonstrance against its title to a place in the Word of God, been expunged by the late revisers. Its false testimony has misled mankind and vitiated their sentiments beyond computation.

John, 6: 53.

"Then Jesus said unto them, Verily, verily, I say unto you, except ye eat the flesh of the Son of man, and drink his blood, ye have no life in you."

This showed that the life he spoke of was not animal life but spiritual life, and might well have suggested that the "flesh of the Son of man" was something of a spiritual nature, as being competent to sustain spiritual life. He had told them that he was the true living bread that had come down from heaven, of which a man might eat and not die, but live forever, suggesting that the bread, the eating and the life were all spiritual.

Verse 56th. "He that eateth my flesh and drinketh my blood dwelleth in me and I in him."

This, again, removes all idea of materiality from Christ's intent, for only the spiritual can interchangeably live in the spiritual.

Verse 57. "As the living Father hath sent me, and I live by the Father: so he that eateth me, even he shall live by me."

This effectually excludes every idea of literal manducation, and shows that the "living" referred to was the same as that spiritual food which Christ spoke of during his temptation in the wilderness, (Matthew 4: 4,) quoted from Deut., 8: 3. Thus, under the Mosaic as well as under the Christian dispensation, the command was "not to live by bread only, but by every word that proceedeth out of the mouth of the Lord." There was to be a feeding not only of the body but of the soul, and soul-feeding was the subject-matter of Christ's discourse all through the sixth chapter of John's Gospel.

Verse 58th. "This is that bread which came down from heaven; not as your fathers did eat manna and are dead: he that eateth of this bread shall live for ever."

Christ tells his hearers that the heavenly manna to which he alluded had the power of imparting eternal life; it was, therefore, not a material substance like the manna of the wilderness, which did not preserve from death. Certainly, these hints and recommendations ought to have prompted his hearers to seek for all the information they could get relative to so great a boon, yet most of them, with alienated hearts and influenced by other hopes and objects than the attainment of eternal life, turned away and with hollow pretence intimated that Christ had talked absurdity and falsehood.

To those of them who were less disaffected Christ did at length furnish a complete solution, though the solution was scarcely other than a repetition of what his previous language had intimated. He told them, then, that it was the spirit which gave life, for that his mere material flesh was ineffective for any spiritual benefit. The words, or doctrine, he taught, was that whereon they must feed in order to attain everlasting life. This was the true manna sent down from heaven, of which if men ate they would live forever.

One remark remains: Peter, or Paul or John, might, indeed, as they really did, verbally dispense to their hearers the bread of life, the true Christian doctrine, but Christ did more. *He* not only taught the truth, but was a living exemplar of it. Not in his teaching only was the heavenly truth conveyed, but it was concretely embodied in his life, so that he was the very substantial truth and life he preached. This perfectly justified his saying, "I am that bread of life"—and no wonder, for the favorite "meat" on which he fed was "to do the will of Him that sent him and to finish his work."

The Lord's Supper.

1st Cor., 11: 23.

"For I have received of the Lord, that which I also delivered unto you. That the Lord Jesus, the same night in which he was betrayed, took bread: and when he had given thanks, he brake it, and said, Take, eat: this is my body which is broken for you: this do in remembrance of me. After the same manner also he took the cup, when he had supped, saying, This cup is the new testament in my blood: this do ye, as oft as ye drink it, in remembrance of me. For as often as ye eat this bread and drink this cup, ye do show the Lord's death till he come."

This statement was directly made to Paul by the Lord Jesus, and not gathered up from among the Christian community as were many other facts. It is an indorsement from the mouth of Christ of the recitals in the gospels; a circumstance not to be undervalued.

Christ stated to Paul that he took the bread and brake it, and handed it in that way to his disciples, likening the broken bread to his body, which, on the morrow, would be voluntarily broken, not for himself, but for them. In doing this, Christ's object was to premonish them of the meaning of his coming crucifixion, viz., that it would be a voluntary offering on his part of his body for their sakes. So with the wine-cup; its contents represented the blood that on the morrow would be shed upon the cross for *them*.

Now there is no element of the Christian faith more to be kept in continuous view than Christ's surrender of his life's blood for the incalculable benefit of his people. Therefore, that so cardinal a fact should not be lost sight of, Christ enjoined that the simple ceremony he had just enacted should be repeated by his followers in remembrance of him; simply, *in remembrance of him*, and not for the purpose of an observance scarcely in itself one remove from insanity, and in spirit utterly contemptuous and defiant of all true religion.

The necessity for such an offering as the pure and precious blood of Christ rested in the insuperable demand of the divine law, not one jot or tittle of which can fail of fulfilment. *Blood as an atonement for sin* was the substance of it, (Leviticus, 17:11,) and the offering must be made by one who had a perfect title to what he offered. Save in the case of Christ alone, no member of the human race was his or her own proprietor. All bore mortgaged and forfeited bodies by reason of their sin. His sinlessness gave him absolute title to himself and all that pertained to him. His offering was, therefore, acceptable and accepted. His blood was everyway appropriate wherewith to sprinkle the Mercy-seat, and be a satisfactory propitiation for sins.

And God, out of His boundless wisdom and goodness, as having respect both to the honor in which Christ deserved to be held and to the inestimable benefit Christ had wrought out for men, caused the New Testament (or *Covenant*) he would make with man to consist in these conditions: That in so far as mankind should in deed and truth accept Christ as their Law-giver, Master and Lord, and cordially believe that God had ratified Christ's work by the attestation of raising him from the dead, should mankind receive remission of sins and be eligible to eternal life. Thus was the cup verily the New Testament in Christ's blood.

This, then, is the FAITH in Christ—saving faith—having for its fruits, 1st, confession of Christ by personal baptism into him as the Son of God; 2d, periodical celebration of the Lord's Supper; 3d and lastly, a living up to the principles of the Christian profession, and perseverance therein even unto life's end.

Thus may the much-needed SECOND REFORMATION be achieved, and the Christian church brought home to its resting place upon the foundation of the Apostles and Prophets, Jesus Christ himself being the chief corner-stone.

The few following texts are submitted as subjects for interesting pulpit discourses, viz.:

1st. The first-commandment-of-all, as mutually understood and settled upon by Christ and the Jewish scribe in

Mark, 12 : 28 to 34 ;—What it is, and to what extent have the churches in general mastered their wills and obeyed this first commandment?

2d. Do the churches in general, and their members individually, comply with the urgent command in Deuteronomy, 6 : 6 to 9?

3d. John, 5 : 19, in connexion with verse 30, relative to Christ's inherent personal capabilities. (See, also, Acts, 1 : 7.)

4th. Does the Son know all things, so that nothing is concealed from him?—Mark, 13 : 32.

5th. Is the Son the full equal of the Father?—John, 14 : 28.

6th. The scope of Christ's authority and personal presence during the period of his earthly ministry—Matthew, 15 : 24, and John, 11 : 15.

7th. At Christ's transfiguration, were the two visitants that appeared in glory divine beings or human?—Luke, 9 : 30 and 32.

8th. True worship is the worship of how many objects—of one, or more than one?—John, 4 : 21 and 23. If only one, who is that object?

9th. Is it not *idolatry* to worship any but the only true God?—Deuteronomy, 4 : 35 ; John, 17 : 3 ; John, 4 : 23.

ERRATA.

Page 40—Sixth line from bottom, for *Vicence*, read *Nicene*.
    42—Ninth line from top, for *Homoonsion*, read *Homoousion*.
    46—Twentieth line from top, for *Arclate*, read *Arelate*.
    55—Third line from bottom, read *Christ, He*
    83—Twelfth line from bottom, read *authoritatively*.
    89—Fourteenth line from bottom, read *or fathers*.
    101—Twelfth line from bottom, read *death* and *descent*.
    104—Twelfth line from bottom, read "*burial into death.*"
    136—Second line from top, for *professed*, read *possessed*.
    143—Twelfth line from bottom, read *three eternal*.

www.ingramcontent.com/pod-product-compliance
Lightning Source LLC
Chambersburg PA
CBHW031815220426
43662CB00007B/655